Family Dynamics and
Female Sexual Delinquency

Family Dynamics and Female Sexual Delinquency

Edited by

OTTO POLLAK AND
ALFRED S. FRIEDMAN

SCIENCE AND BEHAVIOR BOOKS, INC.
Palo Alto, California: 1969

Contributors

Nathan W. Ackerman, M.D., *Psychoanalyst; Director, The Family Institute, New York; Professor of Psychiatry, Columbia University.*

Peter Blos, Ph.D., *Consultant, Jewish Board of Guardians; private practice, New York.*

Alfred S. Friedman, Ph.D., *Director of Research, Philadelphia Psychiatric Center.*

Herbert H. Herskovitz, M.D., *Director, Irving Schwartz Institute for Children and Youth, Philadelphia Psychiatric Center; Training Analyst, Philadelphia Psychoanalytic Institute.*

Elizabeth Herzog, Ph.D., *Chief, Child Life Studies Branch, Division of Research, U. S. Children's Bureau.*

Jerome E. Jungreis, A.C.S.W., *Mental Health Coordinator, Philadelphia Child Guidance Clinic (deceased, May 1967).*

Charles John Kallick, M.D., *Associate Staff Psychiatrist, Norwalk Hospital, Connecticut; private practice, Westport, Connecticut.*

Irving Kaufman, M.D., *Director, Consultation Services, Family Services Association of Greater Boston; Faculty, School of Social Work, Smith College.*

Robert MacGregor, Ph.D., *Chief, Family Therapy Program, Mental Health Center, Chicago, Illinois.*

Salvador Minuchin, M.D., *Director, Philadelphia Child Guidance Clinic; Professor of Child Psychiatry, University of Pennsylvania School of Medicine.*

Gertrude Pollak, Ph.D., *Director, Family Life Education, Family Service of Philadelphia.*

Otto Pollak, Ph.D., *Professor of Sociology, University of Pennsylvania.*

Clara Rabinowitz, M.D., *Research Associate, Wiltwyck School for Boys; private practice, New York.*

Ames Robey, M.D., *Director, Center for Forensic Psychiatry, Ypsilanti State Hospital, Michigan.*

Lora Heims Tessman, Ph.D., *Staff Psychologist, Massachusetts Institute of Technology, Department of Medicine; private practice, Boston, Massachusetts.*

John Warkentin, Ph.D., M.D., *Psychiatrist, Atlanta Psychiatric Clinic; Editor of* Voices.

Carl A. Whitaker, M.D., *Professor of Psychiatry, University of Wisconsin Medical School.*

Harold M. Visotsky, M.D., *Director, Illinois Department of Mental Health; Associate Professor of Psychiatry, University of Chicago.*

Contents

Foreword

Carl A. Whitaker

Modern writing is a team process, just as modern teaching is becoming more and more a team process. This team of editors presents writings covering much of modern experience and theory in work with families; their orientation is that of systems theory. They have backed off far enough from the techniques of treatment to give us the broad perspective of the sociologist, yet have turned the other lens and pictured in clear detail sexual problems, poverty problems, civil rights problems, the practicality of family treatment, and the dynamics of triangular distortions within the family. Furthermore, they include a comprehensive sampling of the multiple therapy aspects of treatment, in which the therapy unit includes a team of therapists working with the team that is the family. Best of all, they even dare to touch the sacred problem of the therapist as a person and his significance in the process of psychotherapy.

A precipitous changeover into work with the whole family is sweeping the country; we must find a theory of family operation and a theory for the treatment of the family. The more we deal with the organism, the more we need a basic perception of what the organism we treat really is. This book approaches the family as a whole and posits that "we belong to three families." To say it another way, "Independence as a family unit is merely the intermediate stage between the early dependent years in our primary family and the later dependent years in the family of our offspring." This book takes the basic focus first presented by Doctor Midelfort* that "the family is the unit of treatment." It brings together case data on family patterns, family pathology, the sociocultural variants that serve to define the family as a system, and the interactional pattern between the parents, between the siblings, and within the cross-generational triangles. The central message seems somehow similar to the message of life; "People can grow." The authors present phases of the relationship between generations—for the older generation, the pain and release of fostering growth; for the younger generation, the problems of growth itself. We are offered old ideas in new gold goblets and new ideas that ring old bells with new harmonics.

The scope of knowledge covered is vast. While it is impossible to encompass the largest areas, we are offered the interface between the disciplines of the social sciences—studies which have many times seemed like separate countries, their borders guarded and few passports issued.

---

*Midelfort, C. F. *The family in psychotherapy*. New York: McGraw-Hill, 1957.

The communication between psychology, sociology, psychiatry, and the grass-roots professional worker is rarely free. Nationalism prevails. The language barrier is massive. The suspicion held by each about the citizens of the neighboring country is a pervasive influence. However, the struggle to maintain a balance of power and to fight for dominance seems to fade when these people, who ordinarily talk with each other only in cliches, meet. Their new language is not an artificial one, an Esperanto of social talk. It is a human language, meaningful across disciplines.

The editors have offered us a record of personal experience aimed at achieving a perspective on the operational processes of growth within our culture. They have blended breadth and perception of the sociologist and anthropologist, with the deep involvement of the psychotherapist and practicing members of the social reconstruction professions. One of the satisfying aspects of this book is the crossruffing between worker, who keeps it human, and theoretician, who makes it visible and perceptible as a set of whole concepts rather than disparate bits of data.

Like Darwin, who was convinced that nothing really counted unless you saw it yourself, these men are clear that good thinking and good theory, while contributions, cannot be substituted for experience. It is as though the authors are saying that science is all right only if warmed by the heart of man. Science is not an organism; it is a method. But the person of the scientist is the essence of its application. The authors are supplying additional data for the ongoing march in the experience of living. Unlike many who think they have "found the answer," the authors see their work as a contribution to a newer perception of family living. They are clear that they have not found the ultimate answer to family living or to the social structure. In leaving their data open to multiple inferences, they are like the modern moviemaker, to whom the presentation is less important than the perceptions of the persons exposed to that creativity. Factual data are less important than the construction, the creation, and the artistry of its presentation. When the perceiver becomes involved, he is himself forced to be creative. The editors leave us with a new experience—not an answer but a stimulus to creative thinking.

I am excited by the fact that this book grew out of a teaching effort. It did not emerge from a series of individually dictated fantasies, but from the moving process of trying to teach the dynamics and therapy of the family to people who were professionals. The teaching was planned not on a theoretical level but within a conceptual framework to organize the workers' ongoing experience. What the therapist writes about therapy is often a kind of monologue understandable only to the speaker, whereas teaching is a dialogue that is geared to the student.

This book tickles my imagination, comforts my despair, stimulates my roving eye, and leaves me with a kind of enthusiasm about pushing my own growing edge. Anyone who works with families, or indeed anyone who really belongs to a family, will come out of this book with a sparkle in his eye.

Preface

This volume had its origin in a seminar on the family system as it influences the personality and behavior of sexually-acting-out adolescent daughters. The seminar was one part of a special training and demonstration project in Family Counseling for Sexual Behavior Problems of Adolescent Girls, conducted during the period from January 1963 through June 1965, under the auspices and partnership of the Philadelphia Psychiatric Center and the Office of Juvenile Delinquency and Youth Development, Welfare Administration, U. S. Department of Health, Education and Welfare. There was also a practicum and demonstration part of this project: Families of girls with sexual behavior problems were treated and counseled in family group sessions by co-therapy teams consisting of a supervisory family therapist and a trainee family counselor, who was usually an experienced social caseworker. The theoretical issues that needed to be considered in the treatment practicum were presented in the seminar, which was conducted under the direction of Otto Pollak, one of the editors. Alfred S. Friedman, co-editor, was the general project director and was in charge of the practicum. Mrs. Gertrude Cohen, our most able executive assistant, helped as factotum to the enterprise—keeping it going where it would have foundered, correcting the recall of the editors, and exercising beneficial control over materials and correspondence.

Some of the participants in the practicum were experienced caseworkers who attended the seminar for didactic material to be integrated with the experiences gained in the practicum. There were also, however, other participants in the seminar—clinical psychologists, school counselors, ministers of various denominations, probation officers, and social workers from psychiatric clinics, family service agencies, and the courts.

The seminar benefited from the diverse backgrounds of the participants, who contributed valuable insights from their professional and personal experience. These were especially helpful in clarifying the particular premarital sexual behavior patterns of various socioeconomic groups. One reason for the broader representation in the seminar was to gain understanding and acceptance for our approach among diverse professionals concerned with the correction and treatment of sexually-acting-out girls through family counseling. Over the three years of the project period, the annual seminar was repeated with different groups of trainees, and it changed and grew in the process of this repetition.

The papers presented here are in part the theoretical lectures given in the seminar. Some appear without change. Some represent elaborations and clarifications of positions presented by guest speakers that proved so stimulating to the audience that we were anxious to have them cast into publishable form. For a more comprehensive presentation, we decided to draw on other unpublished papers that we considered to be significant contributions to our area of concern. We integrated these into a logical sequence with our own seminar material. In consequence, this volume is not just a transfer into print of the material presented orally in the seminar, but is rather the next step in theoretical formulation—one that aims at completion and closure. In that sense, it is the fourth stage of our theoretical seminar.

The arrangement of the papers follows in a general way the order in which the material was presented in our didactic sessions. We began with family dynamics from the viewpoint of system theory, proceeded to socioeconomic considerations and the culture of poverty, and then spent considerable time on various specific constellations of family dynamics and pathology that appear to lead to sexual acting-out in girls. As a corollary to the main theme of the book, we have also presented a brief conceptual framework for conjoint family counseling or treatment. In this way we have proceeded from the level of the person, through that of the family as a small organization, to the web of values and behavior patterns representing the culture.

The reader may wonder why we did not start with individual psychodynamics and then move to higher levels of complexity, such as family and culture. Our choice was determined by our basic orientation in conceptualizing behavior problems. From our point of view, individual psychodynamics derive their content from family experience. We believe that whatever goes on in an individual psyche develops from shared family experience, elaborated by idiosyncratic ideation and fantasy. If a given psychic constellation occurs with sufficient frequency in a population to approximate a majority of modal incidence, we refer to it as a "basic personality structure." Such a personality structure may be maladaptive from the average American middle-class viewpoint of mental health or from the traditional viewpoint of psychiatry and social work. Still, being supported by other reference persons in the client's or patient's environment, it will present more obstacles to therapy than personality configurations considered deviant in the individual patient's subculture as well.

Thus we gradually introduced to the seminar participants the proposition that a system of intervention can make interactional contact with the system of the family most fruitful if both the superfamilial frame of reference, culture, and the subfamilial frame of reference, psychodynamics, are maintained for perceptual orientation.

It is a sad duty before closing these introductory remarks to report the untimely death of Jerome E. Jungreis, who wrote the final chapter of the book and who was the coordinator of the practicum part of the training project. We want to express our sadness over the loss of a colleague who worked closely with us and made a major contribution to this endeavor.

Otto Pollak
Alfred S. Friedman

PART I

Family System Theory

Therapists are often enthusiastic about trying new approaches. Homo sapiens is a reflective species, however, and therapists need theoretical underpinning for their adventures in methodology and for their understanding of why they succeed. A therapy that works without acceptable explanation is unlikely to satisfy the professional mind. Furthermore, experience cannot be transmitted to a wider audience without a supportive theory.

It is true that the shift from individual therapy to family therapy started with the observation that family members who received individual treatment frequently lost their therapeutic gains when they were re-exposed to their family conditions without the counterweight of therapy. It was also observed that improvement of one family member under therapy was frequently accompanied by deterioration of another family member who had remained untreated. Such observations and their practical implications provided the impetus for experimentation with family therapy. But therapeutic inventiveness without theoretical explanation is never permitted to guide professional activity for any length of time without further search for the organizational pattern that may underlie the phenomena of concern. Family therapy found its explanation in family system theory.

The family may be seen as an organization of a limited number of human beings, differing from one another by age and sex, who because of their differences are related in complementarity and can satisfy one another's needs in health and disease. Where the complementarity operates between needs that have been arrested in development, we have family pathology.

Among its various manifestations in behavior, sexual acting-out in adolescent girls appears to have a definite place. Its meaning can usually be grasped in terms of family dynamics and presents a family concern affecting consciously or unconsciously all family members. Moreover, since sexual promiscuity in adolescent girls represents in our culture a behavioral disturbance that threatens the well-being of parents and siblings as well as of the girl herself, it seemed to us appropriate to explore the potential of conjoint family therapy in such instances.

Accordingly, we were concerned with finding an appropriate theoretical framework within which to understand our practical explorations. In searching for a baseline for the chapters comprising this first section, we found it helpful to focus on the conception of the family as a system for satisfaction of its members in the here and now, and for their preparation for the future. Depending on the preferences of the family theorist, the significant aspect of pathology in family interaction can be seen in breakdown of communication, in defaulting of role responsibilities, in stagnation, in conflictual and exploitive family interaction, or in some other way. These represent various sets of attending to, and dealing with, the same phenomena of family arrest and family impairment. This theoretical thinking is presented in the first part of our book.

CHAPTER 1

Marriage—the Cornerstone of the Family System

John Warkentin

Man has found it difficult to follow the ancient advice of Socrates, "Know thyself." Some of us may not want to. In fact, it is not uncommon to find a mother of children who has never even inspected her body nude before a mirror. Nevertheless, through the centuries behavioral scientists have gradually developed a respectable system of knowledge about the human body and the human personality. Sigmund Freud in 1896 laid a cornerstone to our understanding of personality when he identified the *unconscious* of a person as a force to be reckoned with. We have built on that foundation so that the modern psychotherapist can now listen with a perception and understanding never before possible.

On the other hand, behavioral scientists still feel insecure when they face a *group* of patients, or perhaps a married couple, or a family consisting of two or three generations. We easily become confused with the multitude of seemingly unrelated bits of behavior presented to us. At least we as yet have nothing in our formulations of interpersonal dynamics that is comparable to the conception of the individual unconscious or the delineation of the psychosexual development of a child.

When Carl Whitaker and I began working together about twenty years ago, we soon found that we could understand a patient or a married couple much better if we conducted the interview together. We called this *multiple therapy*. Even with the help of this technique, and the many conferences that we have had with each other after a couple or family left the interview, we still often feel ignorant and inept.

The diagnosis, techniques, and goals in working with a family differ profoundly from the conventional medical model. Traditionally, the individual patient comes with symptoms; when these are healed and he is no longer hurting, he is dismissed. By contrast, a disturbed family may present problems in living that are the direct result of their family life style and value system. The therapeutic task then consists of helping them to grow into a more satisfying life style, one that will leave the family less vulnerable to emotional injury. For example, a very repressed family may cultivate a "conspiracy of superficiality," with much emphasis on social appearances. An illegitimate pregnancy in such a family would be a catas-

3

trophe. If they then bring their hurt to a therapist, his value system may differ greatly from that of the family. The discrepancy in values may be so great that the outcome of the therapeutic attempt is very depressing for all concerned.

A case in point was the routine referral of a girl we shall call Gladys Jones by a general practitioner in a small Georgia town. When I called for Gladys in our waiting room, a handsome man of about my own age stood up to shake hands with me, saying that he was Tom Jones and introducing his somewhat flashily-dressed wife as Hortense Jones. Almost as an afterthought, he introduced his small, mousy daughter Gladys. The four of us went to my office, where the tension promptly became so great that it was hard for me to breathe. After some awkward moments, Mrs. Jones said, "Gladys is pregnant!"

Gladys was the second of four children; after her birth her mother had a one-month postpartum depression and developed migraine. The older three children are girls, the fourth is a boy, aged five. The oldest girl, aged nineteen, was married six months before I saw them, and the mother had gone into the menopause four months before that point in time. The childhood history of Gladys revealed that she was a happy "daddy's girl" until age six, at which time she was raped by the older son of the family babysitter; his mother continued to be a very close friend of the family. Mrs. Jones stated that she did not consider Gladys to be a virgin after the raping. From that time on Gladys became quiet, refused to hug her father any more, and developed a problem with speech, a kind of lisping. While still only six, she suffered nausea and vomiting so that she could not eat in the school cafeteria. She also had a brain concussion in an accident. By the time Gladys was ten, her mother complained that she preferred lying to telling the truth, and that she never confided in her mother. Gladys had her menarche the day she became twelve years old. She had not cried at all in recent years, read the Bible every night, and was described as so nervous at night that the mother had to sleep with her about one night a week.

According to our usual routine, I suggested that all three of the Joneses return the next time to meet with Dr. Whitaker and me in a five-way session. They did so, and Mr. Jones this time stated that he was very concerned about his wife; that she had begun menstruating again, that she had had smothering spells after their last baby, and that she had not breastfed any of the children. This time, as the family left the interview, Mr. Jones stayed behind to say privately at the door, "I'm worried about Hortense."

In the third consultation, Dr. Whitaker and I saw the parents alone for part of the time. They assured us that they had developed a good sexual adjustment by sleeping in adjoining rooms after the children came, but Mr. Jones was by now really concerned about his wife's depression. Both of them reported that they had stomach trouble and described themselves as exacting, perfectionistic people. For the rest of this third consultation, we saw Gladys alone and learned that she had been a cheerleader at school for the past two years. She also stated that she was scared to sleep upstairs, afraid of being by herself, but liked the dark because then she could not see what was coming after her. Her major concern about the pregnancy was how it would affect her parents.

The fourth session was another five-way session. We reported briefly that we found no structured psychiatric illness in Gladys, and could therefore not recommend an abortion on psychiatric grounds. We tried to explain the significance of the new life in Gladys, but the parents were not listening. They did not pick up our offer of continued interviews. Subsequently, I got a phone call from an unknown doctor who had seen Gladys, requesting that I give psychiatric sanction for an abortion, which he apparently considered doing in any case.

In this entire case, family and therapist were clearly failing to meet each other in a productive encounter. The inner expectations of the family were clearly contrary to those of the therapist. Our value systems did not coincide. The discrepancy that we experienced with this family was over the whole concept of human nature and how human life operates most effectively.

Repeated such experiences led Dr. Whitaker and me to ponder, and eventually write down, the attitudes with which we meet our patients. In this particular case, we were left with many unanswered questions. For example, Did Gladys get pregnant as a gift to her mother, who had just entered the menopause? Another question, What life experiences and what attitudes make it possible for a family to consider abortion as preferable to a bad reputation? Still another question, How could we possibly have helped them to find a measure of satisfaction in this new life that had come into their midst out of season?

We distinguished five levels in the therapists' participation, all five levels contributing to the total of the "therapists' presence" in the interview:

(1) Our professional training furnishes us with the two more superficial levels of functioning, the first of which is the *tactics of interviewing patients*, which are deliberate techniques. Tactically, we must remember that we have two ears and only one mouth, and the balance of interchange between patient and therapist should operate accordingly. It is the aim of our tactical approach that patients must not leave the interview too greatly upset, that they must have another appointment, and that we must instruct them as to how they can prepare for that next interview. All this is rather elementary.

(2) A somewhat more profound consideration of our professional training applies to a second level, that of *strategy*. This involves such questions as, Should we help the patients to be relieved of their immediate symptoms, or should we leave them with enough anxiety and distress so that it will push them toward emotional growth? Other strategic questions are, What is the motivational push in the patients, and what degree of personal growth can be achieved with the existing push? For instance, in the case described, the parents gradually made it clear that they were consciously motivated simply toward an abortion, with a status quo of

activities otherwise. Gladys sat there like a person who was curious about
what her parents would do next, but without any expressed concern about
her own body or her own future.

(3) Beyond the questions of tactics and strategy, our professional
training is of little help. Our next level of personal functioning as
therapists is determined by *inner assumptions and postulates* about human
nature. These assumptions, or premises by which we live, are only partially
known to us consciously. This chapter is an attempt to formulate the
postulates or assumptions that Dr. Whitaker and I have made about
marriage, and most of the remainder of it will consist of our effort to
present this third level of the therapist's functioning. These statements
arise in part from our professional experience with married couples and in
part from the total of our personal living experiences. They were modified
by our personal therapy, but we must recognize that our assumptions
about living originate above all else from our own childhood experiences.

(4) A fourth level of the therapist's presence in the interview is that of
his *unconscious life styles*. This life style of the therapist expresses his
reverence for life in any form, his unconscious goals for himself, the undefined achievement he is demanding of himself during the unknown but
expected life span, and possibly other aspects of the unconscious value
system within him. He may discover evidences of his life style on occasion,
such as from his slips of the tongue or from dreams. In a larger sense, we
are likely to discover our life style in the manner suggested by a wise man
who said, "I can be sure of what I wanted only after I see what I got." His
life style may be altered only partially by personal therapy, by the ordeal
of creating and meeting crises in his life, and by the rare signficant
moments of his experience.

(5) There is a final fifth level of the therapist's presence in the interview which is probably unmodifiable: his *character structure*. My own
character structure happens to be largely anal. This is the major way I
remember myself, view myself in the present, and will remain until I die.
Even as I mellow with age, I will still be recognizable as having an obsessive-compulsive character structure.

All these five levels of the therapist's presence affect the experience of
the patient in the office. But here our concern is with the middle level—
that of the inner assumptions and postulates about human nature. Let us
first list briefly some assumptions we make about people in general:

(1) *All human beings are imbued with an inexorable drive to become
more than they are*, from the day they are born till the day they die. This
drive to grow may be driven underground in a person, so that it cannot be
detected, but we assume that it is still present.

(2) *Personal growth occurs in phases*, which in the child are physically
quite obvious. In the adult the phases of growth are less predictable, less
easily recognized, and more likely to be set off by experiences that make
the person very anxious.

(3) *A person has major adjustment choices* as to how he or she will
deal with the stress of living: coping, emotional withdrawal, delinquency,

physical illness, or the development of neurotic and psychotic symptoms. During childhood the choice of expression or outlet is determined almost entirely by the family setting and climate. After adolescence, when a person is out of the home, the choice of reactions under stress will be determined increasingly by friends or significant persons such as the pastor and the psychotherapist. When an adult is in therapy, it is often amazing how he will accommodate himself to the attitudes of the therapist, as if he were always trying to act out the therapist's wishes and life style.

(4) *Growth is irreversible.* In the case I mentioned, Gladys had matured to motherhood, and she can never again be a child. We assume that this is true of all emotional growth.

Concerning marriage as a special situation, the assumptions and postulates with which we approach the spouses are the following:

(1) It is not good for man to be alone. We believe that *people are good for each other*, at least in those cases where they become intimate together. Such intimacy may or may not involve a sexual union or a sharing of previously secret thoughts and feelings in words. Intimacy does require a physical presence with each other—it cannot be achieved by correspondence. Martin Buber is reported to have said, "I can be most completely myself only in relationship to another."

It is feeling that binds man to man, or man to woman, or child to parent. When we see an extremely affect-hungry person, we refer to this as the "orphan syndrome," indicating that we recognize his history of no intimacy in living with another. Gladys, in our case above, showed some of the orphan syndrome, and for her sake I was glad that she had found enough intimacy with another to get pregnant, even though this made for a difficult social problem. I wish I could have let her know that her pregnancy was a proud achievement of womanhood, but this was not feasible in the face of her disturbed parents. It is my assumption that deep within herself Gladys was proud of being pregnant, but would probably never acknowledge this even to herself.

(2) *Monogamous marriage is the most ideal arrangement* to provide the opportunity for growing intimacy. Marriage in our society takes place at two levels: the legal commitment and the feeling experience. These are two quite disparate qualities of any marriage, which run along parallel to each other as time goes on and which have certain interconnections. It is clear that the legal commitment, as symbolized by a formal marriage ceremony, has the consequences of common ownership of property, joint checking accounts, living on the same premises, and jointly sharing in all the realities and responsibilities that one might encounter in a business partnership. This legal or social partnership is planned to have a maximum stability, so much so that it is sometimes facetiously characterized as a condition of "being shackled." The rules that apply in the business world at large apply here also—for example, the rule of fairness between the contracting parties. The efforts of the partners are supposed to promote harmonious interaction so that there will be no threat of legal changes in their association. But, simultaneously, there is no provision for growth in

this business aspect of the marriage, other than the gradual accumulation of more real estate and personal property as the years flow by.

The second level of marital relatedness, that of feeling, is different. Onset of the feeling marriage may be dated by the partners before the formal wedding ceremony or after. In fact, the two partners may disagree as to the date when they became "one flesh" in terms of their emotional union. From the first, the partners accept and enjoy the instability of their feeling interaction, the mountain peaks and the valleys of their experiences with each other, and the ever-changing climate of their whole feeling relationship. The laws of society do not apply to their intimacies, and fairness is not an issue since "all is fair in love and war," and marriage is both. It is this constant instability of the feeling relationship that permits growth, a growth in each of the partners themselves and also a growth in the character of their relating.

(3) *Marital partners have chosen each other with great wisdom*, at least with the wisdom of their bodies and of their unconscious motives. We postulate that this is true in cases of "love at first sight," and also in more extended courtships. The exquisite accuracy of marital pairing of personality characteristics repeatedly impresses us. However, we are aware that the partners may be less than well-matched in terms of social background, religious affiliation, educational achievement, and even basic intellectual capacity. However, their unconscious styles of life are almost certainly in close agreement, at least as far as we therapists can determine.

(4) *The marital relationship is the dominant factor in determining the feelings and behavior of all people in the home.* In the usual two-generation family, when the relationship between husband and wife is that of a warm, comfortable ebb-and-flow with a basic honesty and a firm commitment between them, we would expect the children to be essentially honest and sincere people. In a different type of family, where the child has been doing petty stealing since first grade, with increasing skill, and at age ten is arrested for car theft, we would assume that the relationship between his father and mother has much dishonesty and insincerity in it. In private practice we assume that it is going to be difficult to collect our fees from the parents of a delinquent child. This does not depend on how much money they have; their nonpayment of bills is the result of their life styles and their relationship. We would assume that such a husband and wife also fail to "pay their debts" to each other.

(5) *The feeling relationship between the marital partners is kept continuously balanced*, mutual, and reciprocal, both as to type and intensity. As two individuals get married, they seem to agree on a "feeling temperature" that they will regulate between them. To use an analogy, the emotional "thermostat" can then be reset only by agreement of both parties; otherwise, if the one tries to be "too hot," the other will compensate by being "too cold," thus to maintain a stable over-all temperature in the marriage. This does not deny that the behavioral presentation of the two partners may be very different from their underlying feeling tones.

We also use another analogy to describe marital homeostasis. We speak of the "marital see-saw." When a wife becomes particularly anxious, the husband is likely to lose his anxiety symptoms; or, when he becomes physically ill, she experiences a feeling of increased health and strength as she cares for him. Still another example, and perhaps the most obvious, is that the husband seems to be oversexed as long as his wife is definitely frigid; if she then has a year or two of psychotherapy and her sexuality is liberated, he notices suddenly that his sexual desire is greatly diminished and that he has to find explanations for this. A similar sequence occurs at times in the treatment of the alcoholic and his wife. This see-saw will operate only between two people who live intimately together.

(6) *The emotional marriage has a natural growth history.* It progresses through a series of nodal points, or crises, or impasses, as the years go by. The more alive the partners, the more intense is their interaction likely to be at the points of crisis. These nodal points are probably the only times when the marital partners have opportunity to modify their marital relatedness, to reset the thermostat of their marriage, as it were. This refers only to the emotional marriage, since no growth nor impasse is to be expected in the legal marriage.

The two factors that we see as important in marital crises are: the firmness of the legal commitment and the type of significant others who are around when the crisis develops.

It seems as if our society has developed legal monogamy so as to provide a secure setting for the vagaries of the emotional "marriage dance." The legal bond prevents impulsive separation in times of mutual hatred. It is fortunate that the legal marriage is achieved full grown and complete about the time of the wedding ceremony. Obviously, stability in the emotional interaction is not to be expected for many years, if ever.

The second factor in the outcome of a marital crisis is the character of those persons who are meaningful to the marriage partners at that time. The presence of an overindulgent parent may well be sufficient to result in the premature discontinuation of the marital effort. It seems as if parents quite routinely consider their children to have married below themselves in some way. Friends also may provoke the marital couple to follow the example of others and try for a better partner. Professional assistants matter a great deal. The divorce lawyer who is readily impressed with the beauty and charm of the abused young wife may well persuade her that she should get a divorce and marry more successfully next time. This kind of experience may even occur when a marriage is brought to the attention of a psychiatrist who chooses to look closely at the immediate complaints of his patient while neglecting to notice the long-range implications and goals involved in every marriage. Many patients ask questions about the character of their prospective psychiatrist because they sense that his personal attitudes and experiences will significantly influence his impact on the patient.

(7) *Marriage must become characteristically a sexual relationship,* or else it becomes a perverse relationship. Dynamic forces in the field of marriage, other than the sexual, are secondary. For example, a major age difference between two marital partners, if it becomes the primary axis in the dynamics of the marriage, thereby makes it perverse and sick. How-

ever, the marriage can be profoundly satisfactory despite a major age difference if the relationship is sexually loving.

When we speak of marriage as "sexual," we are not referring only to sexual intercourse but to the entire sense of male and female in which the spouses relate positively. Where such a sexual relationship exists between the marital partners, coitus is not a form of reward or punishment, but an expression of their physical and emotional drive toward each other. In a marriage where sex is central, the husband expresses his almost feminine tenderness, while the wife expresses her almost masculine seeking of their union in ever new forms. The artistry of this relationship may be expressed merely by a holding of hands; for marital partners who are sure of their desire for each other, this in itself may be a rich experience.

(8) *In the natural history of marriage specific nodal points, or crises, may be expected at predictable intervals.* The wedding night is often such a nodal point, especially when the two persons have not been having premarital intercourse. Through the courtship they expected that their sexual union would be a crowning joy of togetherness. But on the first night of their honeymoon this may or may not be the way it works out. She may begin to menstruate that day, two weeks early. Or, he may be tremendously embarrassed to find himself impotent that day, or otherwise sexually inadequate. It is surprising sometimes to see how long a shadow the experiences of the wedding night and the honeymoon may cast on the marriage of a young couple.

Assuming that a couple have found ways to surpass the nodal point of the honeymoon successfully, the next period of special stress may well be the first pregnancy. Even though they wanted a child, the young couple find themselves strangely threatened by a separateness of feelings as the pregnancy progresses. They realize that this should be a time of increasing closeness, a time of joy that they can mutually produce new life; and yet they experience a stress in their relating that cancels out all the joy and makes them tense and apprehensive as the day of delivery approaches. She has the normal fear of death as she prepares to give birth, and he may well have a sense of being only a bystander in the tremendous drama about to occur. As the baby is actually born, he may have misjudged the timing and be off with the boys drinking as his wife delivers. In the subsequent period, before the six-weeks' checkup, she may feel overburdened with responsibility and have the "baby blues," while he feels almost like a stranger in a home that now consists of three people. This is another time when the young spouses may question whether they were meant for each other, and whether they really want to stay together until death do them part. It is easy to see how this nodal point in their marriage may present enough stress that they do not wish to go on with each other.

If they weather the nodal point of the first pregnancy, as most couples do, the second baby may pose an even more serious threat, as the couple once more faces the difficulties of pregnancy and delivery. Especially with a relatively immature couple, the second baby may somehow pose a threat that did not quite materialize with the first one. After the second baby, a wife may become desperately afraid of pregnancy, and the husband may become increasingly angry with what he considers to be her problem of frigidity.

Assuming that the legal marriage holds through these three crisis periods, the spouses will have a period of relative peace until the time comes when they have been married for about ten years. This is such a characteristic time of stress that we have come to call it the "ten-year syndrome." During the ten years, the couple have experienced turmoil, change, and interaction. They have probably started whatever family they are likely to have. The transference feelings of "being in love" with which they got married initially are largely exhausted, so that they see themselves now as having "fallen out of love." The areas of mutual irritation have become relatively familiar and painful by this time. The couple may have been "blindly in love" in their early years, but now each sees clearly the character defects in the other. In addition, each is beginning to suspect that he is never going to accomplish his initial desire to remold or improve the other partner. The family squabbles are becoming more repetitive and pointless. It is beginning to dawn on them that neither of them can win against the other, and that each of them has paralyzed the creativity and spontaneity in the other. The freshness of their interacting has gradually faded, and their marital growth has come to a grinding halt. This is the time when married couples most often come for *psychotherapy*.

The stress of the ten-year impasse is frequently expressed as a symptom picture in one or the other partner, while the nonsymptomatic spouse serves as a homeostatic factor for maintaining the outward stability of the home. A symptom of the ten-year syndrome may consist of unfaithfulness, or psychosomatic illness, or job maladjustment, or social withdrawal in one or the other of the partners. Whatever the particular conditions may be ten years after marriage, this is the time when it is especially unwise for the psychotherapist to undertake treatment of only one of the partners. The temptation to simply throw over the investment of living that they have made with each other is so great at this time that individual psychotherapy for either of them can easily be the final straw. At such a point in a marriage, the psychotherapist must exercise all the wisdom he has accumulated regarding the mutual nature of the marital relationship, even though only one of the partners presents himself as the "sick one," and the other plays the part of the plodding worker or even a kind of "psychiatric attendant." We have come to be almost rigid in our insistence that we see husband and wife together, even in the initial consultation, when a married person asks for therapy.

There are various possible outcomes to marital impasses. The pain of a disturbed feeling relationship between the marital partners may motivate them in various directions. They may decide, consciously or unconsciously, to settle for the status quo, even though it is not very satisfactory, and merely to maintain the socially acceptable structure of living in the same house for many years to come.

Other couples, particularly those whose parents were divorced, rather easily think in terms of divorce and the search for a more satisfactory partner. They say to themselves and to each other that the anxiety and distress of a painful marriage is not worth the effort of continuing it, and that their little children would be better off if the couple got divorced. They in effect want to start life over before they get too old. They don't realize that they cannot "withdraw the money from the bank," and that the next partner is likely to be a close facsimile of the first.

Let us consider this analogy of money in the bank somewhat further. It is a metaphor referring to any marriage as being comparable to an irrevocable trust for the lifetime of the participant. The income from it may be withdrawn, but the principal always remains in the bank. When two persons get married emotionally, to whatever degree, they have irrevocably committed feeling to each other that they can then not withdraw again and place elsewhere. They may be able to leave their first partner and subsequently deposit new feelings with another partner, as they build a second marriage. But they cannot take their feeling commitment away from the first partner and give that same feeling to a second partner. A misunderstanding of this matter may result in unnecessary divorce, where the divorcing couple suffers from the delusion that they will be able just to forget about their first marriage.

The resolution or outcome of a marital impasse situation has the highest signficance. Whatever the impasse, breaking out of it constructively constitutes the most magnificent and deepest experience that we know of in marriage. The constructive resolution of an impasse necessitates a "loss of face" in each of the partners. Their individual defensive patterns will no longer be quite the same afterwards. They become aware that they are quite equally matched in their power to hurt each other, and develop a new respect for their profound capacity to love each other. The constructive resolution of an impasse may be so destructive of pride in the partners that they experience it as compromising their personal integrity. Successive resolutions of marital impasses are almost certain to destroy the fantasy constructs that the partners had of each other. They will find an increased acceptance of each other as they really are. If they then feel very naked and defenseless with each other for a time, this is an added bonus to reward them for the struggle that they perpetrated.

In conclusion, I would say that my own character, life style, and verbalized assumptions make a significant contribution to the experience of patients in my office. I believe that this is true for all therapists. We therapists have had greatly differing life experiences, and present greatly differing personalities to our patients. Just as there are no perfect parents, so there are no perfect therapists, but there are therapists who honor their profession with their capacity and willingness to share what they are and think and feel with their patients.

CHAPTER 2

Developmental Difficulties
and the Family System

Otto Pollak

In the course of a normal life cycle, a human being is a member of three families: the family unit into which he is born, the family that he creates through his marriage, and the family of the adult son or daughter to which he eventually relates as a dependent. In our civilization, characterized by nutritional adequacy for most people, sanitation, and medical advances, physical life is frequently maintained for several decades; consequently the individual faces a return to dependency as his primary mode of relating to others, and thus must overcome crises not only of growth but also of decline. In the periods of growth, maturity, and decline the individual needs, and usually has, a family system in which he expresses himself as a part, interacting with other parts, such as father, mother, spouse, brothers and sisters, and collaterals further removed. These interactions have two major functions: satisfaction in the here and now, and preparation for the future. Although subject to many ramifications, these two complexes or functions are interdependent. If gratification in the here and now is not forthcoming, or is excessive, development will be impaired. This impairment can take the form either of partial arrest or of actual regression (1). The anxiety created in either case may be fought by deviance in the form of *acting-out*, such as delinquency, alcoholism, or promiscuity, or in the form of *acting-in*, such as psychoneurosis, psychosis, or ultimately, suicide.

It can be assumed to be a general principle of human development that every phase of the life cycle must be lived out fully and adequately in order to make it possible for the individual to live up to the psychological orientation and instrumental task demands of the next phase (2). Since members of a family act as the chief gratifiers of major need areas for one another, they must be able to give as well as to receive from one another in patterns of behavior that operate under an exchange principle (3). The exchange principle must work sufficiently well to promote and maintain a positive self-image in every member of the family system. It is not a principle of fairness but a principle of adequacy. Every family member must get enough to feel that the world is a place to be trusted (4), that he is a person who adds to the trustworthiness of this world, and that others in this world have the right to receive as well as to give and therefore cannot be used as objects of exploitation (5). It is this interdependent gratification and interdependent development that makes the family a *system*, i.e., "a regularly interacting or interdependent group of items forming a unified whole" (6).

This nature of the family as a system implies that change in one member will require change in all the other members, that the others may resist such change or need help in reorganizing themselves after such a change has occurred, and that an attempt to influence one part of the system must be viewed as an attempt to change the whole. Since the family is a system in which gratification in the here and now is connected with gratification in the future, i.e., with satisfactory development, an attempt to enhance the effectiveness of the human interchanges in the present will affect the human interchanges of the membership in the future. But it should be noted at the outset that the reverse is not true. Changes in the present cannot change the past. This is a fantasy that most people develop to some degree, but that people who are psychologically and socially sick indulge in excessively. The past in all instances is beyond the reach of human intervention. Only the present and the future can be affected. The past is a corpse. Arrests and regression, then, can be viewed as attempts of psychological and social necrophilia, deviant and unproductive. However, we must distinguish pathological regression or arrest from regression in the service of the ego or maintenance of instrumental equipment gained in earlier periods of development (7, 8).

Human beings are open systems. They are equipped for exchanges of physiological and emotional output in such a way that the excess in one fills the deficit in the other. This is most obvious in a mother breastfeeding her child. It is also found, however, in the physiological exchanges that take place in intercourse; in the emotional exchanges that take place in nurture and love; and in the psychological exchanges that express themselves in the sharing of moods or in the readiness of one to serve as recipient of another's cathartic expressions. Ultimately, and perhaps most feasibly, it expresses itself in a division of labor between marriage partners, parents and children, and siblings. The biological equipment of human beings forms the basis of this division. Developmental differences result from different locations on the curve of maturation. Children and parents, by their very difference in physiological maturation, are forced into a division between learning and teaching, developing and making development possible.

Yet parents, even while providing instructive experiences for their children, must also learn the roles and behavior patterns of later maturity and aging. They themselves must develop while making possible the development of their children. In this respect, the maturational and developmental process of the children provides a learning stimulus for the parents. One cannot—without harm to self and to others—retain the behavior pattern of mother of infants when the children are at school; one cannot behave as the mother of children in their latency when they are in adolescence; and one cannot maintain the stance of a homemaker toward sons and daughters when they have left the parental home. Learning to take new roles and to cope with new developmental tasks, learning to let others become independent of them, and ultimately learning to become dependent on others who had once been dependent on them—these are developmental tasks that parents must accomplish. Just as children must learn gradually to give up their fantasies of omnipotence, to subordinate their strivings for autonomy to the adult power of their parents, and gradually to increase their independence, so too must parents learn to make ego and superego demands on their growing children, later on gradually to give up these demands, and ultimately to submit to the ego and superego demands that their adult sons and daughters make upon them. From this viewpoint, then, the developmental lines of parents and children are orchestrated, in the sense that the developmental attainment of one supports the developmental deficiency of the other, which in the course of time reverses the location of attainment and deficiency in the family system.

The division of labor within the family system and the resulting patterns of exchanges follow not only from different locations of the family members on the developmental curve, but also from differences in sex, natural endowment—such as physical strength or congenital activity pattern (9)—or educational experiences, and from the pattern of task assignment dictated by the culture in which the family has to operate. The division of labor according to sex represents a substantial heritage from our agrarian past. Man as the warrior and woman as the nurturer, man as the provider and woman as the homemaker, man as the person in charge of the field and woman as the person in charge of the garden, these have been time-honored arrangements that have contributed significantly to self-images related to sex. In our time, with the advent of modern technology, the differences in physical brawn usually associated with sex differences have disappeared, creating a developmental problem. A similar developmental problem has been created by the disappearance of educational differences based on sex. In consequence the traditional division of labor between husband and wife has been blurred, and the structural clarity of the family system has been lost.

Concomitant with this development, the existence of unconflicted ego ideals based on sex has suffered great interference. Instead of a division of labor based on maleness and femaleness, we now frequently have a sharing of tasks and a pooling of effort. Both husband and wife go to work; in early stages of a marriage it is sometimes the husband who spends his time studying and investing the use of his time in preparation for the future, while the wife through her participation in the labor force bcomes the breadwinner. Even so, however, the system character of the family asserts itself when one of the two spouses drops his assignment. The arrangement for both then will have to be changed; life plans will have to be revised and emotional realignments made. Whether labor in the family is shared or divided, the organizational principle of a system is in operation, with the result that a change in one part will bring about change in all the others. He who shares task performance with others will react unavoidably, but not necessarily predictably, against a change in his partner's contribution. He may react toward a decrease or a cessation of contribution either with hostility or with relief. He may assume a greater part of the total burden, or he may decrease or stop his own contribution. He may gain or lose in his self-image by these changes.

For purposes of classification it is convenient to divide the family system into three subsystems: the spouse system, the parents-children system, and the sibling system. Each system serves a variety of functions that can be directed toward satisfaction in the present or toward preparation for the future. The functions of the spouse system seem to fall into the following categories: interpersonal reorientation, sexual satisfaction and procreation, collaboration in the economic sphere (income acquisition and income use), and ego support. In the first area, the spouses use themselves to provide each other with new anchors of intimate association as differentiated from those provided by their parents. Later on they permit each other to find such anchors partly in their children. They thus furnish each other with help in interpersonal reorientation that is related to the past, the present, and the future. In the sexual area, they provide each other with testing grounds of their readiness for biological completion and procreation, and with an opportunity for approved gratification of a major biological urge that otherwise can be gratified only at the price of social risk. In the economic sphere, they provide each other with a measure of economic security not attainable in single life. In our society, at least, they pool the earning potential of two adults, providing each other with the experience of tangible property and with some relief of the burden that comes from a division of labor in property use and property maintenance. Most important, perhaps, they support each other in the maintenance of their ego strength, both defensive and autonomous.

Probably one of the most damaging failures in ego support results from a marriage in which the defenses of one person interfere with the maintenance of the defenses of the other (10). Unresolved oedipal conflicts will frequently lead people into marriages with partners whose very personality expressions mutually invite the return of the repressed. Chance, however, may lead to similar unforunate combinations, particularly in arranged marriages or marriages of convenience. In the sphere of autonomous ego function, spouses help each other to learn spouse roles, parental roles, and ultimately, the roles of retirement from both parenting and jobs. Throughout, each helps the other to express his identity. Failure in these areas of course will produce dissatisfaction in the present and therefore unreadiness to prepare for the future, because attempts at remedying the present will preoccupy both marriage partners and monopolize their thought, their work, and their emotions. Over a period of time, this will negatively affect their ability to give to one another, through the impairment of their self-images.

In the literature of human growth and development the functions operating in the system between parents and children have been presented with an emphasis on what parents have to do for their children, but with little attention to the reciprocal functions on the children's part. It is axiomatic that parents must provide nurture to their children in age-appropriate dosages. They must submit unconditionally to the nutritional and emotional demands of their infants; they must engage in toilet training during the anal period; they must respond to the oedipal reaching-out of their children with reassuring affection and restraint, provide the proper school experiences in the latency period, in preadolescence, and in adolescence. They must be available to meet their children's developmental needs, but must also control demands from their children that might impede the growth process through symbiotic attachments. They must prepare their children for adult life and then be ready to let them go and start families of their own. In the psychoanalytic frame of reference, mothers particularly are exhorted to spend the first five or six formative years with their children, to give up their employment and the utilization of their professional training until the children are ready to assume membership in an absorbing peer society.

All this is presented as a one-way passage in which children are not asked to render return services to their parents; and it should cause little surprise that under such conditions many mothers find it difficult not to be rejecting of their children. That so many of them manage is due to the fact that children do have functions serving the needs of their parents and that they fulfill them, albeit without knowing that they do. First of all, they give the experience and the status of parenthood to their fathers and mothers; they attest to the virility of the father and the fertility of the mother, thereby confirming the sexual adequacy of the parents in the appropriate dimensions. In the ages of pubescence and adolescence, they usually assist in home maintenance in one form or another, although parents are sometimes confused about their right to accept such services and pay for dish-washing after parties or for lawn-mowing (11). The children also support the self-image of the parent as adult by the contrast their own physiological, emotional, and mental status presents. In adolescence and adulthood they represent the harvest of the human crop; they increase the social network of the parent (12). Through their school contacts, their contacts on the job, and their marriages, they promote the articulation between the family system created by the marriage of their parents and other social systems. Finally, they embody the promise of security and support for the old-age dependency of their parents. In some religious systems children represent the absolution for the sexuality of their parents; and for the irreligious they represent the promise of biological continuity beyond death. Throughout the growth process they furnish the parents with a certain relief of loneliness, beginning with the repetitive comfort of their positive body responses as infants through their reliable presence in the home before they attain independence. Ultimately they furnish most parents with the gratification of being creators, or at least stimulators, of personality development in other human beings, and with the superego pleasures of serving the needs of others more than the needs of self. It should be noted, however, that most functions of children toward their parents are related to the automatic factors of existence and maturation, while most parental functions are expressions of ego adaptation and thus depend on the exercise of volition.

The functions of the sibling relationship for individual health have long been underrated or simply disregarded. First of all brothers and sisters release one another from a growth environment in which they are under the shadow of unreachable models. Mothers and fathers are so far advanced in physiological and intellectual attainments that any hope to match them must appear unrealistic, or too distant in time to support the child's ego in the here and now. Siblings, however, are by nature of their age reachable models. In most instances a child can see it will take only a few years before he is at the point in development where his brother or sister is now. Anchor points provided by the school system support this manageable perspective. Not only do brothers and sisters provide models; they also provide competitors who can be defeated. They provide one another with baselines for identity formation. Identity means to be similar and yet different. What better framework of orientation could be found for the attainment of such a goal than that provided by the personalities of one's brothers and sisters? Although nobody wants to be completely like somebody else, he does not want to be completely different either. The perception of a brother or sister provides the growing individual with both a feeling of likeness and a feeling of difference—i.e., with a feeling of identity to which in healthy development he can say yes, in preference to the identity of another.

A brother and a sister provide for each other an encounter with the other sex on the level of one's own generation—an opportunity to perceive persons of the other sex as human beings who do not have the adult's claims to superiority. Siblings also provide one another with the only permissible associate for intimate discussions of their parents. They provide one another with biological continuity and unity after the death of their parents. They form a special community of familial destiny that nobody else can enter. They teach one another to live with scarcity, emotional and economic. Perhaps most important, they teach one another that expressions of hostility can be survived both by the one who expressed it and by the recipient. Thus they teach one another the powerful arts of making war and making peace. They learn from one another that peace follows war, but also that war follows peace; in other words, they teach one another realism in a way parents cannot. They also learn interpersonal relationship rank order on the peer level. To be the oldest brother of brothers, the youngest brother of brothers, the oldest brother of sisters, the youngest brother of sisters, the oldest sister of brothers, and so on, would seem to have a remarkable interpersonal orientation impact for later life (13).

In such a welter of simultaneously operating relationships among spouses, several children, and possibly dependent aging parents as well, dysfunctions are likely to occur. Every increase of complexity is likely to increase the risk of functional failure. Every failure in one area of family functioning will affect the functioning of family members in other areas. It would be unrealistic to make the smooth functioning of all members in all three subsystems of the family a criterion of normality. We must assume that all family systems can tolerate a measure of dissatisfaction in the here and now without impeding the future development of their members. It is known that every physiological organism has the capacity for self-repair (14), if no infection sets in; and sometimes even an infected wound will heal. The common cold—albeit without known remedy—will disappear; schizophrenics burn themselves out. The capacity of spontaneous recovery is one of the most remarkable qualities of organic systems. Apparently a similar mechanism is also at work in the social system of the family. Frequently one can notice a tendency on the part of family members to change their behavior in response to change in one member in such a way as to maintain the basic operating theme of their system. No self-repair or reestablishment of the homeostatic system is ever complete, for its very occurrence represents an element of stress which, in accumulation, will finally kill the system. In recovery from mutilation, we have only the dramatization of a universal phenomenon; the loss connected with recuperation may be great or small, noticeably disabling or inconspicuously weakening, but there is always some expenditure of system vitality that is not recovered (15).

In the study of system pathology it is therefore necessary to pay particular attention to the length of time over which dysfunction occurs, because a dramatic occurrence need not be more damaging than the repetitive and prolonged impact of a minor dysfunction. In the study of human development, we have identified certain well-known constellations of dysfunction in the family system that have been associated with failure in maturation and development. The rejecting mother and the colicky baby, the seemingly normally responsive parent and the autistic child, the parent who acts out his own impulses through an adolescent son or daughter—these have become almost classical syndromes in the etiology of developmental failure. Underlying all these constellations is a system failure that produces repetitive stress, and an accumulation of deficits or excesses over time that cannot be absorbed in the process of normal wear and tear. Every mother rejects her child on occasion, but a "rejecting mother" does it frequently, probably regularly, and in massive accumulation over time. Occasionally every parent fails to respond to his child's demand for attention; it would be difficult to find a father or mother so ever-present and ever-ready that no response which the parent-child relationship calls for would ever be missed. But the autistic child seems to have parents who are permanently and hopelessly incapacitated in connection with other human beings on a primitive level (16). The girl who acts out sexually, on the other hand, frequently has a mother who routinely admonishes her to protect her sexual integrity on dates, or a father who routinely warns her about the depravity of boys. In differentiating herself from the superego of her parents or in identification with the parent's id, such a girl must engage in promiscuity, thereby fulfilling the parent's unconscious sexual striving. She also represents a developmental victim of parental system failure.

We should be careful, however, not to perceive developmental failure as a result solely of parental misfunctioning. Children also have functions in the parent-child relationship, and it might be a failure on their part that stimulates the functional failure of the parent. The child's congenital activity type may have stimulated the original reaction (8). The child's sex may stimulate latent homosexuality in a parent or frustrate his need for the continuation of the family name into the next generation. Limitations in the child's intellectual endowment may represent severe blows to the self-image of one or both parents. The self-image of the mother may be supported by the weakness and dependency of the infant but threatened by the daughter's gain in maturation and development. We know that a foster mother may have to be changed when children reach a certain age, because after a certain developmental stage has been attained the children fail to satisfy the need of this woman to nurture infants, and may actually threaten her feelings of adequacy. In natural families, however, such changes are not feasible, and children are considered for placement only after dramatic developmental damage has been done. In a much greater number of instances, we have simply situations of infantilization and symbiotic imprisonment that impede the growth process in less dramatic but also ultimately disabling ways. Such children frequently find it impossible to break the ties with their parental family, or are driven into aggressive forms of separation, such as delinquency, promiscuity, and running away, all of which have the characteristics of overdetermination in the reaction to parental dysfunction.

So far only direct failures in the exchange principle in the family system have been considered in their impact upon growth. There are, however, also indirect effects of failures in the marital system that affect growth and development of children. An unsatisfactory marital relationship will drive the spouses almost of necessity into seeking emotional compensation in the relationship with their children. The husband who is belittled by his wife, who feels that he does not get sexual responses from her that support his self-image, will be permanently tempted to seek substitute emotional gratifications from his daughter, thus driving her into an incest anxiety against which she may defend herself by promiscuity and extramarital pregnancy. The mother who is disappointed in the transference expectations that had led her to hope for a sexually satisfactory father-figure in her husband may further transfer these expectations onto her son. She may drive him into exaggerations of masculinity by the conscious or unconscious expressions of such expectations. In these instances, the children represent objects of exploitation. They are used for gratifications that the spouses should find in each other. Since they are physiologically inferior owing to age, psychologically helpless owing to the lack of development, and socially inexperienced owing to the lack of contact with other persons of significance equal to their parents, they lend themselves defenselessly to such exploitation. In unresolved oedipal striving, they may welcome this exploitation. The price they will have to pay will show up most significantly in their adolescence when, in the crisis of early encounters with heterosexuality on the level of their own generation and under the developmental demand of separation from their parents, they may be driven into panic reactions, such as sexual acting-out or psychotic withdrawal.

Thus failure in one subsystem of the family can lead to failure in other subsystems of the family and ultimately also to failure in other social systems, such as the school or employment. The juvenile delinquent or the school drop-out may be the result either of failure in the parent-child relationship or of failure in a spouse relationship of the parents, but he will appear as failure in the school system, the police system, or the community system.

REFERENCES

1. Rank, B., & Macnoughton, D., A clinical contribution to early ego development. Vol. 5. *The psychoanalytic study of the child*. New York: International Univer. Press, 1953.
2. Slawson, S. R. Extra familial parthogenesis in social science and therapy for children. In O. Pollak and Collaborators (Eds.), *Social science and psychotherapy for children*. New York: Russell Sage Foundation, 1952.
3. Homans, K. G. *Social behavior: In elementary forms*. New York: Harcourt, Brace & World, 1961.
4. Erikson, E. H. *Childhood and society*. New York: W. W. Norton, 1950.
5. Brammer, L. M., & Shostron, E. L. *Therapeutic psychology*. New York: Prentice-Hall, 1963.
6. *Webster's third new international dictionary*. Springfield, Mass.: G. & C. Merriam, 1963.
7. Kris, E. On inspiration. *Int. J. Psychoanal.*, 1939, *20*, 377–389.
8. Hecker, F. J. The discriminatory function of the ego. *Int. J. Psychoanal.*, 1962, *43*, 399.
9. Fries, M. E., & Woolf, P. J. Some hypotheses on the role of the congenital activity type in personality development, Vol. 8. *The psychoanalytic study of the child*. New York: International Univer. Press, 1953.
10. Pollak, O. Sociological and psychoanalytic concepts in family diagnosis. In B. L. Greene (Ed.), *The psychotherapy of marital disharmonies*. New York: Free Press, 1965. Pp. 15–26.
11. Pollak, O. Irresponsible parenthood. *Tenn. Pub. Welf. Rec.*, 1965, *26* (2), 27–32.
12. Bott, E. *Family and social network*. London: Tavistock, 1957.
13. Toman, W. *Family constellation*. New York: Springer, 1961.
14. Murphy, G. *Personality*. New York: Harper & Brothers, 1947.
15. Goddard, D. R. Concepts of biology: A symposium, *Behav. Sci.*, 1958, *3* (2), 151.
16. Meredith, D. Some observations of five psychotic young children. Doctoral dissertation, University of Pennsylvania, 1965.

CHAPTER 3

Family Structure: Its Implications for Mental Health [1]

Otto Pollak

Among the many definitions that Webster offers for *structure*, the one that might most profitably be used as a conceptual basis for the study of families is that of "an interrelationship of parts as dominated by the general character of the whole." Both interrelationships and character represent a wide range of variations when seen in sociological perspective. From that viewpoint, the different ways of life that are found in people from different positions in the class structure appear to be of great significance. These differences express themselves in the number of people comprising the family and the number of generations to which they belong. Even more important, they express themselves in the attitudes of the family members toward the present and the future. For this reason it is difficult to propose an ideal type—or, to use modern scientific lingo, a "model"—that could claim universal relevance. Social workers and psychiatrists, being members of the middle class, tend to gear their diagnostic thinking to the framework of a family structure composed of the parents and a few children, of both sexes. Actually there are still subcultures that operate on a three-generational basis, including grandparents in the family organization.

In the socioeconomically disadvantaged groups—which we have come to designate with the unfortunate term "lower-class"—we often find fatherless families dominated by a mother or grandmother, and relatively large numbers of children who frequently do not have the same biological father. Furthermore, we have middle-class families in which, due to divorce, the father is absent from the home, but the number of children corresponds to the model. Ultimately, we have childless families on all levels of socioeconomic stratification. Increasingly, also, we have a family structure that has not yet been discussed to any sufficient degree in the literature: the family with a retarded child who, due to birth damage or congenital defects, cannot adequately respond to the push and pull of

---

[1] This chapter is an expanded version of an article in the *Social Worker* (Canada), 1964, *32* (4).

maturation and development, but is kept at home for a period long enough to influence the developmental experiences of brothers and sisters.

In this chapter an attempt will be made to present the implications of these various family possibilities for mental health. This will be followed by an analysis of a second aspect of family structure—namely, the power relationships among the various family members and their implications for mental health. Here one word should be added about the general character of the family as a whole. Currently, parents in middle-class families are essentially conservative and try to prepare their children for the conservation of the status they have achieved. They force their children into the bureaucratic mold of our society and try to keep them performing at an educational level that will ultimately lead to college and professional training. Adolescent rebellion frequently represents only a temporary dissonance in this essentially conservative character of the middle-class family as a whole. Lower-class families, however, have a choice between living existentially or preparing for upward mobility of the children. It is the essential existentialism of the culture of the poor that challenges and occasionally defies interventive effort.

In the relatively small middle-class family, we would assume completeness of membership if both parents shared the home with a small group of children of both sexes. Here, obviously, the limitation of the membership does permit an intensity of emotional commitments to one another that cannot be found in any other organization for living. People have emotional time for one another, and there are few competitors for anybody's attention. This makes for intensity of love as well as of hate. It also furnishes only a limited number of foci for perception in human interaction. The attention of a mother is focused on a small number of children. She can afford to invest a large measure of concern, care, conflict, and even clear-cut antagonism in one or another channel of the mother-child relationship. She also is not likely to find among her children a helper in child-rearing for younger children, because the children will be close enough in age and limited enough in number to present a child-care group rather than a child-care organization. An older sister, say in her early teens, caring for a baby brother or baby sister, is hardly ever encountered in American middle-class life today. The mother is therefore faced both with a great intensity of feelings and with the concentration of a child-care demand that represents a drain on her vitality significant enough to deserve attention from the mental health point of view. It is true that the culture pattern of this group calls upon the father for a sharing of the child-care function, but it should not be forgotten that modern arrangements make his absence from the home during working hours imperative and therefore leave the mother for significant periods of time without any adult assistance in coping with the emotional demands or purely physical tasks of child-rearing. It might also be worth noting that the company of children, with their relatively low impulse control, presents an invitation to regression. A mother whose vitality is sapped through the demands of the situation would need to have her defenses strengthened by the presence of another adult. In middle-class life today, however, she is likely to be without such assistance, and she may frequently be stimulated into acting out, or at least into conflict, by a return of repressed material that the behavior of her children has stimulated.

From the children's side, the lonely presence of the mother furnishes an initial association of adult power with femininity and maternity, which is unlikely to be completely dispelled during the whole experience of the life cycle. As far as this family structure is concerned, the father plays the role of the weak male—not necessarily due to his personality characteristics, but simply due to the cycle of his absence during his hours of vitality and his return at a time when his emotional and physical resources are depleted, by coping with the demands of his job and by commuting. A father's day on the job, in an organization society, is likely to be spent under the impact of some supervisory or hierarchal arrangements in which needs for autonomy and decision-making have almost of necessity been frustrated. When he comes home, he is therefore likely to be ready either to regress into dependency or to release feelings of aggression and hostility that he had to keep under control while he was on the job. This point has to be stressed, because the recurrent concern of the clinician with the weak father is somehow based on the assumption that this is an expression of pathology and that strong fathers exist in healthy families or can be restored in client and patient families under the impact of therapy. A strong case can be made, however, that the structure of the modern middle-class family—in or out of therapy, before and after therapy—does not permit strong father-figures to come into being. Our culture, our living arrangements, and the interpersonal experiences provided in our formative years work in concert against the development of forceful masculinity as such, and particularly against its expression in the home.

The diagnostic bent in our discussions of such situations frequently dulls our perception to the strength-producing impact of existing social arrangements. Taking another viewpoint, it is possible to consider that what has been presented here and in other places as family weakness is only the price of significant achievements in personality formation, the emotional benefits to be derived from such a family structure, and its contributions to the strength of our civilization. Intensity of emotional experience prepares people for attitudinal commitment, for the empathic competence on which all adequate performance in human interaction ultimately depends, and for the willingness to sacrifice that is an essential condition of civilization.

Middle-class society has been described as anxiety-prone, unable to enjoy sexuality as it should be enjoyed and mortgaging the present too heavily in the interest of the future. This indictment overlooks the fact that guilt is one of the sources of creativity, the emotional fuel that propels men to compensate for the imperfections of the past by contributing to a better future, and ultimately one of their baselines for communication with God. For those who have a purely secular orientation, it should still be suggested that without suffering, ecstasy could not be perceived nor experienced.

From a purely sociological point of view, it should be stressed that the modern middle-class family, with its quasi-matriarchal structure, represents a reaction to the patriarchal arrangements that, for most of recorded history, have provided the mold of human existence. The power that the wife and mother enjoys in the middle-class family structure today is probably necessary for a transition to arrangements of real equality between male and female. Seen from this vantage point, the setting of therapeutic goals may have to shift from its current emphasis on strengthening the male and weakening the female—which, in a misleading fashion, has been called "helping people to accept their sex"—to a relationship between the sexes in which difference can be acknowledged without the need to associate it with a relationship of superiority and subordination. The very phraseology used in proposing that one should accept one's sex implies that biological destiny is hardship rather than potential for fulfillment. One is always asked to accept the unacceptable, but it is highly questionable whether being either male or female can truly fall into this category.

Most important, perhaps, the intensity of feeling and the importance of dynamics in the close interrelationships of the middle-class family structure present a unique counterweight to the shallowness of affect, the fleeting nature of human association, and the damage to the self-image that organizational life in our society creates. In an organization, a human being must be replaceable. Prima donnas or people with unique abilities are more harmful than beneficial. Their moods, their mobility, and ultimately their mortality are all threats to the smooth flow of organizational life. Where the outcome of a process depends on the coordination and appropriate sequence of a multitude of effort, the individual human being must be replaceable and therefore insignificant as an individual. One of the greatest ego pleasures, however, and one of the basic conditions for one's feeling of adequacy, is a positive self-image—a feeling of being needed and irreplaceable. The modern middle-class family, by being a hotbed of emotions, provides the perfect counterpoint to organizational life which can do without shallowness of interpersonal relationships only at the peril of being disrupted.

If we now turn to the three-generation family, we will find other advantages and other disadvantages. Where grandparents, parents, and children are present in the home, it is obvious that the whole life cycle is represented in the membership. People who grow up in three-generation families are less surprised by aging and less scared by the phenomenon of death than are people who have grown up in two-generation families. Not only does dependency appear to be a condition of development that is bound to be redeemed by independence in maturity; it is experienced in its reality as the beginning and the end of the life cycle. Thus independence gains its proper place in the perception of the life cycle, as an intermediate period between growth and decline, but not as a heaven of human development that succeeds the purgatory of childhood and adolescence.

Three-generation families are likely to be found among people who still have sufficient religious beliefs to experience the dimension of time in the perspective of a life after death. Aging then becomes preparation for transcendence, and dying a transition. It liberates life experiences from the burden of reality-testing, because the ultimate outcome of man's ambition and striving is projected into the hereafter. Grandparents in such families are not seen as representing decline in human experience, but as ascending toward a more meaningful future.

It is of course true that any family, whether a two-generation or a three-generation family, can have only one mother figure. In three-generation families, maternal authority must either be abdicated by the grandmother or not be claimed by the biological mother. If a house divided cannot long endure, maternity divided can produce nothing but havoc. For this reason, the joining of a two-generation family by the aging mother of either husband or wife is likely to create a family structure that represents pathology rather than a cultural alternative to the two-generation family. People who have grown up in two-generation families have not learned to give up power, or not to claim it, upon attainment of social and biological maturity. Dependency in old age has to be learned while one is still young. A family structure comprising three generations can therefore be experienced as acceptable and strengthening only by those who have grown up in it. It is one of the tragedies of our time that advances of medicine, and probably also the benefits of our relative abundance, have prolonged the life span for people who have grown up in two-generation families and are now experiencing a dependency that makes them needful of living in a three-generation family. This is a condition of living for which neither their adult sons or daughters nor they themselves are prepared.

This situation is aggravated by the fact that, in two-generation families, parents frequently consider the relationship to their children as a one-way passage in which parents serve the children, but children do not have to render any service in return. "Collecting" from people whom one has reared in the expectation of "owing nothing" is always a precarious undertaking, and many aging parents find out too late that this is so.

Another mental health consequence of living in a three-generation family is a balance among the claims of the young, the mature, and the aging for emotional attention and allocation of material goods. When parents have only to consider the allocation between themselves and their children, the weakness of the young becomes seductive. In the so-called "child-centered" family, it seems normal to allocate more to the children than to the parents—in other words, to put offspring first. Where grandparents as well as children have to share in what is to be allocated, a balance of perception may well suggest not only a more even distribution between young and old but also a more equitable share for the mature and middle-aged who carry the responsibility and burden for the whole structure. Where such conditions of balance exist, a decrease in allocation to the young and old may not seem too high a price for greater equanimity of the parents and spouses who represent the center and baseline of the organization. Self-sacrificing parents are likely to be resentful parents.

Resentment, however, vitiates the effects of giving, and if the hypothesis that the balancing of demands in the three-generation family produces greater allocation to the parents and spouses is valid, then it is equally likely that these adults will carry their responsibilities with a degree of emotional comfort that will make whatever they have to give less conflicted, and therefore more productive, than it could be under conditions predicated upon different family structures.

Another mental health effect of the presence of grandparents in the home may be the sense of continuity that they will derive from permanent and intimate contact with grandchildren. This will probably support them in coping with the inroads of aging upon their own ego functions, and support their self-image by the gestalt of a family constellation in which they do not have to compare themselves only with adults at the height of their maturity but also with children at various levels of maturation and development.

Finally, their presence may relieve a mother from the acting-out stimulation that intimate and exclusive contact with children is likely to produce, which I have highlighted as one of the emotional hazards of the mother in the middle-class two-generation family.

Fatherless families are found in various forms. The father may be missing because he played only a biological and ephemeral role, never married the mother, and has disappeared from her life. The father may be absent because he deserted the mother after marriage. He may be absent as a result of divorce and assignment of the children to the care of the mother, as is customary in most instances. He may be absent because of death. The family structures that are created by conceptions out of wedlock can appropriately be designated as "uncompleted" families, and should be differentiated from "broken" families where a father was once present but has disappeared from the family membership.

The uncompleted family, in which we have an unmarried mother and children, who may be only half-brothers and half-sisters because the mother had relationships with several men, can occur on the two-generational or three-generational level. In some instances, the grandmother represents the family head while the mother remains in a daughter relationship to her, and the grandchildren look to her as the ultimate maternal figure. Here the mother is probably conflicted between tendencies that make her feel like a sibling of her own children and tendencies that make her wish to fill the mother role. Role conflict is likely to occur and to produce shifting behavior that must confuse the children as to the person of the mother and the nature of maternity.

Girls growing up in such homes are likely to gain two impressions that make for a perpetuation of such family structure. They will gain very negative and devaluative impressions of men, because they will have encountered them mostly as fleeting contacts of their biological mother—exchangeable, unreliable, and possibly not the exclusive partners of their mother, even for the period of their appearance. They may also have encountered them as brothers, who, surrounded by women of three generations while themselves confined to the formative years, will appear to be drowning insignificantly in an ocean of femininity, truly the material of which the paramours of mother seem to be made. The male children in such families will grow up without the superego formation resulting from the fear of the family in oedipal conflicts, and be sexually mobile far into adult life; but they will also be driven by a burning hatred of women, likely to break out in frequent bursts of violence.

It is not possible, however, to grow up in such a family and not know that in our society there are other and more desirable family structures, and that one belongs to a structure that is looked down upon by many people who seem to be better off economically and emotionally than the members of one's own family. There will be added to the negative evaluation of masculinity a negative self-image, and there is the likelihood of an attitudinal development that borders on depression, relieved only by a more-or-less permanent pattern of immediate impulse gratification, when and where an opportunity appears. Here the pleasure principle reigns supreme; promiscuity is likely to be found in the young, obesity in the middle-aged and the old, and physical aggressiveness at all levels of maturation. If it were not for these pleasures, questionable as they may seem to be from the mental health point of view, one might well ask whether depression would not destroy these lives, producing either psychotic conditions or suicide. Such pleasures may not produce mental health, but they will sustain the capacity to hang on to physical existence.

In the broken family, a woman is left with children, and she, as well as her sons and daughters, has to cope with emotions about the father's disappearance. If the father has deserted, there is no certainty that he will not reappear, so the disorganization created by his absence cannot be combatted with definite plans of reorganization. The feeling that desertion represented an act of irresponsibility may mean for the mother that she made a mistake in mate selection or failed in giving her husband enough gratification to make him wish to stay with her. The self-image of the deserted wife is unlikely to hold up well under the impact of such self-questioning. It will probably be further burdened by difficulties in keeping the family going without the support of an adult male, without the freedom to consider remarriage, and, in many instances, without an adequate economic basis.

The children of a father who has deserted may either reproach the mother for not having been able to hold the father, or blame themselves for not having been able to do so. Oedipal fantasies may come into play, if the desertion has occurred after a child has reached the age of three, and may be revived even if it has occurred at a stage when the oedipal involvement can be assumed to have yielded to repression. Daughters may ask themselves whether they have failed the way mother did and have driven the father away. Sons may wonder whether their death wishes for the father have produced his disappearance. The future adult attitudes of the children may be affected in similar ways. A daughter may wonder whether she will be able to hold a husband. A son may consider the marriage situation as something from which he in turn will be able to escape.

Compensatory reactions may also occur. Children may form over-determined wishes to achieve better success in marriage than their parents did, and thus set a baseline for patterns of marital interaction in which they will proceed not according to the demands of the situation but according to apprehensions of failure that originated in the interaction pattern of their parents.

The mental health impact of deserting fathers who return is likely to be even more confusing. What kind of father image or husband image can be developed in such situations, and what type of ego ideal can be developed? It would seem to me that in situations such as these, healthy personality development can be based only on a utilization of negative feelings that are used to score against the unreliable father and, by implication, the inadequate mother, through the formation of an ego which is distinguished from the ego of the father by greater reliability and from that of the mother by greater effectiveness.

In the family broken by divorce, similar feelings between mother and children will of course be aroused, but there will be a lesser amount of uncertainty. The whereabouts of the father will usually be known. The legality of the situation will provide a baseline for reorientation. However, the visiting rights of the absent father may well provide a complicated situation. A visitor is always on his best behavior, and so is the host. The relationship between the children and the father during the visit can hardly be a true father-child relationship. It will not occur in the mainstream of daily life. It will have holiday implications or, in more unfortunate situations, the implications of a battle, an occasion for the children to fight the battle of the mother and an occasion for the father to fight the battle against his wife. And the children, instead of being guests, will be used as auxiliaries in emotional warfare, their hostilities exploited for purposes of gratifying the hostility of the parents.

At home the disappearance of the father in broken families will produce inappropriate role assumption and, in consequence, role confusion and role conflict. Mothers will try to be fathers as well as mothers to their children. Sons will try to be husbands as well as sons to the mother, and maybe even fathers to their siblings. Almost without a possibility of escape, mothers and sons in broken families will be forced into roles inappropriate for their age and sex. One is almost driven to say that the only human beings in such a family who are not immediately affected by the role confusion are the daughters of the divorced couple, because the mother is still present. However, if the mother also tries to be father to them, their concept of masculinity may be indeed confused beyond the ranges of developmental tolerance.

The family in which the father has disappeared from the family structure through death will have to cope with the same role confusion and role conflict as the family in which he has disappeared through divorce or desertion. But there will not be—at least on the conscious level—the same degree of self-reproach on the part of either the mother or the children. There will also be the outside support of sympathy on the part of family, friends, and representatives of the wider community. Unconsciously the

widow and the children may blame themselves for the apparent fulfillment
of whatever hostile wishes they had against the father. They may also have
to suffer self-blame for not having been kind enough to the departed, not
loving enough, not giving enough. They may blame themselves for having
hurt him and damaged him, and they may have to do all this under the
shadow of irrevocability. Still, community support will come to the
bereaved family and provide a basis for repression. There will be neither
the disturbances created by visiting of the divorced father nor the apprehensions about return of the deserting father, and ultimately there will
also be the conscious recognition that death is beyond the control of
human existence, while divorce, desertion, and pregnancy out of wedlock
are not.

It is important to point out that here we have a significant difference
between the uncompleted and the broken family. In the broken family
people try to make up for the absence of the father. In the uncompleted
family they do not. In the broken family we have phantom fathers upon
whom fantasies can project desirable and undesirable traits. In the uncompleted family there is no recipient for projection. The uncompleted family
is truly the fatherless family.

As has been intimated at the beginning of this chapter, structure does
not imply only an inventory of membership; it implies also a distribution
of power and of function. It is difficult to discuss the differential power of
family members in a democratic society. As a matter of fact, it is difficult
to discuss the family in a democratic society, because the family is by its
very nature an organization of unequals separated from one another by
unalterable differences in age and sex. A mental climate that advocates
equality is almost by definition unsuited for correct, or at least unconflicted, perception of the distribution of power in the family and for acknowl-
edging mental health aspects of such power distribution. In the last
decades we have seen strange attempts to adapt democratic concepts to
family life. There was a time when Margaretha Ribble (1) presented the
world with the proposition that infants had rights, a time when Hilde
Bruch (2) assured parents that they need not be afraid of their children,
and more recently a phase when people writing on parent education began
to elaborate the theme that parents also had rights. There is a kind of
pathetic humor in these attempts to reconcile civic ideals with the reality
of generational and sexual heterogeneity. The family council in which
family matters are supposedly discussed between parents and children is
another, and in most instances patently dishonest, attempt to bring the
political concept of democracy into the nonpolitical organization of
family structure.

If we want to retain our diagnostic sanity, we have to free ourselves
from the spill-over of political ideals into a nexus of nonpolitical phenomena. As far as we know, patriarchal arrangements have been the expression
of family power for most of recorded history. There is some suggestion
that in prehistoric times matriarchy dominated family structures, and
there exists some empirical evidence that this is so again in many families.

There is no question that ideologically we should like to think of egalitarian power constellations between husband and wife. In terms of mental health implications, however, it would seem to me that we must first evaluate patriarchal versus matriarchal forms as possible molds for personality development. In the perspective of history, the status quo has always proved to be wrong, and the farther back we go in history the more unacceptable the arrangements of the human condition appear to us. In this perspective alone, mankind has reached its verdict about matriarchal arrangements.

As a matter of fact, it is just this rejection of matriarchy, which is somehow ingrown in our system of social development, that makes for the vindictiveness of the clinical indictment against the strong mother and the weak father. But it is interesting to note that very little dynamic analysis has been devoted to the mental health aspects of patriarchal arrangements. A number of propositions might be considered in this respect. Both male and female infants encounter adulthood in terms of femininity, and this specifically in terms of maternity. Even the transitional "love objects" identified by D. W. Winnicott (3) are part of the female body structure. Therefore, from the most primitive level of perception almost up to the genital stage of psychosexual development, femininity represents exclusive power to the growing child. Social arrangements in our school system perpetuate this impression well into high school age. The fact that women have to bear the burden of the physiological consequences of conception has brought us to make young girls the guardians of morality in their social contacts with young men. In marriage, with husband absent, they are forced to fill the demand for authority existing in every family structure.

Under such conditions, it is difficult for the male child ever to acquire an adequate self-image if he compares his sexual identity with that of the other sex. It requires almost an overdetermined compensation for these formative impressions to produce an adequate self-image in the male, and family power arrangements of patriarchy seem to have provided that. Patriarchy has always been a phenomenon somewhat akin to reaction formation, but at least it provided balance to the one-sided impact upon male personality formation of having to encounter adulthood first of all, and in essence for most of his life, in terms of femininity associated with maternal traits. It is the adequacy of the male that permits him, as a father, to be sufficiently secure in response to the oedipal reaching-out of his daughter to make her feel a worthy love object of an adequate male. It is my impression that patriarchy was probably most beneficial in permitting daughters to feel like girls and future wives rather than like future mothers. Actually, one could propose that, for both sexes, adequate self-images as desirable love objects may well have been more easily attainable under patriarchal arrangements than under matriarchal arrangements, because under matriarchy males must remain boys and females are not permitted to be girls. Under patriarchy, both sexes can go through the full cycle of development. Boys can become men, and mothers are permitted to start out as girls and possibly remain girls in relation to their husbands.

Patriarchal arrangements, however, have been possible basically only under conditions of civilization in which the superiority of muscular power with which the male is equipped had social and economic significance. Under conditions of mechanization, this social and economic advantage is lost. Under political conditions of democracy it is made morally questionable, and at any rate the wheel of history does not turn back. It is therefore a moot question whether patriarchal arrangements are more conducive to mental health than matriarchal arrangements. The question that we must ask ourselves for the future is how the current condition of quasi-matriarchy can be turned into a truly egalitarian arrangement. Ideally—and hypothetically—the mental health demand posed by sexual diversity in the family structure could be formulated in the following desideratum: An egalitarian structure of the family would have to be confined to husband and wife. There cannot be equality between maturity and immaturity. Equality, however, is also incompatible with difference, and it might be well to propose equity as the governing principle of human relations within the family structure of the future. Seen from the baseline of our experience of past failures, it might be suggested that it would be equitable for a male in the family to grow up into adulthood and for a female not to be prematurely forced into it. Femininity, then, would be that type of behavior on the part of a female that would permit a male to grow up and to act as a grown-up. Masculinity would be behavior in a male that would permit a female to act young, to abandon the maternal stance in the marital relationship and even in the courtship relationship, and ultimately to give the male a future and the female a past. On that basis, specificity on various levels of development can replace arrest in power positions that in the flow of time must either have been or must become inappropriate.

When women will permit boys to become men, and men will be able to help women to be girls, the power structure of the family of the future may become equitable on the spouse and parental level. Equality of the family structure for the children, however, would again not mean priority in allocation, as we are inclined to practice it now, or equality in decision-making, as we frequently pretend, but support through opportunity and encouragement in the development of the autonomous functions of the ego and limitation and protection against impulse stimulation in the development of the defensive functions of the ego. In the constellation of encouragement and control, the child will be more equitably provided with the pleasures of development. A barrage of opportunities and a lack of impulse control created by insecure and frequently immature parents is no recognition of equality in children; it is the abdication of the responsibility of decision-making that power always implies. In that sense, a refusal to accept power differentials between parents and children seems to be an abdication of responsibility in decision-making that is one of the great dangers of our times.

REFERENCES

1. Ribble, M. A. *The rights of infants.* New York: Columbia University Press, 1943.
2. Bruch, H. *Don't be afraid of your child: A guide for perplexed parents.* New York: Farrar, Straus and Young, 1952.
3. Winnicott, D. W. *Mother and child: A primer of first relationships.* New York: Basic Books, 1957.

CHAPTER 4

Delinquency and the Family System

Alfred S. Friedman

Those concerned with the increasing and difficult problem of juvenile delinquency in this country have listed among its varied expressions: antisocial behavior, acts of violence, organized prejudice, bullying and scapegoating, sexual rebellion and promiscuity, compulsive search for new thrills, drug addiction, alienation, withdrawal from society and from its accepted standards and values, tendencies to anarchy, severe conflict with parental attitudes and the goals of family life, overconformity with the delinquent peer group, confusion over personal identity, and vulnerability to adolescent mental breakdown.

Part of the confusion and disagreement regarding its etiology has been due to viewing delinquency as an entity, which it is not. Various types of persons and problems have been lumped together wholesale under this term. Some of the diverse types characterized as "delinquents" are: the socially deprived, those who grew up in a delinquent family, the neurotic "criminals from a sense of guilt," the mentally handicapped or retarded, the character-disordered, the sex deviant, the psychotic, and the so-called "pure psychopath."

Delinquent behavior is found in combination with other types of personality disturbance as often as it is found in the "pure" form of asocial, antisocial, or illegal behavior—if such "pure" cases ever really occur at all. Delinquents are frequently reported to have character defects, neuroses, sexual perversions, paranoid personality, borderline psychosis, or psychosis in remission. Delinquency may be a component reaction, which in some circumstances occupies the center or the core of an individual's character and behavior, and which under other circumstances appears only at the periphery. The "pure psychopathic personality" is usually considered to have the following traits: antisocial conduct, impulsiveness, defective control and judgment, egocentricity, immaturity, no consideration of the rights of others, lack of guilt reaction, inability to empathize, and shallow emotionality.

In the psychodynamic view, delinquent acting-out behavior is a substitute for, or an avoidance of, development of a symptom. There is an inability to internalize conflicts or to convert the inner tensions related to primary instinctual tendencies into acceptable substitute modes of behavior. Instead, the inner conflict and related anxiety are avoided by experiencing it as a conflict between the self and the environment. Conflict is provoked or engaged in with the environment—which is perceived to be like a person who is withholding gratification—as a means of tension reduction. One might ask whether this battle between the self and the environment is really just a defensive reaction—a displacement to avoid inner tension, as considered in the psychodynamic view—or whether there is also some reality basis for the grievance and the battle with the environment. After all, many nondelinquent, as well as delinquent, individuals try to change the environment rather than changing themselves.

Seen from the family system point of view, the adolescent delinquent externalizes, rather than internalizes, the unresolved, suppressed, and unspoken parental conflicts. His acting-out serves as a release valve for unstable, unendurable family tension, and may even function as a homeostatic stabilizing procedure for the family. But at other times his acting-out behavior takes a form that is unacceptable to his parents or to himself and thereby precipitates a family crisis.

When the choices provided within a family by parents and siblings might tend to psychotically overwhelm a child, and the neighborhood and larger community do not provide any constructive opportunities or substitutes, it may then be a more positive outcome for that child to escape psychosis by engaging in a struggle to change his environment, even if this results in delinquent behavior. This observation obviously holds only for some of the more extreme cases, since not every delinquent is threatened with psychosis. There are many other delinquents, however, who while not vulnerable to psychosis are still not provided with constructive outlets and substitutes for their inner tensions.

Another current view in the mental health field is to regard delinquency less psychodynamically and less in terms of the abnormal, psychopathological, or bizarre, and more in terms of immaturity in emotional and social development. This includes a low tolerance of frustration, willfulness, a feeling of being cheated, and an angry, shameless, demanding attitude. According to this view, depth psychotherapy which uncovers the unconscious is considered to be less indicated for most cases than a long-term re-education of attitudes, character, and emotions.

There are still other observers who consider that focusing on traits, pathology, and deviancy—whether these are viewed as consciously or unconsciously determined, and whether the delinquents are regarded individually or in groups—is a misplaced emphasis which misses the main point. They see delinquency as a problem in the organization of our society and look to solve it by implementing social, economic, and political change. One current point of view (1) is that other delinquent peers, and not the parents, supply the important frame of reference, sources of support, and identification models for the delinquent adolescent. Accordingly, to concentrate on changing the delinquent's relationship with his or her parents would mean: (*a*) to treat him as an unstable isolate without a meaningful reference group; (*b*) to fail to recognize the intrinsic nature of his membership in the delinquent system; and (*c*) to fail to treat that system.

It appears to us that while there is some merit to this view, it deals with only one side of the problem. We consider the young delinquent still an integral part of his family system, not an isolate. Whether his family wants to reject or isolate him, or whether he wants to divorce himself from his family, he is psychologically still an integral part of that family system. But we do not, at the same time, minimize the importance or the force of the delinquent peer-group culture. The lives of many delinquents, particularly those from low-income families, are conditioned by environmental stimuli and situations that limit their access to the conventional successes and satisfactions of our larger society. They lack the skills and the opportunities for participation, and they are frustrated and ambivalent toward the values of the society. Membership in a delinquent system is then seen as an alternative means for attempting to acquire social, economic, and emotional satisfactions (2). Delinquent acts are not necessarily private and secret deviations; others may participate, provide techniques, and give sanction, and the perpetrator of the act may thereby gain status in the group.

We differ with this conceptualization only when it denies the possible ongoing importance of the family in the delinquent's life, negating the family system completely in favor of the peer-group system. The intergenerational conflict is not always the overriding factor, and the break and separation between the delinquent and his or her parents is not always complete. The problems and patterns of one generation actually appear to follow almost inevitably into the next. The parents as well as the children—whole families, groups of families, and large segments of neighborhoods—are often caught up together in what is allegedly a "delinquent" group culture. The delinquency is the product of development over two or three generations of socioeconomic conditions, values, and attitudes—toward human relationships, toward work, toward sexual relationships, and toward law and constituted social authority—most of which are detrimental to the individuals involved. Parents and children share attitudes and behavior that do not conform to the standards, or comply with the vested authority, of the larger society or of traditional middle-class morality. Certainly a part of delinquent rebelliousness and contempt for middle-class values stems from being deprived of the opportunity to afford the better learning opportunities and better living conditions implied in these values.

Regardless of the relative merits of the differing points of view presented above, we postulate here that juvenile delinquency is multiply determined, influenced by a multiplicity of interdependent and interpenetrating factors—social, economic, political, historical, cultural, geographic, familial, and personal. Also, a particular delinquent individual may tend to be either more "psychologically" delinquent—i.e., internally motivated to act out his or her delinquency—or more "sociologically" delinquent, in which case his or her delinquent behavior is primarily determined by the social environment.

The recent pilot programs started in California and New York City—in which the offender, the *product* of the social problem, participates in *solving* the problem—are apparently consistent in their concept with the theoretical sociological formulation described above. They imply that the social authorities, as well as the delinquent boys, must change in their attitudes and approaches to the problem. The offender is recruited into the "professional corps," given a training or research role, a status, and a salary, and given the responsibility for solving the delinquency problem. The question arises whether this is just a trick or maneuver to take the leadership away from the delinquency subculture, in the guise of appearing to give it leadership and responsibility. Whenever anyone accepts a request from another person to take over a problem or solve a problem, he is giving up a degree of freedom of choice and of authority in that relationship. This then can be seen as a maneuver (similar to that employed at times in psychotherapy, when the therapist refuses to comply with the request to provide practical solutions) which may work because it saves face for the alienated or defiant delinquent. This approach may be more constructive, however; it may facilitate a dynamic interaction between the representatives of the delinquent subculture and the representatives of the larger culture, leading to modifications in philosophy and structure both in the offenders and in the institutions of the community.

We address ourselves not only to the effects of the emotional and behavioral conditioning of the delinquent adolescent historically, within his particular family, but even more importantly to the current, ongoing effects of the family system on the delinquent adolescent, and to his current role relationships and assignments within the family. We consider juvenile delinquency in one of its aspects as a manifestation of a disordered or deficient family system.

Healy (3) stressed the etiological importance of the "family drama" in delinquency as far back as 1915. Reiner and Kaufman (4) studied and treated a series of eighty parents of juvenile delinquents at the Judge Baker Guidance Center in Boston. They found that a majority of the parents fell into the category of "impulse-ridden character disorders," and they reported some success with their long-term casework and counseling approach to these difficult cases. They speculated that the delinquency was an attempt to deal with early deprivation and object-loss, by striking out at and taking from the environment. They saw the goal of their psychotherapy as helping the delinquent and his parents go from their denial of affect to an awareness of their underlying depression.

Nathan Ackerman (5) has reported that while he, like others, found the "delinquent" psychopathic adolescent virtually untreatable in isolation from his family and community, he could "successfully alleviate psychopathic behavior in adolescents when oriented to it as a family process, with the adolescent representing a symptom of the psychopathological warp of his family group, or a component of psychopathic behavior in the family structure." This conviction was derived from clinical experience, and obviously has yet to stand the test of a controlled evaluation.

Among attributes observed clinically in the multiple-delinquency-producing families of low socioeconomic status studied and treated by

Minuchin et al. (6) at Wiltwyck School were: lack of consciousness of themselves as constituting an integrated family unit; lack of organization, structure, and cohesiveness in regard to family role relationships; global, vague, and undifferentiated perception of childhood experiences and development in these families; paucity of verbal symbols, lack of communication, or limited, stereotyped communication; lack in parental functioning, specifically in regard to providing executive control and guidance and in setting limits. When the parental roles of responsibility and authority are defaulted, the sibling subsystem often takes over the socialization process and gains more power than it can properly handle. Mothers, in their understanding of their role, often rely heavily on the function of nurturing, and feel guilty if they do not provide material supplies even beyond their realistic capabilities.

We arrived at similar clinical observations when we conducted intensive conjoint family treatment in a special demonstration project with families of sexually delinquent adolescent girls. In addition, we noted the absence of an adequate family image, although the family image and the role relationships were not usually as distorted as we had found them to be in families with schizophrenic members. Poor parental marital relationships and negative components of the parent-child relationship—such as emotional deprivation, hostility, rejection, and excessive separations—appeared to exist in these families to a greater extent than in the average. Most family members were seen to be at particular levels of arrested development and immaturity beyond which the family could not foster growth. The parents at times abdicated their role responsibilities or oscillated from overly strict, punitive, and restricting attitudes toward the children's behavior to closing their eyes and ignoring the behavior altogether. They at times adopted a helpless dependent position in relation to their children, reversing the parental role and expecting emotional support, healing, and guidance from relatively young children.

Adelaide Johnson and S. A. Szurek (7) have developed a psychoanalytic family-relationship thesis of delinquent behavior, documented clinically from their concurrent therapy of adolescent children with behavior problems and their parents. This thesis is that the parents' unwitting sanction, indirect encouragement, or provocation is a major cause of, and the specific stimulus for, such antisocial behavior as unacceptable sexuality, stealing, setting fires, and truancy of young delinquents. "In every adolescent brought for treatment in whom simultaneous intensive study of the parents was possible, the child's defect in conscience was traceable to a like defect in the parent's own poor resolution of unconscious impulses to similar anti-social behavior." The child's ego and superego development is found to be weakest in those areas that correspond to the unresolved conflicts within one parent or within the parental marriage relationship. In this thesis, the delinquent "acts out" the repressed or thinly suppressed wishes, impulses, or fears of the parents. These delinquencies often arise in apparently "normal" middle-class families of good reputation, as well as in lower-class families, and are not primarily determined by poor economic and living conditions. There are many such cases, however, and they constitute an important community problem.

Following is a brief review of research studies that report evidence supporting the presence of familial factors in delinquency, i.e., significant differences found between families of delinquents and families of nondelinquents:

Gregory (8), in an anterospective study of a state-wide sample of Minnesota ninth-grade children (N = 11,329), concluded that "family status of the parents remained a significant antecedent variable in delinquency, after socioeconomic status and intelligence level were taken into consideration: Delinquency in boys was much more frequent than average among boys who lost their fathers by death, as well as among boys who experienced other varieties of parental loss in childhood. Delinquency in girls was most frequent among those whose parents had been separated or divorced, those who had lost their mother by death, those who were living with father only, and those who were living with neither parent. These findings suggest that the identification model provided, and the control normally exercised, by the parent of the same sex are more crucial in preventing delinquency among boys and girls than any aspect of the relationship with the parent of the opposite sex.

Cohen (9) similarly suggests that the relatively high rate of juvenile delinquency in the lower classes is related in part to the father's frequent physical and/or psychological absence from the home and to the aggressive "masculine protest" syndrome to which this gives rise in the sons. Using a cross-cultural design, Bacon et al. (10) found that in societies in which the father's effective presence in the household is at a minimum, there is also a relatively high rate of theft and personal crime. These correlated factors could both, however, be variables dependent on some broader economic factor. Siegman (11) found a similar effect in male medical students, presumably not from lower socioeconomic backgrounds: "father-absent" students (whose father was away in the army for at least one year during the student's early childhood) admitted more antisocial behavior on an anonymous scale than did "father-present" students.

The Gluecks' (12) classic delinquency research study compared 500 delinquent boys with 500 controls, equated for age, IQ, ethnic derivation, and residence in underprivileged neighborhoods. Some of the significant differences in families of delinquents that they reported were: (a) the family backgrounds of the parents revealed more mental retardation, more emotional disturbance, more drunkenness, more criminality; (b) more fathers were poor workers and poor wage-earners, and more families were on public relief; (c) there was more incompatibility and conflict in the parental marriages; (d) more mothers failed to provide adequate supervision for the children, and parents knew less about the activities of their delinquent sons; (e) fathers were more lacking in warmth, sympathy, and affection toward their sons, and the boys did not perceive their fathers as suitable objects for emulation; (f) the picture of the mothers' relationship to their delinquent sons was less clear and consistent than that of the fathers, in that some mothers were overprotective while others were indifferent and rejecting; (g) the total impression gave compelling evidence that the family backgrounds of the delinquent boys were less positive than those of the control boys.

Andry (13) conducted in London one of the better-controlled studies of delinquent boys, in which both the matched delinquents and nondelinquent controls lived in the same low socioeconomic geographic area, in homes with both parents. He concluded that the role of the father was as crucial as that of the mother, and questioned the theory of "maternal deprivation" (14) as a universal factor in delinquency. The delinquent boys reported: (a) less open and strong love from their parents, especially from their fathers; (b) less adequate communication from their parents, especially from their fathers; (c) a more tense home atmosphere; (d) less adequate parental training, especially from their fathers; (e) their deviant behavior was less known to and less dealt with by their parents. The importance of considering both parents is thus highlighted by this study.

McCord et al. (15) found that extreme parental neglect and punitiveness, coupled with a pathologically aggressive paternal mode, produced aggressive antisocial behavior in boys. They found the delinquent boys they studied had apparently "passive" mothers, but not "passive" fathers, more often than controls. They also found inconsistent discipline, rather than any specific form of discipline, to be more characteristic of these homes.

Bennett (16) reported a comparison of fifty delinquent children, boys and girls, with fifty neurotic children. The delinquent youngsters were found significantly *more* often to have had: (a) interrupted father-child relationships; (b) interrupted mother-child relationships; (c) unsettled home, frequent moves; (d) parents separated; (e) time spent in foster homes; (f) more than three siblings; (g) overcrowded home conditions; (h) disturbed mother-father relationship; (i) a father or mother with an antisocial or morally unstable personality; (j) inconsistent discipline; (k) less than four months of breast-feeding. The delinquent youngsters *less* often had parents who had "neurotic traits," less often manifested difficulties in adaptive behavior in the first two years of life, and less often were subject to overly strict discipline by parents.

A recent study at Devereux Schools (17) of a group of delinquents from families of higher socioeconomic status found that they had an intrafamilial experience different from that of a matched nondelinquent control group. Consistent with earlier findings of Glueck and Glueck (12), Nye (18), and others, one or both parents was found to be indifferent or openly hostile to the delinquent, or one parent was found to be overly permissive. This particular group of delinquents did not come from broken homes or grossly unstable family backgrounds more often than the controls, but this finding obviously cannot be generalized to lower-class families and neighborhoods.

Keller (19) speculated from a brief review of the literature that the

causal influence of the family (i.e., the family system, the parental personalities, etc.) on delinquent behavior may not be as crucial for lower-class
families as it appears to be for middle-class families: "In the middle-class,
where children are wholly dependent on their parents and on the general
family milieu during their formative years, the family probably does have a
decisive influence on the manifestations of delinquent behavior patterns.
Those with inadequate or unstable families may therefore experience
greater relative deprivation by comparison with their schoolmates and
friends from intact families. In the lower class, however, 'broken' and
'unstable' families are so common that the relative deprivation suffered by
the children is probably smaller, and the family's causal influence on delinquent behavior may be correspondingly reduced."

Stabenau et al. (20) have reported perhaps the first controlled comparison of whole delinquent families with normal families and schizophrenic families. The sample studied was very small, only five in each
group (attesting to the practical difficulties involved in such a controlled
study). The delinquent behaviors included sexual promiscuity, running
away, and car theft. Results obtained by the Thematic Apperception Test
and Revealed Differences Test showed that the family organization of the
delinquent offspring was unstable, and roles were not reliably executed by
the parents. The demand was for expedient action and for immediate
submission to a goal; and when the parents' standards were not met, the
child was automatically rejected. Parental affect was artificial. In the
stories told by parents of delinquents, the involvement of the parents with
the children appeared superficial and impersonal. Although the parents
were depicted as strictly demanding, coercive, and punitive, characteristically seeing immediate submission of the child as a goal, they appeared
to be superficially "proper" and "respectable" in their behavior.

In summary, the above-reviewed research and clinical studies appear to
us to develop a fairly consistent picture regarding familial factors in delinquency. If, for example, we take the Glueck study as a reference point, we
observe that most of the other studies report findings that deviate from it
only in relatively minor ways. Attributes of both the mother and father
individually; their early family backgrounds, including their parents;
qualities of their marital relationship; and the total family experiences,
past and present—all appear to be implicated. Accordingly, we consider a
family-system and family-dynamic point of view, and the treatment of the
total family situation, to be one of the appropriate approaches to the
juvenile delinquency problem.

In our past preoccupation with the individual psyche, we have not
sufficiently considered the social, emotional, and mental-health problems
of family life. Clinical examination of the whole family as an entity has
been impeded by long-standing cultural taboos. In the family treatment or
counseling approach, there is an opportunity to gain a deeper understanding of the individual members involved—in terms of their most fundamental human relationships, those of the family—as well as to gain
additional understanding of the delinquent adolescent's behavior.

REFERENCES

1. Empey, L. T., & Rabow, J. The Provo experiment in delinquency rehabilitation. *Amer. Sociol. Rev.*, 1961, *26*, 679–696.
2. Cloward, R. A., & Ohlin, L. E. *Delinquency and opportunity: A theory of delinquent gangs.* New York: Free Press, 1960.
3. Healy, W. *The individual delinquent.* London: Heinemann, 1915.
4. Reiner, B. S., & Kaufman, I. *Character disorders in parents of delinquents.* New York: Fam. Serv. Ass., 1959.
5. Ackerman, N. *The psychodynamics of family life: Diagnosis and treatment of family relationships.* New York: Basic Books, 1958.
6. Minuchin, S., et al. The study and treatment of families who produce multiple acting-out boys. Paper read at Amer. Orthopsychiat. Ass., March 1963.
7. Johnson, A., & Szurek, S. The genesis of anti-social acting-out in children and adults. *Psychoanal. Quart.*, 1952, *21*, 322–343.
8. Gregory, I. Anterospective data following childhood loss of a parent. *Arch. gen. Psychiat.*, 1965, *13*, 99–109.
9. Cohen, A. K. *Delinquent boys: The culture of the gang.* Glencoe, Ill.: Free Press, 1955.
10. Bacon, H. K., Child, I. L., & Barry, H. A. A cross-cultural study of correlates of crime. *J. abnorm. soc. Psychol.*, 1963, *66*, 291–300.
11. Siegman, A. W. Father absence during childhood and anti-social behavior. *J. abnorm. Psychol.*, 1966, *71* (1), 71–74.
12. Glueck, S., & Glueck, E. *Unraveling juvenile delinquency.* New York: Commonwealth Fund, 1950.
13. Andry, R. G. *Delinquency and parental pathology: A study in forensic and clinical psychology.* Springfield, Ill.: Charles C Thomas, 1960.
14. Bowlby, J. *Forty-four juvenile thieves: Their characters and home life.* London: Balliere, Tindall, & Cox, 1946.
15. McCord, J., McCord, W., & Howard, A. Family interaction as antecedent to the direction of male aggressiveness. *J. abnorm. soc. Psychol.*, 1963, *66*, 239–242.
16. Bennett, I. *Delinquent and neurotic children: A comparative study.* New York: Basic Books, 1959.
17. Herskovitz, H., et al. Anti-social behavior of adolescents from high socioeconomic groups. *J. nerv. mental Disease*, 1959, *129*, 467–476.
18. Nye, F. I., *Family relationships and delinquent behavior.* New York: Wiley, 1958.
19. Keller, S. The American lower class family: A survey of selected facts and their implications. Research document, New York State Division for Youth, Albany, 1965.
20. Stabenau, J. R., Tupin, J., Werner, M., & Pollin, W. A comparative study of families of schizophrenics, delinquents, and normals. *Psychiatry*, 1965, *28*, 45–59.

PART II

Socioeconomic
and Cultural Factors
in Sexual Delinquency

The papers presented in this section gain special significance in the perspective of the war against poverty, which has become the central effort of domestic reform in the mid-sixties. The refocusing of concern upon the poor has led to significant increases in awareness of the differences that distinguish middle-class culture from the culture of poverty. Additionally, the significant representation of the Negro in the poverty sector of our population has brought political questions of racial tension and discrimination within the orbit of the family therapist. These differences have been described along various dimensions, sometimes with special concern for the implications for methods and goals in therapeutic intervention.

The poor are said to be more concerned with the present than with the future; they are likely to have poor self-images because of their failure in a society that makes success a criterion for personal worth; they are said to expect from professional helpers "pills and needles" rather than talking; they are said to be more closely related to peers than to parents; and they seem to be unresponsive to representatives of the middle class such as teachers, social workers, and psychiatrists. All this creates problems in communication and in goal-setting between the professional helper and the client. Still, the poor hold out the greatest challenge. The fact that, in spite of these many handicaps, middle-class professionals can register successes with clients from socially deprived backgrounds testifies to the power of therapeutic intervention.

CHAPTER 5

Sexual Delinquency
among Middle-Class Girls

Nathan W. Ackerman

The theme of this paper is the relation between family disorder and sexual acting-out in the teen-age girl. How shall we understand the emotional disturbance of the girl and of her family? How shall we identify the special type of family equilibrium that evokes sexual delinquency in the female child?

Let us pinpoint the problem at the outset by presenting a few brief clinical vignettes. One such family, from a middle-class suburb, consists of the two parents, a son of fourteen, and a daughter of thirteen. The girl was caught with a boy in a parked car, virtually naked and engaging in sex play. This episode was merely the culmination of a whole series of such activities. She had been running off to teen-age clubs and bars, and hobnobbing with questionable characters, some of whom had police records and were addicted to drugs.

The girl's father has a relatively small printing business, earning about twenty thousand dollars a year. He is intelligent, emotionally constricted, conformist, obsessed with the goal of success, but plagued with a gnawing sense of disappointment; his status as a businessman is mediocre. The mother stays at home but chafes at her confinement. She is bright and more spontaneous than her husband, but her expressiveness is choked off by the constraints of her marital bond. Privately she cherishes a romantic dream of a more exciting, fuller life—getting out on a job and cultivating a wider set of friends—but she has compromised for the reward of a "secure" home life.

Between husband and wife there is an undercurrent of chronic tension. Sexually, the husband is demanding, can never get enough; the wife resents this, and rations her sexual response. Occasionally, he presses her to submit to sex contact other than intercouse, but she mostly fights him off. Between them there is a continual power struggle, though they are collusive in muting the overt manifestations of this competitive war.

The fourteen-year-old boy outwardly plays the game, conforming superficially to the rules of his family, but he is evasive, wily, and hypocritical. The mother laments her inability to control her daughter. She feels she cannot reach her and retreats from the battle. In so doing, she incites the father to step into the breach to enforce discipline. His approach to his daughter is detached, rigid, fault-finding, and overbearing. He rips her down for disrespect of her parents' authority, but seems blind to the child's emotional hunger and loneliness, blind also to her appealing, pretty face. In a covert, disguised way, the mother pushes her daughter toward the father and, at the same time, reproaches him for his coldness, lack of empathy, and unresponsiveness to the girl's charm and beauty.

In the meanwhile, the brother hides behind the cloak of his role as the "good" child, siding with his parents while they exploit his "goodness" as the basis for chastising his sister.

The parents make it plain that their daughter's conduct is a threat to their way of life. Their status in the community is thrown into jeopardy. They fear disgrace and react violently, virtually imprisoning the girl in her home.

In the family interview, the girl presents a picture of abject wretchedness. She sits pathetically alone, her head bowed. At first she darts poisonous glances at her parents. Feeling some acceptance and support from the therapist, she launches a caustic attack on her parents. She reproaches them bitterly for their utter lack of understanding, their unfair punishments. She exposes the empty, dull, joyless atmosphere of the home, the absence of any show of warm feeling between her parents. She vividly describes their trumped-up hypocrisy and false pretense of respectability. She shows utter contempt for the sniveling ingratiation and sneaky lying of her brother.

In another family, there are two daughters. The older one, seventeen, is involved in a liaison with a boy now in jail for car theft. She visits him in jail at irregular intervals. The boy comes from a broken family on "the other side of the tracks," is physically handicapped, and has a long history of clashes with the law. The girl had been intimate with him, became pregnant, and had an abortion arranged by her father. Prior to this involvement she had engaged in loose sexual contacts with many boys, but is now loyal to the "one and only."

The family resides in a comfortable home in a good neighborhood. The father, a business executive, married late after a period of free and easy sexual indulgence with women for whom he had no feeling whatsoever. His own mother had been a volatile, explosive woman whom he tried to avoid. When he decided finally to settle down, he consciously sought out a wife who was intelligent, reasonable, and calm, with a family background much like his own. He felt he had found just such a woman, extraordinarily steady and controlled. It turned out not to be so. To the age of twenty-six years, when she married, this woman had been a virgin. She had earlier broken an engagement with a man of a different religion, of whom her parents disapproved. Her husband initiated her into a sex life, but it meant little to her. She was merely doing her wifely duties. She conformed to her husband's pattern of life, had only rare outbursts with him, but indulged in bitter, screaming tirades with her daughter. She was rigid, unaffectionate, and carping. Mother and daughter were never close. Father and daughter were closer and more empathic. The father alleged he had a "liberal" attitude toward sex; the mother superficially copied this attitude. Despite this the parents were intensely suspicious of their daughter and checked her every movement. They accused her of lying and concealing her sexual activities. The mother forced her to submit to a vaginal examination—and yet each day both parents reminded her to be careful and checked to be sure that she took her contraceptive pill. They were frightened of the girl, placatory, and at the same time accusatory.

The girl was herself open and direct. While feeling inwardly guilty and damaged, she assumed a posture of superiority to her parents. She took them to task for their contradictory attitudes. She was flagrantly contemptuous of their fumbling, righteous efforts at self-justification. She bluntly asserted her mistrust of her parents and her conviction that her boyfriend loved her for herself, not for sex. She appreciated his kindly devotion to her. She admitted she did not enjoy sex but wanted to keep her boyfriend happy. She was saving money to rescue him from jail and hoped to keep him "on the straight and narrow."

In a third family, the father had nearly beaten his daughter to death when he caught her "making out" with a Negro boy on a park bench. The family lives in an interracial neighborhood, and when the father looks out from their apartment window and sees a Negro boy and white girl walking arm in arm, he goes into a frenzy. He is a sick man who has been in the hospital twice for a bleeding ulcer. The girl's mother is a depressed, agitated woman who has been hospitalized for her mental condition. She lives in terror of her husband's proneness to violence, goes into panic, and sobs uncontrollably. The sexual relationship between the parents has deteriorated to nothing. Father feels totally deprived, frantic. He has occasional spontaneous emissions. The daughter is desperate; she wants to leave home.

The term "delinquency" is basically a sociological concept. It refers to certain actions that are viewed as deviant and dangerous, and therefore are proscribed by the community; persons engaging in such actions come into conflict with the law or other representations of authority. Delinquency is, therefore, in no sense a psychiatric diagnosis. In its broader ramifications it is relatively nonspecific; it has multiple forms and determinants. It may be psychological, sociological, or both. In some of its manifestations, it overlaps with psychopathological conditions, but these fall into a wide range of categories: neurosis, character disorder, and psychosis. This is a significant qualifying consideration in clinical assessment of the relations of individual "delinquency" and family psychopathology.

Sexual delinquency in teen-age girls has a different significance in families of the lower, socially deprived classes than in families of the advantaged middle class. I am here concerned mainly with female sex delinquency in the middle class. In general, delinquent behavior occurs less commonly in girls than in boys. When it occurs, however, it is apt to be more extreme, less tractable, and rather more likely to have a malignant outcome. Sexual acting-out in girls is part of a deeper and broader pattern of revolt against authority. The sexual aspect becomes the vehicle for an explosive discharge of aggression. It is a common observation that a teen-age girl of this type is not yet awakened sexually, that she carries a secret prejudice against sex, is frigid, and does not enjoy the experience. On the other hand, she has somehow discovered the lure of her female body and the power of its use as an instrument for manipulating boys. She leans on sex not as pleasure but as a way of holding onto a boy, a way of assuring interest and protection, a way of denying dependency on mother, and a way of destroying female rivals.

Hidden beneath all this is a hungry, lonely child with a deeply-injured self-esteem. In paradoxical fashion, while seeking a balm for a damaged sense of self, the girl engages in sexual contact that only degrades her all the more. Often she attaches herself to a boy who, in social and familial terms, is "beneath her," one who is delinquent, emotionally deviant, and occasionally even physically deformed. It is in this setting that a white, middle-class girl sometimes gets involved with a Negro boy. The girl feels rejected, wounded, scapegoated by her family, and in reaction to this, attaches herself to one who she feels has suffered in the same way. The boy thus selected epitomizes in his personal and social identity a violent clash with the values and standards of the girl's parents and family. Boy and girl "mother" one another; they cuddle to supply one another with compensatory warmth. They form a hostile alliance against family and society.

The core sentiment underlying frantic acting-out is despair and depression. The girl gives up a desperate, failing struggle to find an acceptable place for herself in her own family. Feeling scapegoated and humiliated by them, she flees the living space of family to enter a new life space with her boyfriend. Family hurts girl, girl retaliates by degrading family through her acting-out. But in the choice of a particular boy, the girl reflects her profoundly damaged sense of self and her urge to self-destruction.

The special middle-class family setting is interesting in a number of ways. At one level, one detects a factor of emotional complicity on the part of one or both parents. While the parents overtly react to the girl's sexual activity with shock, indignation, and anger, they stimulate and facilitate the acting-out. One or another parent makes a sly aside, a belittling slur, or expresses an attitude of "I knew it!"—"I told you so!"—"She acts like a little slut!"—etc. In effect, the parents brainwash the child; they project to the girl their suspicious expectation that she will be bad, and the girl fulfills the prophecy. Then they punish her for it. In this setting, the girl lives out in her sexual behavior something implicit, covered-over and choked off in the life of her parents. In a basic sense, the parents are partners in the sexual drama. They are in collusion with the girl's delinquency. From another point of view, one is impressed again and again by the dramatic contrast between the defensive hypocrisy of the parental pair, on the one hand, and the deep emotional honesty of the acting-out girl, on the other. Often it is as if the girl in her very acting-out is hurling the lie to her parents, puncturing their loud and false pretensions to goodness and respectability. The denials of the parents become all too transparent. The directness, the simple human candor, of the girl is impressive. Her need to show up the falsity of the parents often follows an earlier, failing effort to make them more sincere, more the kind of parents she needs. The pain of disillusionment in her parents, and her failure to make them over, drive her to extreme actions.

Yet despite the destructiveness of the girl's acting-out, she often shows elements of emotional health, in which her parents are strikingly lacking. In family therapy interviews, one is struck again and again with the realization that the parents are in some respects sicker than the child. The delinquency of the girl is a signal that the unity, integrity, growth, and health of the family is in danger. The acting-out induces a crisis, which demands that the family take a deep look at itself; it must change or it will fall apart.

From still another point of view, acting-out of teen-age girls is a transitional phenomena, serving as a defense against depression or an acute psychosis. The girl's flight, her desertion of family for the arms of a boyfriend, offsets the threats of a mental crisis. Were she thwarted in the attempt to leave the living space of the family, she would be at the mercy of a flood of anxiety threatening disintegration of her personality.

There are several considerations that merit intensive study. As indicated above, the flight from the living space of the family is a defense of personal integrity. The acting-out pattern is a sequel to an earlier failure to heal the emotional warp of the parental relationship. The girl's actions are a diagnostic clue to the psychosocial pathology of the family unit. It is a form of extreme protest, which implicitly contains a valid diagnostic judgment of the distortions and emotional deficits of her family group. Reading between the lines, one can glean something of the following:

(1) The acting-out is a resistance to a spurious pattern of control and conformity in the family. There is a deep split betwen the external facade of the family, the mask that the family presents to the wider community, and its inner life. The family looks respectable on the outside but is rotten on the inside.

(2) The nuclear family poses as being integrated to the larger community, but is really alone. It is emotionally cut off from grandparents and extended family, yet has not replaced the continuity of family tradition with appropriate horizontal supports in the community. The parents crave acceptance and approval by the community, seek it by way of surface conformity, and yet remain relatively isolated. They do not achieve close friendships with their social peers.

(3) Each parent is caught in an unresolved conflict in the simultaneous roles of child and parent, continuing to need the satisfactions of dependency and protection, while being required to function as strong, self-sufficient parents, genuinely and sacrificially concerned for the welfare of their children.

(4) The essential functions of the family are out of balance. The parents give their allegiance to security, stability, and social approval. They are hitched to the goal of success, money, status, good social conditions.

At the same time, in the inner life of the family, there is a critical neglect of support of the affectional bonds among family members. The vital spark of family life is sharply reduced. There is little love, little sharing, little joy. The inner energies of the family are dedicated to maintaining a superficially smooth operation, while the heart of the family dies.

(5) The complementarity of the parental partnership is defective. There are failures of complementarity at the sexual, emotional, and social levels. In a basic sense, the parents are alienated, and yet before the world they pretend to be together. Beneath the surface, one of the parents is in secret revolt, and in a covert way spurs the child to act out this rebellion.

(6) Complementarity of parent-child relations is damaged. The emphasis is on the child *looking* good rather than *being* good. The prime value is placed on appearances, on a ritual of conformity to conventional standards of achievement, while parent-child relations fail in the areas of need satisfaction, support of self-esteem, quest for solutions to conflict, and respect for individual difference and creativity.

(7) The frustration in the sexual partnership of the partners results in a trend toward parental seduction of the child. This seduction expresses in disguise a suppressed and hidden tendency to sexual delinquency in the parent.

(8) Complementarity in child-sibling relations is disturbed. Disturbances in the parental partnership and the excessive importance of approval instill exaggerated rivalry among the children. The compliant, conforming adaptation of a sibling is used as a shield for the parents' denial of the deeper currents of strife and alienation. The parents alienate the children by setting the "good" one against the "bad" one.

(9) At the surface level, the acting-out of the bad female child fortifies the defensive alliance of the parents. This is a highly precarious alliance, but the parents use it to exclude the "bad" child from the family.

(10) With these progressive failures of complementarity, family contact deteriorates to endless bickering, mutual blame and punishment, or to progressive distancing and alienation. Temporarily this may lend support to an unstable, tenuous equilibrium for the relations of parents and the "good" child, but it is a dead end for further family development.

These trends prevent constructive change and lead to incomplete pathological healing of family conflict. They induce recurrent family crises and magnify the danger of family disintegration. A critical gap develops between the family as it functions in real life and the ideal of family living, bringing in its wake a progressively bitter disillusionment and the urge for escape. The family must find a way out of this impasse; it must learn to grow or it withers. The emotional destiny of the sexually delinquent girl is inextricably linked to the family's capacity and incentive for healing its inner warp.

CHAPTER 6

Developing Standards
of Premarital Sexual Conduct
among Deprived Girls

Gertrude K. Pollak

This paper is based on a number of discussion series with culturally deprived adolescent girls, conducted as part of the Family Life Education Program of Family Service of Philadelphia. The purpose of this program is to offer the leadership of the agency's professionally trained staff to community groups who wish to discuss questions and problems of family relationships and social adjustment. The program has been in existence for fifteen years; in the last year, leadership was offered for 213 meetings of this type. A variety of community groups make use of this service (1, 2, 3), and a considerable number of them are teen-agers who come from economically, educationally, and culturally deprived segments of the population.

The teen-agers from deprived groups who use Family Life Education discussion leadership repeatedly, and therefore in a more intensive fashion, meet in various settings. Some groups meet in branches of the Free Library; some meet in a housing project; several groups are members of special education classes offered by the Board of Education to mentally retarded girls and meet, therefore, in the public schools. Work with these teen-age groups dates back to 1959; group discussion leadership has been offered to them by the author, by the three family life educators in the department, and by some of the senior counselors who participate in the Family Life Education Program.[1]

Some of these teen-age groups were composed of Negro girls, others of white girls, and some groups were of mixed racial membership. The groups with which the author and the family life educators worked were, with very few exceptions, groups of girls, while a male counselor offered discus-

[1] The author gratefully acknowledges the contributions and the observations made by the three family life educators: Mrs. Sooch Rannells, Dr. Dorothy A. Meredith, and Mrs. Arlene B. Zane, as well as those of Mr. Henry H. Marter, Administrative Director of Family Service of Philadelphia.

sion leadership to groups of boys. The ages of group members ranged from eleven to sixteen in the different groups, with fewer at the extremes of this age range.

Since we found it more effective to work with the same group of teen-agers repeatedly and fairly consistently—usually two discussion series per year—it has been possible to get to know some of the group members very well. Thus it has been possible to draw some conclusions about the special problems that these young people tend to have, the particular impact of their environment, and some of the ways in which Family Life Education leadership can be of help to them in the growing-up process. For a variety of reasons, we have started working with younger groups lately, offering Family Life Education leadership to ten- and eleven-year-old girls. Leadership has been held constant; the same person meets with the group as long as a Family Life Education discussion series is in process.

TASKS OF ADOLESCENTS AND THE CULTURE OF POVERTY

If one has repeated contacts with adolescents, and particularly if these contacts are of a therapeutic nature—be they individual therapy, group counseling, group therapy, or whatever—one becomes aware that most of the problems of these young people fall into four categories: relationships to members of the other sex, relationships to parents, relationships to peer groups, and planning for the future. In the area of problems of hetero-sexual relationships, dating problems are usually brought out, along with the problem of whether to engage in premarital intercourse or not; groups of older adolescents also discuss planning for marriage, and may even wish to discuss some of the adjustments that one may have to face in the early years of marriage. What each group will discuss depends of course on various factors, such as the age of group members, their specific interests, their personalities and personality problems, to name only a few; but one can safely assume that at least some of the above-mentioned problems will be brought out by some of the young people. This is in line with the growth and development of the adolescent—"the three tasks of the adolescent personality" (4) which need to be carried out more or less successfully, if the young person is to attain adulthood. These tasks are:

(1) Developing predominantly satisfactory relationships to members of the other sex, which will eventually narrow down one's choice for a future love and marriage partner.

(2) Making a choice in the area of one's life work—that is, deciding on the place one wishes to take in this society, in which earning a livelihood is the accepted norm for a man and more and more so for women, especially for unmarried women.

(3) Breaking the primary family ties—that is, developing one's own set of values, one's goals for oneself, and one's philosophy of life, which may or may not be identical with the goals, values, and philosophy of one's family. If identical, they should be so because the individual has come to them by a process of thinking through and accepting them, rather than by unquestioning identification.

In comparing the problems that middle-class adolescents seem to encounter in facing these developmental tasks, with the problems and questions raised by members of economically, educationally, and culturally deprived groups, we have found some interesting differences. While all adolescents are, of course, preoccupied with problems of relationships to members of the other sex, adolescents from deprived groups begin to cope with these problems at a much earlier age. In the area of relationships to parents, however, there seem to be fewer problems—that is, there is less conflict with parental authority; on the other hand, the relationship to the peer group seems to have a more intensive and a more positive meaning in the growing-up process. In line with their more limited educational opportunities the deprived groups show less concern with choices than we encounter in middle-class groups. Since many adolescents from deprived groups tend to marry at an early age and many marriages are unplanned—that is, due to an unwanted pregnancy—the problems of selecting a marriage partner, which adolescents from middle-class groups discuss, are less likely to be discussed spontaneously by our lower-class groups. Problems in marriage, on the other hand, get discussed very freely, as most adolescents from deprived groups tend to come from homes where the marriage of the parents has not been a positive experience, so they are very familiar with such problems.

These differences in the concerns of adolescents from deprived groups are due to various factors: Young people from these groups tend to be exposed, at a very early age, to diverse experiences, which leave them few if any illusions about the relationships between the sexes. It is quite usual for many of these adolescents to have witnessed intercourse, to have been approached by older members of the other sex, or of the same sex, and sometimes by members of their own families, for sex relations. Most experiences related to sexual relationships, therefore, are likely to be of a negative nature. It is a rare adolescent from a deprived group who makes a spontaneous connection between love and sex, or between sex, love, and marriage.

Again, the nature and quality of the relationships to their parents affect their preoccupation—or lack of preoccupation—with problems of parent-child relationships. They tend to come from very large families, where incomes are usually low and earning capacity is marginal; along with this, there are more health and other problems (5, 6). In many instances, the daily fight for survival consumes all available energy of the parents; if only one parent is home, the demands on that parent are still greater. Many mothers find it difficult, under these circumstances, to offer a warm and understanding relationship to their children; the developmental needs of children, especially their dependency needs at an oral stage (7), tend to be poorly met. It is a rare parent who, in this situation, does not use the older children, often at too early an age, to care for the younger children. Also, as these children grow up, they experience little of the sustained authority and guidance that children in more fortunate homes often receive during the growing-up process. It seems to be more in situations where the parents' own tenuous state of satisfaction is affected, that parental authority will be suddenly exercised—often with a beating or cursing. When these young people undergo the process known as "adolescent rebellion" (8, 9), it does not seem to be accompanied by as much guilt and anxiety about parental reactions as when teen-agers with closer family ties bring out their concerns about their relationships with their parents.

Because of the lack of closeness between the generations, or even because of pronounced parental apathy—due to the unending fight for survival—the adolescents from deprived groups seem to find more strength and more support in their peer group than many young people from middle-class families do. Relationships to members of one's peer group do not always run smoothly, of course, and some of the usual squabbles and gossiping of teen-age girls, particularly, are quite prevalent; nevertheless, the involvement of these adolescents with their peer groups tends to be much stronger. There is more concern about coming to the meetings together, leaving together, and just being together, in an over-all sense. There is more actual sharing of whatever little extras life may offer—a bottle of coke goes from hand to hand; chewing gum, cigarettes, are passed around. There seems to be even more need for physical closeness, more readiness to share a chair with another girl, if one comes late to a meeting. It may well be that if one finds little strength and support in the relationships to one's parents, one looks for support from other sources. Since many of the adolescents who come from deprived groups are, unfortunately, also in conflict with the sources of authority that society presents to them—in the form of the school or the church, for instance—the peer group seems to offer most of the available support. As older siblings, in many instances, act as parents to younger brothers and sisters, a transference phenomenon may also account, in part, for the closeness among the group members, as shown in the discussion meetings.

The points mentioned above, seem to apply—again, with the usual exceptions, as far as individual members are concerned—to the girls as well as to the boys from deprived areas. In the area of attitudes toward marriage, however, there seems to be considerable difference between the sexes. While young girls as well as young boys have hardly any concept of what marriage can mean in a family where there are healthy family relationships (10, 11), to many of these teen-age girls marriage seems to be "the only way out." This is due partly to the fact that many of them engage in premarital sex relationships, which quite often—one wonders for what unconscious reason—lead to pregnancy. Another important factor, however, in the writer's opinion, is the general hopelessness of their life, its lack of choices. Seeing marriage as "the way out" is understandable in view of the economic deprivations that most of the young people suffer and the lack of positive experiences of love relationships within their own families. "What else can I do?" is a comment these teen-age girls make fairly frequently. It is true that adolescent girls from middle-class families also experience pressures toward early marriage—familial pressures or internal pressures; however, the reality within which middle-class teen-agers live offers them more choices and more opportunities for spending pleasantly any interval between adolescence and marriage. Not only are there more financial resources available to them, but their social life is usually infinitely richer in opportunities and contacts than that of teenagers from deprived groups.

As for the male members of these groups, their attitude toward marriage was, in general, one of wariness. Marriage was seen as involving heavy responsibilities but without offering many emotional or other rewards. Since many of the teen-age boys came from broken homes and had not had opportunities to identify with a father or to establish satisfactory relationships with other adult males, their negative attitudes toward marriage and parenthood were quite understandable. While the findings of the Moynihan Report (12) refer only to the family structure in Negro families, which tends to be characterized by the lack of a father figure, family breakdown of a similar nature is, of course, quite prevalent among white families in deprived groups of the population. Frequently, the promiscuity of the parent—or parents—with whom one lives adds to the devaluation of the marriage relationship.

PROFILE OF ADOLESCENTS

If one attempts to sketch a profile of adolescents from economically, educationally, and culturally deprived groups, it will—with individual exceptions, of course—show the following components:

(1) Adolescents from deprived groups tend to have unsatisfied oral and other dependency needs, for various reasons, of which the parents' own unsatisfied oral needs, marital conflict, and struggle for physical survival seem to be the most important. To this one can add the tendency of parents to use children in adult roles, particularly the tendency to have older siblings take care of the younger members of the family before their own dependency needs have been satisfactorily met.

(2) The self-image of most of these young people tends to be a poor one. Again, this is due to the lack of positive experiences in relationships with their parents, from which most of the young people suffer. The self-image of the parent of the same sex, which is usually a poor one also, seems to reinforce this development. Most of the young people have no feeling that they have value as human beings or as members of their own sex. They have not had the experience of being cherished by their parents or of receiving recognition for any success they may have attained.

Unfortunately, the experiences of the environment often reinforce such a negative self-image. Many children in school have, as is well known, a class system of their own. Quite often, young people from housing projects or from homes in the slum areas of the town find that this is a stigma that other, more fortunate young people in the high schools will attach to them, leading to their exclusion from these other young people's activities. In defense against such experiences, those from the most deprived groups tend to "band together" and form their own peer groups.

This, in turn, limits their experiences of social interchange with different groups of the population, experiences that could otherwise enrich their social life and broaden their outlook.

(3) Adolescents from deprived groups of the population tend to have negative images of family life and, along with this, few goals for a better family life for themselves. It is difficult for most young people who grow up in unfavorable environments, as these young people do, to visualize what a marriage relationship, or relationships between parents and children, can offer in positive and satisfactory experiences to the individual and to the members of the whole family. Where the young people have not moved beyond these negative images, they will show a certain cynicism, often deep hopelessness.

(4) Problems with authority and conflict with society—in whatever organizational form the young person meets it—are other characteristics of adolescents from deprived groups. Again, this is partly transferred from the parents, many of whom are themselves in conflict with the sources of any authority they encounter (1). These negative attitudes are reinforced by the many experiences that the young people will have, in their encounters with the schools, where many of them tend to be difficult in the classroom or to be truant, and with the police, when they engage in antisocial activities, such as stealing or destroying property. Since most parental authority tends to be inconsistent, motivated by the needs or problems of the parents rather than by the needs of the children, other sources of authority are likely to be regarded as sources of negative experiences also.

Because of the pressures under which teachers and police officers operate, and because of their own often justified anticipation of negative experiences from the adolescents of deprived groups with whom they come in contact, a vicious cycle of interaction is often started, so that the conflicts of the young people with authority increase and become part of what they expect from life. Judging from past experience, one can expect that when these young people grow up and get married, they, in turn, will transfer their expectations of negative experiences with authority to their children, as their own parents transferred such expectations to them.

(5) Adolescents from deprived groups tend to be physically less developed than young people of the same age from a middle-class background. It is not unusual for a fifteen-year-old to look like a twelve-year-old from a more advantageous background, as far as height and body development are concerned. There also tend to be various health problems, such as poor skin or poorly-cared-for hair, which the girls sometimes make more obvious by elaborate hair-do's.

THE SOCIAL DYNAMICS OF THE CULTURE OF POVERTY

Many of the factors outlined above are, needless to say, directly related to what is frequently called "the culture of poverty" (13). To be poor, in the real sense, leaves a deep impact on the personality of most young people. If one must struggle daily in order to meet the bare necessities of life for oneself and for one's family, considerable inner strength is necessary to be able to look beyond this daily struggle to see the needs of children or to set one's goals toward a better life. If insecurity about what the next morning may bring is the central theme of one's life, how realistic may it seem, under those circumstances, to struggle for improvement of today's life situation? The result may be apathy, hopelessness and—in reaction to the undue pressures of the environment—acting-out, as far as resources for today are concerned. It is a well-known phenomenon that where money is short, and should (as middle-class values presuppose) be spent wisely, it may be squandered—spent on a TV set, or on convenience foods, or on new dresses, perhaps for oneself, perhaps for the children. Resentment against a society that permits the individual to suffer these hardships leads to some of the acting-out and is at the basis of some of the destructiveness and antisocial behavior that seems to be part of the culture of poverty. The well-known reluctance of members of deprived groups to use the community resources that society provides—clinics, social agencies, recreation centers, churches, to name only a few—is based partly on this resentment toward society, and partly on the expectation of negative experiences in further contacts with the environment.

Many concepts that members of the middle class take for granted are foreign to people who have grown up in the culture of poverty. Time is one of them; the well-known inability of many members of this group to keep appointments is partly an expression of hostility toward the other person, needless to say. It is also related, however, to the fact that time, as such, is usually not a very valuable commodity for many members of deprived groups, who intermittently tend to be unemployed. The usual schedule for family activities—meals, doing the laundry, cleaning the house, shopping—which is a characteristic of many middle-class families, is often lacking in the families from the deprived sector of the population. The disorganization of family life seems to be pervasive, in many of these situations, and affects not only marriage and parent-child relationships but also all the other aspects of family life, such as sharing a home, coming or going at more or less expected times, sharing meals at more or less expected times, etc.

The usual roles in a family do not seem to apply to many members of families from low-income groups. The role of mother is often passed on to the oldest daughter or daughters. Any son who happens to be a wage-earner may get drawn into the role of provider, especially if the father is a poor provider or is absent from the home. Even the roles of a husband and wife as sexual partners tend to be undefined and are often assumed by other sexual partners. This, unfortunately, does not always exclude the adolescent children, especially not teen-age daughters.

Relationships between members in many of these families tend to be fluid and labile. This is due partly to the lack of models for stable family relationships and to the lack of the structured internalized patterns and attitudes that are prerequisite for a stable marriage or parent-child relationship. But, in the author's opinion, a desire to escape the drabness of life, "to feel alive" (14), is often at work here also. In a variety of contacts with the members of the deprived group, adults as well as teen-agers, one is struck by the desire that many of these persons have to create "a commotion," to be present whenever there is an opportunity for excitement, such as a brawl, or a fight, or an accident. One is often reminded of some of the social relationships of very young children. If one married partner craves excitement and attention, what better way is there than to announce that one is through with one's marriage, has found another mate, or is "going home to mother"? Furthermore, since privacy is an unknown luxury in most families of this kind, there is always room for another member of one's family; and while this undoubtedly offers an experience of support and strength to those members of the family who are under real stress, it also seems to encourage the fluidity of family relationships, the lack of investment in marriage relationships, the ease with which relationships are abandoned and the way to new attachments paved.

Lack of privacy also means, of course, that children are exposed at a very early age to various auditory and visual experiences that leave them in no doubt about the nature and quality of the relationships between the sexes. Lack of privacy also seems to discourage pride in oneself and in one's appearance within the circle of one's family. Since efforts to be attractive are ego-supportive in nature, their absence provides another negative experience for many persons who live under the impact of poverty.

PROFESSIONAL RELATIONSHIPS AND LEADERSHIP

With a realization of some of the character traits of adolescents from deprived population groups, in what ways does group discussion leadership aim to help young people?

The first step must be to offer a supportive and positive relationship. Many of these young people have not had the experience of growth-fostering relationships in their homes; or any such experiences that they may have had were usually incomplete, interrupted by the loss or absence of a parent, by the birth of a sibling, by illness, or by other problem situations. We have found therefore that many of these young people respond very quickly and positively if such a relationship is offered by the group discussion leader. Prerequisite for the development of such relationships is—as in any situation in which the goal is to help—acceptance of the young people at the level in which they are, as a first step. This does *not* mean, needless to say, that the discussion leader accepts this level as far as his or her goals for the group are concerned. It is essential, however, to accept the level at which the young people seem to function in the beginning stage of the relationship, before one can hope to help them to move toward better levels. This requires intensive work. The policy we have developed for work with these groups includes offering them repetitive experiences of group discussion with the same leader—usually two discussion series per year. This policy is probably as helpful to the leader as to the group members, because the former need not feel any undue anxiety about achieving goals quickly.

Considerable knowledge of "the culture of poverty"—the family situations from which the young people come and the social environment in which they live—is another prerequisite for this kind of work. In addition to the great amount of published material on these topics, we have found that group discussion leaders accumulate a fund of knowledge of their own, as the result of the problems and concerns that the young people themselves have brought out in the discussions. No book, no article, no pamphlet can give as vivid a picture of what it means to grow up in these situations, as do the comments that are made, often quite casually, by the young people who *live* in these situations! Assigning the same leader to the same discussion group for the duration of our repetitive work—which often has extended over several years, on a twice-a-year basis—has helped in the accumulation of such a fund of knowledge.

It is also extremely important that the leader offer the young people the experience of an accepting and understanding, but *professionally* controlled, relationship. It is sometimes easy even for professional people who have considerable experience to overidentify with the young people. The opposite reaction, rejection of the group, is apt to be much less frequent among experienced counselors. Here, as always in a helping situation, empathy is better than sympathy. However, the discussion leader does not become just one of the peer group. Since the young people are seeking the support of a relationship with an adult who is stronger than they are, any relationship that would blur the professional limits or negate the role of the group leader as a social authority representative would be detrimental.

Techniques

Along with offering the experience of such a relationship, we use a variety of other techniques that we do not use with middle-class adolescents. Some of the discussions center around very elementary questions of personal hygiene: many of the young girls have never had a washcloth of their own, for instance, when they start coming to the group discussions. Since one of the things we try to do is to help the young people develop a better self-image, any help we can give them with improving their appearance—even with very elementary devices, such as discussing how to use a washcloth or a toothbrush—has meaning beyond the physical aspects involved in the use of these tools. Another area in which we use special techniques is that of the party, which terminates the Family Life Education clubs for girls. All teen-agers like to have a little party at the end of such projects; here, the party also serves the purpose of assisting the girls in developing some table manners and of giving them an object lesson in how to set a table, how to pass food, and when to say "please" and "thank you." Acquiring these skills again serves a variety of purposes. The greater social acceptability among friends is one, but the increased self-confidence and the praise of others are equally essential, and have effect also on an improved self-image of the young people. It is interesting, incidentally, to see how the character of these teen-age parties changes, from the one given by a group of very young girls, who may be ten to twelve years old, to that which the same group will give two years later. The food served has usually progressed from something like hot dogs with mustard to a little dinner party; the material used, not only for the food, but also for the table setting tends to show a sense of color and improved taste. Some of the "social graces," such as saying "please" and "thank you" without being prodded, have become fairly well ingrained; furthermore, as the experience of being part of the group progresses, the members tend to take more and more responsibility for planning these parties. This, again, increases self-confidence as well as social skills, and the young people are exposed to some of the satisfactions of a job well done.

Another interesting development in many members of the groups, which occurs after they have had repetitive experiences in these situations, is their wish to recognize the contributions made by the discussion leader and by the management aide, who is instrumental in planning these programs when we offer them in a housing project.[2] The groups of retarded educable girls in the school system, to whom the author has offered leadership for group discussion, have reacted in somewhat comparable fashion; they, too, seem to have developed greater self-confidence, greater social skill, and a greater desire to express their appreciation to the group discussion leader and to the cooperating school personnel.[3] Since the projects with the senior girls in the school setting were not planned as repetitive projects—the girls are about to leave the public school system—some of the previously described developments could not be seen as part of the service offered to the girls under the Family Life Education Program. Judging from the author's experience, there is no doubt, however, that being exposed to the school situation has had similar effects on members of these groups over the years.

Goals

The goals toward which we are working, in Family Life Education Projects with culturally deprived people, are not only an improved self-image but also a strengthening of the ego, which will, among other things, help the young people develop increased capacity to take responsibility for their own lives. We believe that this can be achieved only if one is able to postpone the immediate gratification of premarital sex relationships in favor of a planned marriage, which will not be entered upon because of pregnancy. In line with this is the ability to live in a family situation which

[2] The author, as well as Mrs. Zane, who has offered leadership to these teen-age girls' groups, acknowledge with gratitude the help received from Gertrude E. Bush, Management Aide, Tasker Homes.

[3] The author acknowledges with pleasure the invaluable help of Alethea D. Watson, Principal; Lillian C. Homelsky, Counseling Supervisor; Sunnie Warrick, School Counselor, in her work with the senior class of the Retarded Educable Center in the Stephen A. Douglas School.

will be a little better organized than the family situations from which most of the young people come. Developing better aspirations for oneself, one's family, and one's own children, is also a part of these goals. Such a development, where it will occur, will narrow the gap between young people from the "culture of poverty" and the middle-class goals of the society in which they live.

After they have expressed their ideas, concerns, and points of view about premarital relationship and marriage, young people are helped to see possible alternatives to the choices they are making, which are usually based on impulse gratification. This needs to be done very slowly and skillfully; without expressing any distress or, worse, any feeling of shock at the points of view expressed, the discussion leader raises questions about the avenues into which one or the other decision may lead. Realizing that one can make choices, and that these choices will greatly affect one's future life, is an important step forward for many of the young people. A question such as "Would you like to marry John?" may get a frank reply of "No, but if I am pregnant, I'll be glad if he marries me!" A question addressed to a young man: "What do you think parents should do for their children?" may lead to such comments as "Give them a gallon of wine!"—a comment which was not made facetiously, by the way—but may also lead to some more realistic evaluation of what parents can contribute to the child's happiness and development. This, in turn, may lead the young man to look at early marriage, with the usual necessity of dropping out of school and getting an unskilled job, in a somewhat different light. Another frequent by-product of such examination of oneself, one's goals, and one's future is an increased hopefulness about the future, which in turn enables the young people to strive toward a better life than that which their parents had.

Because the young people we work with are faced with so many handicaps, attempts to help them to move out of the vicious cycle of early marriage—marginal employment—poor family relationships need to be repeated. Anyone who has worked in a helping relationship—which, where these young people are concerned, is an attempt to support the ego against the forces of the id, and to help the superego develop, where such development is lacking—knows that a great deal of continued effort is necessary. Young people from deprived groups need repetitive experiences of supportive and ego-strengthening relationships, and this is what we try to offer to them in the Family Life Education Projects.

After a young person has realized that he or she has opportunities to make choices, at least within some limited sphere, and that these choices will, in turn, determine to a great extent what his future life will be like, the next step is to develop the capacity to plan for such a future life. This involves the realization of the importance of starting married life with some solid basis, which includes a job for the husband, perhaps opportunities for further education along with the job, some savings so that an apartment or a house can be rented and furnished, and some working together of the young couple toward achieving these goals. We do not wish to imply here that these socioeconomic opportunities are always readily available for the poorly educated and culturally deprived segments of our population. Finding a job is sometimes difficult, and they need guidance and encouragement in this effort.

Planning for one's future life will also include some anticipation of what children may mean—in terms of changing roles from just husband and wife to those of father and mother, in terms of financial and other responsibility, and in terms of the care and nurturing that children need. Very often, the deprived experience which the young people themselves had, during their growing-up years, can be cited as a negative example: "I don't want my children to go hungry and barefoot, as I did!" Where this happens, movement has occurred, and young people have taken a step forward on the road to responsible adulthood and sounder family relationships. These, in turn, will in all likelihood offer them greater gratifications and more satisfying life experiences.

To help young people from economically, culturally, and socially deprived groups move forward means really to help them internalize the goals of the middle-class society around them. This particular point tends to arouse violent emotions whenever the author has presented it in seminars or in institutes for professional staff. This is understandable, because many representatives of the middle-class society themselves question the goals of this society and the hardships which these goals work on those who cannot reach them or cannot conform to middle-class standards. Catherine S. Chilman (15) has observed that whether one is in agreement with the middle-class goals of our society or not, all of us agree that it is better to eat than to be hungry, to be housed well, and to have a job and the self-respect that goes with employment.

What we are attempting to help these young people achieve requires a great deal of determination on their part—a hard struggle with themselves, with others, and with the environment—and not all of the young people are able to develop sufficient strength to follow this road toward greater self-control and different goals. We have not attempted any planned research on these projects, but enough individual stories of achievement have come our way to make us feel that our investment of time, effort, and leadership skill is justified. In one of the library branches, a young girl with whom the Family Life Educator had worked regularly, decided to become a nurse; she was the only one from this group who had such aspirations, and she followed through on this decision. It is interesting to note, in that connection, that this family life educator had had professional training as a nurse. One of the young men who participated in Family Life Education Projects in the housing projects found employment in a large department store. Quite recently we received a wedding invitation, very formally worded, informing us that one of the young girls in this housing project, and one of the young men who also lives there, were planning to get married. They had saved toward this, had acquired some furniture and rented a house; both told the management aide that if they had not had the opportunity to participate in the Family Life Education Projects, they would not have been able to do this. "We would have gotten married like everyone here and stayed here in the project!" This young couple is getting off to a better start, whatever their future lives may hold.

Most young people from deprived groups suffer from unmet dependency needs and operate on the pleasure principle. One of the most important purposes of programs like our discussion groups for deprived girls is to provide a sustained professional relationship that will be ego-strengthening and will encourage better superego development.

REFERENCES

1. Pollak, G. K. Family life education for parents of acting-out children: A group discussion approach. *J. Marr. Fam.*, November, 1964, pp. 489–494.
2. Pollak, G. K. New uses of a family life education program by the community. *Soc. Casework*, 44:335–342, 1963.
3. Pollak, G. K. Family life education: Its focus and techniques. *Soc. Casework*, 34:198–204,
4. Erikson, E. H. The problem of ego identity. In G. S. Klein (Ed.), *Psychological issues*. New York: International Universities Press, 1959.
5. Geismar, L. L., & Ayres, B. *Families in trouble*. St. Paul, Minn.: Family Centered Project, Greater St. Paul Community Chest and Councils, 1958.
6. Philip, A. F., & Timms, N. *The problem of the "problem family."* London: C. Tinling & Co., 1957.
7. Benedek, T. Parenthood as a developmental phase: A contribution to the libido theory. *J. Amer. Psychoanal. Assoc.* 3:389–417, 1959.
8. Blos, P. *On adolescence: A psychoanalytic interpretation.* New York: Free Press, 1962.
9. Pearson, G. H. J. *Adolescence and the conflict of generations.* New York: W. W. Norton, 1958.
10. Pollak, O. Design of a model of healthy family relationships as a basis for evaluation research. *Soc. Serv. Rev.*, 31:369–378, 1957.
11. Pollak, O. Sociological and psychoanalytic concepts in family diagnosis. In B. L. Greene (Ed.), *The psychotherapy of marital disharmony*. New York: Free Press,
12. New crisis: The Negro family. *Newsweek,* Aug. 9, 1965, pp 32—35.
13. Cohen, J. Social work and the culture of poverty. In F. Riessman, J. Cohen, & A. Pearl (Eds.), *Mental health of the poor.* New York: Free Press, 1964.
14. Reiner, B. S., & Kaufman, I. *Character disorders in parents of delinquents.* New York: Family Service Association of America, 1959.
15. Chilman, C. S. *Growing up poor.* Washington, D. C.: U. S. Dept. of Health, Education, and Welfare, 1966.

CHAPTER 7

Families Out of Wedlock [1]

Elizabeth Herzog

Vital statistics show that an increasing number of children are born without a publicly and officially recognized father. Some of them (approximately one-third in 1965) quickly move into two-parent families through legal adoption.[2] Most of the others remain in a family situation that may or may not provide the elements necessary to growth and development but that, in either case, lacks recognized status as a family. Yet, along with the problems specific to this lack, it shares many problems of other families, intact or broken.

We know very little about such out-of-wedlock families and their members, and we know least of all about the children born out of wedlock. A slightly greater amount of information is available about unmarried fathers. And somewhat more—although still a meager amount—is known about unmarried mothers. There are obvious reasons why we know more about unmarried mothers than about their children and the fathers of their children. The mother carries the child and bears it. She is the one who needs pre-natal care, for her own sake and that of the child. Her plight is visible, responsibility for the child rests on her, including the decision (free or forced) whether she will keep it or place it in adoption. Accordingly, this discussion will focus on a few of the things we do know about unmarried mothers.

If people talk about unmarried mothers at all, they are likely to exclaim about how many there are and how much the numbers have increased. Both statements are true. The number of births out of wedlock has risen radically in the past twenty years, from about 89,000 in 1940 to about 291,000 in 1965. Whether that increase be defined as evolution or revolution is not merely a semantic question, for the definition conditions the perception of the problem, and the perception of it conditions the response to it. We constantly see references to "the alarming rise" in

---

[1] Adapted with permission of the publisher from E. Herzog. The chronic revolution. *Clin. Pediat.*, 1966, 5, 130–135.

[2] An estimated 88,000 of the children adopted in 1965 were born out of wedlock, amounting to about one-third of the total number of out-of-wedlock births in the previous year (1).

illegitimacy. Alarm could be directed to increase in numbers, or to the imputed causes of the increase, or to the consequences—actual, probable, and possible. And the word "alarming" could reflect unadulterated fear, or it could reflect fear compounded with hostility and resentment.

From the context of the many statements referring to the "alarming rise" in illegitimacy, it appears that all these elements are present, plus another one. The recurrent word "alarming" seems to reflect a belief that the reported rise in illegitimacy is recent and sudden; that it reveals radical changes in the behavior of large segments of our population; and that these changes mean that people—especially young people—are more wicked than they used to be. It appears, further, that this belief is associated with a strong urge to clamp down on the alleged eruption of misbehavior and to punish those who indulge in it.

Actually, of course, the urge is to punish only half of those responsible. One hears few burning indictments of unmarried fathers, and few suggestions of prison terms or compulsory sterilization for them. This is a subject in itself, but for another time.[3]

Because hostility and fear are so often associated with the crisis view, it seems worthwhile to examine the extent to which the present picture should be regarded either as a crisis or as the current point in a chronic situation—that is, as revolution or as evolution. The answer to that question will not change current statistics. It could, however, change the way they are viewed. And this, in turn, is bound to influence perceptions of what could and should be done in relation to births out of wedlock and the problems associated with them. Because of these considerations, it is important that the undoubted increase in numbers of births out of wedlock be viewed in context and in perspective. The difference between seeing statistics in and out of context can be illustrated most easily by two sets of simple charts. The comment on them will be brief, and there is no need at this point to be concerned with absolute numbers.

The statistics on which these pictures are based are from 1965. First, the trend line for births out of wedlock from 1940 to 1965 (Figure 1) leaves no doubt that since 1940 the numbers have tripled. This is the picture most often impressed on the public. When we see this same trend line as part of *all* live births (Figure 2), the rise is still clear. We see a gradual, steady increase—actually somewhat less steady than it looks here, because the nature of the chart did not permit showing a slight jog downward from 1947 to 1948. The long-run rise is definite. In this context, however, we see it as part of a twenty-year rise in the number of total births. The rise in both reflects (among other things) the rise in total population, especially in the number of women of child-bearing age. After 1961, total births declined, while the number of births out of wedlock continued to rise.

---

[3] The differential is time-honored. Calhoun (2), writing of our Colonial period, tells how "the father of a bastard was sentenced to go before the congregation and confess. The mother was to receive thirty lashes on her bare back."

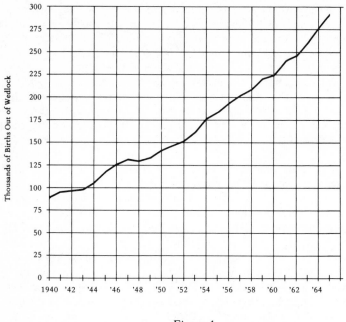

Figure 1
ESTIMATED LIVE BIRTHS OUT OF WEDLOCK:
UNITED STATES, 1940-1965*

*Beginning 1959, includes Alaska, beginning 1960, includes Hawaii.

Source: U.S. DHEW, PHS, National Center for Health Statistics, *Vital Statistics of the United States—1964. Vol. I, Natality*, Table 1–26 (1966) and *Vital Statistics of the United States—1965. Vol. I, Natality* (in press).

Why the number of births out of wedlock has not followed the decline in the number of all live births is a fascinating question to which there are some complicated answers, involving computations and predictions that the future will confirm or refute. The relevant point for the present is that the increase in the number of births out of wedlock has been gradual rather than abrupt. It is not that, suddenly and erratically, illegitimate births have shot up, and that this is an isolated aberration. It is rather that, over a considerable period, births out of wedlock shared with other births a gradual tendency to increase, and have maintained this gradual tendency even after in-wedlock births decreased. We must cope, not with a crisis, but with a long-term trend.

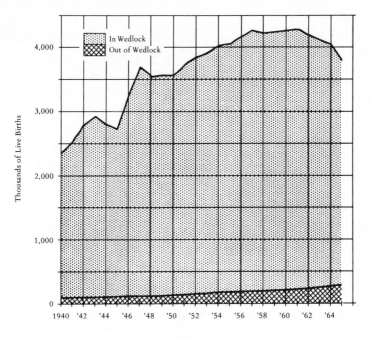

Figure 2
TOTAL LIVE BIRTHS and
ESTIMATED LIVE BIRTHS OUT OF WEDLOCK:
UNITED STATES, 1940-1965*

*Beginning 1959, includes Alaska; beginning 1960, includes Hawaii.

Source: U.S. DHEW, PHS, National Center for Health Statistics, *Vital Statistics of the United States—1964. Vol. I, Natality*, Tables 1-1 and 1-26 (1966) and *Vital Statistics of the United States—1965. Vol. I, Natality* (in press).

Seen in context, it becomes clear that the problems arising from births out of wedlock are due primarily to a phenomenon that has been with us for generations. Had the births out of wedlock not increased more than the births in wedlock, the top of the black segment at the right-hand edge of Figure 2 would be lower than it is. The problem, however, would still be with us and would probably trouble us just as much as it does now. We are faced, in other words, with the results of evolution rather than revolution.

One more set of pictures will finish this effort at putting numbers in context. We are constantly hearing about the alarming increase in teen-age illegitimacy. The figures most often quoted tell us that the number of out-of-wedlock births to mothers under twenty is larger than the number in any other age group. And sure enough, a comparison of age groups

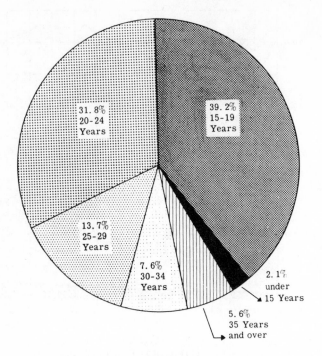

Figure 3
ESTIMATED LIVE BIRTHS OUT OF WEDLOCK,
BY AGE OF MOTHER: UNITED STATES, 1965

Source: U.S. DHEW, PHS, National Center for Health Statistics, *Vital Statistics of the United States—1965. Vol. I, Natality* (in press).

(Figure 3) bears out the statement. This often leads to the remark that "most unmarried mothers are under twenty." That one just isn't true. (See Figure 4.) The majority of unmarried mothers are not teen-agers.

Some other points are more important, however. Figure 5 shows the unmarried women of child-bearing age, and the teen-agers in that group. The teen-agers bulk large as a proportion of unmarried mothers, but they bulk much larger as a proportion of all unmarried females.

In comparing the present with the past, even the recent past, it is necessary to think not only of numbers but also of *rates*—that is, the number of births out of wedlock per thousand unmarried women of child-bearing age. We hear frequent statements about the increase in rates during

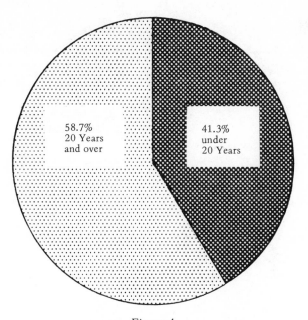

Figure 4
ESTIMATED LIVE BIRTHS OUT OF WEDLOCK,
BY AGE OF MOTHER: UNITED STATES, 1965

Source: U.S. DHEW, PHS, National Center for Health Statistics, *Vital Statistics of the United States—1965. Vol. I, Natality* (in press).

the past forty years, and these statements are true.[4] To the extent that estimates for the past forty years are accurate (and the accuracy varies through time), the rates have definitely increased. What we do not hear so often is that during the last six years reported, although numbers have mounted, the over-all rate has oscillated at about the same level, rising or falling one or two points, or less, but in effect representing a six-year plateau. Any year, of course, it could resume the rise. But, by the same token, any year it could decline. Thus, the current picture is a rise in numbers and a leveling-off of rate.

---

[4]*Ratios*—the number of babies born out of wedlock per thousand live births—have also increased. The ratio is important for answering certain kinds of questions. However, it has little utility as an indicator of changes in human behavior, because it is drastically influenced by such factors as composition of the population, marriage rates, and rates of fertility among married women. The *rate* is also influenced by such factors. Despite its limitations, however, it is more meaningful than the ratio as a reflector of the proportion of "women at risk" who become unmarried mothers, and of changes in that proportion through time. For all its defects, the rate is the best available indicator of behavior trends in relation to non-wedlock pregnancy (3).

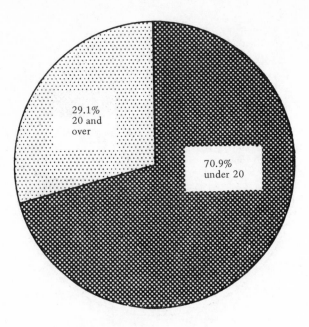

Figure 5
UNMARRIED FEMALE POPULATION,
14-44 YEARS OF AGE, BY AGE GROUP:
UNITED STATES, 1965

Source: U.S. Department of Commerce, Bureau of the Census, *Current Population Reports*, Series P-20, No. 144, Nov. 10, 1965.

I have been discussing over-all rates. If we look only at the teen-agers, their rates have increased less than the rates in other age groups over the past twenty years, and in the last nine years reported, their rates have fluctuated within one or two points. The rates for those fourteen and under have not increased since 1947. The population explosion has exploded since then, and numbers in that age group have multiplied; but rates have remained relatively stable. Granted, these rates are based on estimates, and there are a number of reasons for wondering about them. But all our national figures on unmarried mothers derive from estimates, and we have as much reason to trust one part of them as to trust another part.

If we talk about trends through time, we are obligated to take into account not only numbers and rates, but also relevant changes in the composition of the population, in marriage rates, in fertility rates, and in the ages at which women bear children. This requires a real grasp of statistics and demography. However, there is a very simple solution: we are not obligated to talk about trends. It is enough to recognize that the number of births out of wedlock is too large, and that it has long been too large. Even back in the 1870's it looked like a crisis (1).

When I ask why an increase in numbers is always heralded so loudly, and a leveling-off in rates receives so little fanfare, I am sometimes told that the public will only support services if people are scared. Such an approach to the problems of births out of wedlock is hardly compatible with precepts of mental health. It has fostered, among other ills, a fixation on figures, an obsession with trends, delusions about the younger generation, and paranoid ideas about the effects of births out of wedlock on the taxpayer's pocketbook. And it has impeded constructive coping with real and severe problems.

Our present approaches, I think, suffer from undigested statistics. When the organism is unable to digest some item of food, doctors often recommend eliminating it from the diet, and that would appear to be a sensible prescription in the present circumstance. A trend-free diet of public information should help to promote rational efforts at problem-solving and to diminish the punitive component in such efforts. We do not have much evidence on this point, but what we do have shows that with-holding services and support does not decrease births out of wedlock and that giving services and support does not increase them. They do appear to be increased, however, by administering services and support in a way that puts a premium on fatherless homes.

I have been trying to show that problems connected with births out of wedlock have increased not primarily because people are behaving differently but primarily because there are more people (4). This does not mean that one can belittle the problems related to non-wedlock births, for these problems are present and severe. More people need more services, but there has not been a service explosion comparable with the population explosion.

Although unmarried mothers represent a small proportion of our female population, that small proportion represents a very large number of unmarried mothers—some 291,000 in 1965. If each of those mothers and her baby were in a hospital bed, and if the beds were laid end to end, the line would stretch from Chicago down through all of Indiana and Kentucky, and half-way to the Tennessee border. How many nurses and doctors and social workers and other professionals would be needed to give each of those mothers and each of those babies the services we think they should have? Without stopping to figure, one can say confidently, a great many more than they are serving them now. A rough estimate is that probably less than one-third of our unmarried mothers receive social services near the time of the child's birth. Presumably still fewer receive them at other times.

One must also say, unfortunately, that the insufficient services we do have are not distributed evenly or efficiently. I focus mainly on social services here, but the picture with regard to health services is also distressing, as described in a Children's Bureau publication (5). With regard to social agency services, it has been estimated that as of 1961 about one unmarried mother in six received services from a public or voluntary child welfare agency (6). Three-fourths of the mothers served by such agencies in 1961 were white, although the majority of the children born out of wedlock in that year were nonwhite. From this we can estimate that nearly one-third of the white unmarried mothers and less than one-tenth of the nonwhite were served by public or private child welfare agencies.

On the whole, the unmarried mothers served by voluntary child welfare agencies, maternity homes, and family service agencies tend to be of higher socioeconomic status (including somewhat higher education) than the average for all unmarried mothers in the United States. They also tend, as do those served by public child welfare agencies, to be younger and more likely to place their children in adoption. It is roughly estimated that about 70% of the white babies born out of wedlock and less than 10% of the nonwhite are legally adopted.

It is striking, too, that those who do receive service from agencies with specialized programs for unmarried mothers are likely to be in contact with more than one agency—the average in a New York study being 2.7 (7). This finding documents a point made by one or two commentators: that there is a tendency to multiply services for those who do receive them, while many go unserved in a field plagued by manpower shortages (8, 9).

Failure to receive services does not necessarily mean that service has been sought and refused. On the contrary, a major deterrent to receiving social services is that the unmarried mother-to-be sees no need of service. It should be added that her definition of her needs and her conception of the kind of help social agencies give seldom coincide with the agency's definitions. Moreover, if all unmarried mothers did seek agency help, the agencies would be unable to cope with the demand.

Another major reason why many unmarried mothers do not turn to social agencies is their wish to conceal the pregnancy, and the fear—not always realistic—that the agency will prevent concealment. On the other hand, some turn to the agency for help with concealment, especially if they wish to place the child in adoption. Less frequent deterrents may be equally potent when they do operate. Among these are problems of eligibility for service and lack of referral, or inadequately followed-through referral, by members of related professions.

Although the primary focus here is on social services, it should be added that all too few mothers, married or unmarried, receive adequate prenatal medical care, and many receive none at all. Fewer unmarried than married mothers-to-be receive prenatal medical care, and the deterrents are much the same for medical as for social services. However, in the case of medical services, problems of eligibility and of arranging for care bulk far larger than with social services. Problems of arranging for care include difficulties with transportation, inability to get to the clinic during the specified hours, the need to make arrangements for care of children during the mother's absence (if there are other children), the length of time one must wait for service at the clinic, the problems—financial and psychological—of taking time away from work, especially when a woman is trying to conceal her pregnancy as long as possible. Moreover, some women, married or unmarried, dread a medical examination, are afraid of doctors, are uncertain what is expected of them. Dread of doctors and medical procedures is compounded by the conditions of overcrowded clinics, where one is likely to see a different doctor each time, and where the harried clinic personnel (as women in one study remarked) "don't talk nice to you."

Whatever the reasons for not receiving services, the fact remains that the great majority of our unmarried mothers do not receive them, and that certain selective factors strongly influence who does receive services and what kind she receives (4). For all their infinite variety, unmarried mothers can be grouped with regard to specified characteristics in which the members of one group resemble each other more than they resemble other groups, even though they may differ widely with regard to other characteristics. Such groups are commonly referred to as "populations." Review and analysis of facts, figures, reports, and professional discussions concerning unmarried mothers make it clear that, with regard to the planning and availability of services, several distinct populations of unmarried mothers must be recognized. For convenience in describing two of them, I will call them *Population A* and *Population B.*[5]

Population A is middle- or upper-class in social status and economically self-sufficient (or with a family that is economically self-sufficient). Its members are predominantly (though not invariably) white, and under twenty-five years of age. Members of Population A are likely to go to a maternity home in their own or a different community; to have contact with casework agencies; to have private prenatal care, although not usually private hospital care at delivery; to evince concern about concealing their pregnancies, to be expected to have concern about concealment, and to have help in effecting it; to place the baby in adoption with the help of a social agency; and to leave the unmarried mother status shortly after delivery. It is widely assumed that unmarried mothers in Population A are likely to have only one child out of wedlock, although there is no firm evidence on this and some questions have been raised about it. It is also widely assumed that unmarried mothers in Population A do, or should, feel guilty about their non-wedlock pregnancies.

Services for Population A are geared to individual diagnosis and treatment, with emphasis on psychological and psychiatric problems and their alleviation. The social services are likely to include casework or psychiatric treatment, to be received from a trained practitioner and in a setting that includes a high ratio of staff to service recipients.

The community, through its voluntary agencies and organizations, is ready to invest money and effort for bringing more Population A mothers into services and placing their babies in adoption. In fact, the objective of most demonstration programs relating to Population A is to draw more of

---

[5] For this formulation I am indebted to Rose Bernstein. It concides with some of the main points made by Helen Harris Perlman (10).

them into medical and social services, often by attempts to make the services more palatable and more accessible to unmarried mothers. (8, 9, 10). Caseworkers often try to engage the unmarried mother in psychological counseling after the child has been placed, but for the most part such efforts have proved unsuccessful, if we can judge by our review of available reports.

Population B is of low social status and low income, although not necessarily on public assistance. Its members are predominantly (though not invariably) nonwhite, and their ages vary widely. The proportion of first births is probably lower than in Population A. Members of Population B are not likely to conceal the pregnancy, and the popular stereotype assumes that they do not care about concealment, though in fact they often do. Prenatal care—if any—is likely to be obtained at an outpatient clinic. Medical complications of pregnancy are far more frequent than with Population A. The unmarried mother in Population B is likely to keep her baby, though not necessarily because she wants to do so. She is less likely than members of Population A to leave the unmarried mother status, although she may move in and out of it. She and her family are generally assumed not to feel great concern about her non-wedlock pregnancy, although increasing evidence challenges this assumption.

For members of Population B, contact with, or knowledge of, social agencies is primarily in connection with public assistance, and a substantial number of them, with their babies, are likely to join the AFDC (Aid to Families with Dependent Children) rolls. They are likely to receive social services from an untrained rather than a trained practitioner, in a setting that includes a very low ratio of staff to service recipients. The diagnosis is likely to emphasize group characteristics (social or economic) rather than individual psychodynamics, and the goal of treatment is likely to be defined as socioeconomic rather than psychological rehabilitation and to involve vocational training and assistance in obtaining employment. That is, the focus is on sociological rather than psychological or psychiatric considerations.[6]

The community objective in supplying social services for Population B is to get the unmarried mother out of service rather than into it, especially to get—or keep—her off the relief rolls. With medical services, the community objective is to bring all mothers, married or unmarried, into prenatal medical care. In the past, the means have usually depended on exhortation rather than on attempts to make the medical services palatable or accessible. As a result of recent legislation, there are efforts to make changes in the way these services are offered.

---

[6] Legislation passed in 1962 opens the door to providing more social services for recipients of public assistance. Efforts are now under way to give fuller social services to unmarried mothers and their babies under AFDC, to decrease the size of caseloads, and to improve the training of AFDC staff. It is too soon to know the effects of such efforts in changing the picture for the minority of unmarried mothers who receive public assistance.

By far the majority of this country's unmarried mothers fall into Population B, although this population receives a very small proportion of the services specifically designed for unmarried mothers. If received at all, such services typically end soon after the unmarried mother-to-be becomes an unmarried mother. Studies and reports give little attention to the problems of unwed mothers as mothers, or to the needs of non-wedlock children kept by their mothers; and little information is available about these children after the age of six months. Thus, for Population B as for Population A—though for different reasons—special services end shortly after the child's birth.

If the majority of services for unmarried mothers are given to those who are white, above the poverty level, and likely to place the child in adoption; and if the majority of unmarried mothers are nonwhite, of low income, and not likely to place their children in adoption, then adjustments would seem to be needed. I have no blueprint to offer, but clues to possible directions of change are implicit in models at home and abroad.

One clue concerns basic planning of services. For the most part, our services for unmarried mothers function as an array of discrete operations, each of which serves a segment of need, and may involve separate social agencies, schools, vocational training centers, hospitals, clinics, courts, etc. Notable attempts have been made, from time to time and from place to place, to coordinate a few of these services, and in some instances such projects seem relatively successful. However, they involve complex collaboration between agencies and require constant effort to bring together activities originally set up as separate entities. Moreover, so far such projects are scattered, reach relatively small numbers of special groups of unmarried mothers, exist as islands of local activity rather than as part of a comprehensive plan, and may be discontinued after a period of operation glowingly described as successful. A number of people, including Helen Harris Perlman (10), Alfred Kahn (11), and Clark Vincent (12) have urged that we need a broader base and an altered conception of the purposes and tasks involved. Kahn, especially, has emphasized the need to conceptualize services for unmarried mothers as a coherent network rather than as a multiplicity of more or less related parts.

This is the kind of planning now being attempted in many communities, in connection with the poverty program and juvenile delinquency. These efforts are new and growing, but the basic idea of comprehensive, integrated, accessible services seems likely to survive a number of false starts. In considering services for unmarried mothers, we can profit by both the mistakes and the triumphs of analogous programs.

Some clues can also be found abroad. Our patterns of service are and will be and should be strictly indigenous. Nevertheless, it is useful to survey the general purposes and the specific services that have developed elsewhere, and to consider whether some elements of them might usefully be applied here. In Denmark, for example, an unmarried mother is expected to receive help in establishing adequate living quarters, adequate day care for her child, and adequate training for herself, sometimes for several years. We are told also that more than 90% of the mothers so helped eventually marry and, presumably, establish stable homes (11). Illegitimacy rates in Denmark are reported to have decreased during recent years. Apparently the kind of help that opens up a vista of stable family life and economic independence does not tend to increase illegitimacy.

Because of the often-expressed fear that effective help for unmarried mothers might encourage illegitimacy, we need to repeat that in this country, also, the evidence is all in the other direction. This is one of the points where perception of a problem conditions the nature of efforts to solve it. The crisis view, with its components of anger and fear, fosters a punitive element in our programs—at least in programs for unmarried mothers who are likely to become a drain on the taxpayer's pocketbook; and this element interferes with efforts to meet practical needs in a way that will diminish the likelihood of future drain. The punitive element is not overt enough to make many propose such measures as sterilization or imprisonment; but it is strong enough to make many oppose measures, especially expensive ones, that could promote self-sufficiency but might seem to reward wrongdoing. There is a question, as Kahn points out, whether it is wise or even expedient to regard services as a proper vehicle of moral judgment. The question is reinforced when the latent purpose of retribution conflicts with the manifest purpose of habilitation.

Whatever the patterns we develop, it seems obvious that we must find ways to bring needed services to a larger proportion of our unmarried mothers, with less selectivity based on those painfully intertwined factors of class, color, and income; and that these services should be designed, not only to tide unmarried mothers over the period of pregnancy and child-birth, but also, where indicated, to provide support and training that will lead toward the possibility of their becoming adequate mothers and adequate citizens—citizens who will participate in, rather than burden, the society. Although no one claims it will be cheap, the return on the investment can be enhanced by more effective, coherent planning, more diagnostic discrimination, and less socioeconomic discrimination in determining who gets what kinds of services, and more efficiency in utilizing available manpower. Such efficiency involves avoidance of over-service to a few as well as under-service to many, and also involves job analysis to separate out professional, subprofessional and nonprofessional components. And such efficiency calls for unemotional concentration on practical problem-solving.

I have been talking about services for unmarried mothers, and not at all about prevention. Talk about prevention would be a very different story, and would not be focused on unmarried mothers or on the agencies that provide services to them. Social agencies are not in a position to do much about prevention, even though prevention of repeated non-wedlock pregnancies may be among their stated aims.

To discuss prevention, one would have to discuss our economy, including the consequences of poverty for the poor and the consequences of affluence for the rest of us. One would also have to discuss our values–the values we talk and the values we live, and the effects of discrepancy between them. It has been aptly remarked that if the values to which we pay homage conflict with the values we live by, then we must change either the one set or the other in order to be whole and healthy. That topic deserves discussion, too, but it is for another day.

REFERENCES

1. U.S. Department of Health, Education, and Welfare, Welfare Administration, Children's Bureau, *Adoptions in 1965.* Supplement to *Child welfare statistics–1965,* Statistical Series 84, 1966.
2. Calhoun, A. W. *A social history of the American family.* Vol. 1. *Colonial period.* New York: Barnes & Noble, 1960. (Reprinted)
3. Campbell, A. A. Illegitimacy. In C. V. Kiser, W. Grabill, & A. A. Campbell, (Eds.), *Trends and variations in fertility in the United States.* Cambridge, Mass.: Harvard Univer. Press, in press.
4. U.S. Department of Health, Education, and Welfare, Public Health Service, National Center for Health Statistics, Monthly Vital Statistics Report, *Highlights,* June 14, 1966.
5. Herzog, E., & Bernstein, R. *Health services for unmarried mothers.* Department of Health, Education and Welfare, Welfare Administration, Children's Bureau. Washington, D.C.: U.S. Government Printing Office, 1964.
6. Adams, H. M. *Social services for unmarried mothers and their children provided through public and voluntary child welfare agencies.* U.S. Department of Health, Education, and Welfare, Social Security Administration, Children's Bureau, Child Welfare Report No. 12, 1962.
7. Bernstein, B., & Sauber, M. *Deterrents to early prenatal care and social services among women pregnant out-of-wedlock.* Study made by the Community Council of Greater New York. Albany, N.Y.: State Dept. Soc. Welf., 1960.
8. Bernstein, R. Gaps in services to unmarried mothers. *Children,* 1963, *10* (2), 49–54.
9. Bernstein, R. Perspectives on services for teenage unmarried mothers. *Child Welf.,* January 1964, 5–13.
10. Perlman, H. H. Unmarried mothers. In N. E. Cohen (Ed.), *Social work and social problems.* New York: Natl. Ass. Social Workers, 1964. Pp. 270–320.
11. Kahn, A. J. *Unmarried mothers: A social welfare planning perspective.* Paper presented at the Northeast. Area Conf., Florence Crittendon Ass. Amer., Boston, Mass., October 19, 1964.
12. Vincent, C. *Unmarried mothers.* New York: Free Press, 1961.

CHAPTER 8

A Community Project
for Unwed Pregnant Adolescents

Harold M. Visotsky, M. D. [1]

Social disorganization, especially as it is reflected in the behavior of today's troubled and often alienated youth, is cause for increasing concern. The school drop-out, the adolescent unwed mother, the teen-age narcotics addict, the juvenile delinquent, as well as the frightening incidents of senseless violence and vandalism, all are symptomatic of an extensive sickness whose effective treatment involves an equally extensive effort on the part of all of us—federal, state, and local government, public and private agencies, and members of the community at large.

The Community Services Project for the Unwed Pregnant Adolescent is the story of one community's efforts to deal with a serious social problem through the coordinated services of a number of agencies and resources. Designed as a demonstration program, it is just finishing its second year of operation, so its story is far from complete; but we hope that a sharing of our experience to date, the lessons we have already learned, and the future directions in which we plan to move will be of help to other communities faced with a similar problem.

In the city of Chicago, the largest proportion of teen-age, out-of-wedlock pregnancies occurs among Negro girls who come from culturally, socially, and economically disadvantaged backgrounds. Often illegitimately conceived themselves, many come from fatherless homes. For the most part, their immediate historic past is the rural South, whose values, mores, and beliefs are still an important part of their parents' way of life.

They are part of a group that exists as a subculture within the larger culture. Even those girls whose families have lived in the urban North for at least a generation have often remained isolated from the community around them. A southern heritage of functional illiteracy and minimal labor skills, coupled with inadequate educational and vocational opportunities in the North, where Negroes are notoriously "the last to be hired and the first to be fired," have helped to build a wall that many have been

---

[1] This chapter was written in collaboration with Paulette Hartrich and Mattie Wright of the Chicago Board of Health.

unable to penetrate. Segregated housing, which has confined the majority of Chicago's Negro population to congested slum areas, has also tended to strengthen the isolation of disadvantaged families. At the same time, the overcrowding and anonymity of tenement living have resulted in a breakdown of traditional family controls and an exposure even of small children to many kinds of social disorganization.

Ironically, while the highest incidence of out-of-wedlock teen-age pregnancy occurs among Chicago's culturally disadvantaged Negro families, this same group has received a minimum of service. On the one hand, attitudes of fear, suspicion, and hopelessness often prevent these families from seeking help; on the other, there are serious lacks in the services available to them. The Community Services Project was planned to demonstrate ways of bridging this gap. Although it was designed to deal with the problems of girls coming from a particular segment of the population, we feel that almost every aspect of the program can find some application to other community programs dealing with the problems of the unwed pregnant adolescent, regardless of her socioeconomic background. We believe this to be true not only of the community organization, medical, and educational facets of the program, but also of the psychiatric and social services.

An intimate acquaintance with the sixty-seven girls and their families already known to the project has reinforced our conviction that, academic stereotypes to the contrary, there are no sociological pigeonholes in which to file away feelings of helplessness, guilt, and inadequacy—a depreciated self-image—or an adolescent's desperate reaching-out for recognition and affection.

The lack of adequate community services for pregnant unwed adolescents was originally brought to the attention of the Mental Health Division by Board of Health nurses. They were concerned about the increasing number of young girls coming to the infant welfare stations for pre-natal care. From September, 1961, to August, 1962, 750 illegitimately pregnant girls of compulsory school age were reported as excluded from public school in Chicago, the majority being under sixteen years of age.

This figure did not reflect the total number of teen-age pregnancies out of wedlock in Chicago during that year, since not all were reported to school authorities. Previous experience indicated that probably less than 30 percent of the girls excluded from school because of pregnancy returned after the enforced absence. In considering the problem, the Mental Health Division recognized that, in addition to augmenting the number of school drop-outs, these young girls would be ill-equipped for the responsibility of parenthood about to be thrust upon them. The disastrous results an interruption in schooling could have on the girl, her child, her family, and the community-at-large were obvious.

The girls were part of a disadvantaged group, Negro girls, predominantly in the lower socioeconomic class. They came from seriously deprived areas of Chicago where they were exposed to the multiple problems of poor housing, crowded schools, family disorganization, and minimal job opportunities. They seldom maintained a plan of regular medical care and usually ended up at the County Hospital at the point of delivery, confused, frightened, and unprepared. They belonged to a group that has historically been isolated from community resources. They were rarely known to a social agency, except when seeking public assistance. Instead of receiving their care in a maternity home, they remained in their own homes during pregnancy.

After discussion with other professionals in the field of social welfare, the Community Services Project came into being. It had two major objectives: (a) to transfer these girls to an educational program consistent with their condition and to maintain an emphasis on responsibility—both theirs and the school's—for continuous school attendance; (b) with this structure, to maintain these girls during a stressful period and to make them available to psychiatric, social, educational, and medical intervention.

These objectives took care of two major problems: (a) that these girls were excluded or excused from school, with all the implications of rejection that this involves; 70 percent of girls who are excused from school because of pregnancy never return to school, and remain as dropouts from the school programs; (b) that in providing a program against an educational background, we could involve the girls in psychiatric, social, and medical programs, along with significant members of their families.

The project is limited to girls in elementary school who have not reached their seventh month of pregnancy, are in good physical health, and wish to continue their schooling during pregnancy. The maximum number of participants who can be included in the total program at any one time is thirty. Over the three-year period the project expects to serve approximately one hundred girls.

The staff includes the project co-director, two psychiatric social workers, a half-time psychologist, and a consultant psychiatrist. Nonprofessional services are handled by an administrative assistant and a secretary. The mental health education director for the Mental Health Division serves as a program coordinator and liaison between the project and the Mental Health Division. Two teachers are provided by the Chicago Board of Education, and currently, a nurse in a master's degree program in psychiatric nursing has been placed with the project for a community-centered fieldwork experience.

The educational phase of the program, offering both an accredited academic and home arts curriculum, is carried out in a large YWCA classroom without cost. In addition to teaching staff, the Board of Education provides many of the educational supplies. The Board also provides carfare for the girls and a nutritious hot lunch. The school program approximates as nearly as possible a regular classroom setting and routine. Girls who complete the eighth grade while in the project are graduated from the project school.

The program is enriched in a number of ways: an arts and crafts class is given by a volunteer; individual piano lessons and trips to plays and concerts are made possible by community groups who have a special interest in the program; the YWCA staff has given help through offering leadership for such after-school activities as typing, knitting, and handcraft classes.

Medical services for the participating girls, including prenatal and delivery care, are given by the Board of Health infant welfare stations and participating local hospitals. For those girls who have had their babies and are keeping them, instructions in baby care are given by Board of Health nurses. Follow-up home visits made by the nurses are augmented by the psychiatric nurse.

The project office is in the Ida B. Wells Housing Project, situated in a culturally and economically deprived area that is predominantly Negro and has a high rate of illegitimacy.

The mental health services encompass individual and family counseling, psychological testing, and psychiatric consultation. In addition to individual counseling, weekly group meetings are held with participating girls. Under the leadership of a social worker, the girls are encouraged to discuss common concerns. These may range from questions of school adjustment to discussions of conflicting feelings related to being pregnant and the problems that often develop after the baby is born. Discussions on prenatal and postnatal care, with particular emphasis on feelings and attitudes associated with pregnancy, are led by the psychiatric nursing trainee.

Mothers of participating girls are also involved in regular interviews and biweekly group meetings. These meetings serve multiple purposes of fostering communication between the girls and their mothers. They also gave the staff some understanding of the mothers' attitudes toward men and sexual behavior.

Men are seen by the girls' mothers as providers of a whole host of gratifications. These women feel intense insecurity and a great need for material support. Much of their pathology stems from their massive lack of security, self-esteem, and material well-being. This is their predominant focus, and their own sexual activity is often a way of securing satisfaction of these needs or of making payment when these are fulfilled. Because most of them are in a constant state of depressed self-esteem, the women demand little in the relationship over and above sexual gratifications. There is a tendency to separate sexual activities and emotional investment in the individual male.

They generally believe that "you will go crazy" if you don't have sexual relations before adulthood. (The same attitude has been expressed by participating girls.) They also believe that regular sex relations are necessary for the physical well-being of women. They assume that all women will inevitably have sexual relations, whether married or not, and that if a woman has not engaged in sex by the age of eighteen or nineteen something is wrong with her (undersexed, abnormal, physically or mentally ill, "crazy").

Men are rarely seen as a part of the sustaining continuity of family life. Fathers generally are not expected to be active within the family in disciplining or guiding children. A good father is seen primarily as a good economic provider.

In their attitudes toward themselves and sexuality in their children, the mothers see themselves as having little control over their own fate and have little confidence in controlling their daughters' sexual behavior. Because of congested living conditions and lack of privacy, children may frequently be sexually stimulated at an early age by observing sexual acts involving older children as well as adults. Often this results in the young child's imitating the observed sexual behavior.

There is a tendency to deny that masturbation occurs with their offspring in childhood. The girls as a group likewise report no masturbatory experiences during adolescence.

The girls' mothers view sex as not a "nice" topic to discuss. Giving factual sex information to preschool children is generally disapproved of, and at the same time it is assumed that children will learn from each other when they reach school age. On a conscious level, the mothers set up many verbal prohibitions against sexual acting-out prior to adolescence. On an unconscious level, however, the mothers' prohibitions, along with their own sexual experiences, serve to stimulate and provoke sexuality in the girls. They tell the girls of the "awful" things that will happen if they allow boys to touch them, especially at the onset of the girls' menses.

There seems to be acceptance by the mothers of the likelihood of sexual relations occurring at the onset of menstruation, regardless of age. It is enforced by strong prohibitions, restrictions, and controls on girls' behavior when they start menstruation. Many warnings are given about not exposing themselves under their clothes. A common practice is to check every month to see that the girl is menstruating. The onset of menstruation means she can have a baby. This is the important consequence to prevent, rather than loss of virginity itself, or the part this plays in the total development and maturing of the girl. The comment of one mother was, "Sex relations are not as serious at eight years old, because then girls can't have babies." They are often less permissive than the middle class about dating, anticipating that this is likely to result in sex relations.

The girls' attitudes toward sexual intercourse, pregnancy, and peer-group values indicate that being attractive and feminine is often achieved by engaging in intercourse (strong narcissistic qualities operating with girls). There is a marked lack of information and/or distortion in understanding male and female physiology and how conception takes place. For example, it is believed that: (a) pregnancy will not occur at the time of first intercourse; (b) pregnancy will occur only when intercourse occurs during menstruation, or (c) only after many sexual experiences, or (d) when the boy is older.

Within the peer group there is marked pressure to have sexual relations, coupled with other factors that serve to over-stimulate adolescents to act out sexually, and a corresponding lack of adequate substitutes to satisfy these impulses. Ego development in the girls is less well integrated. Correspondingly, their drives are stronger, particularly sexual ones, as opposed to their regressive and dependency drives, which their mothers will not permit them to express.

Boys consider it a status factor to have visible proof of potency. It is often a prestige (ego-enhancing) factor to have fathered several children. Girls seek to please boys by having babies. (The peer group expects the girls to keep their babies and take responsibility for them.) There are strong feelings that a baby belongs to both parents, and that the father has certain ownership rights.

Promiscuity on the part of girls is frowned upon—that is, engaging in sex relations with a number of boys, as opposed to one boy. Going steady and getting married gives a girl status, in terms of proof that she can "keep her man." She is expected to have sex relations with a boy of her own age. It is considered more acceptable to have intercourse in an appropriate place, such as a home. The girl who has intercourse in public places, such as a fire escape, roof-top, etc., is not approved of.

The immediate reaction of the mother to a girl's pregnancy is one of shock, dismay, and disappointment. This is viewed as a crisis situation, and often evokes tremendous guilt, anxiety, and angry feelings in the mother, tied in with some discomfort about her role in the girl's dilemma. Gradually, one sees the mother erecting defenses against these original reactions by taking a position such as, "It's fate; it's their [the girls'] nature which we [the mothers] can't control."

The mothers often expect the girls to keep their babies, as the consequences of their behavior. Mothers also feel that a girl's having to take responsibility for her baby will be a deterrent against a second pregnancy.

A strong sense of family ties is evident. The mothers believe that only relatives or close friends who are actually extensions of the family—godmother, play-aunt, and others—will take good care of the baby. There is the often-heard statement: "You don't give babies to strangers." And adoptive placement is equated with "throwing away your own flesh and blood." In addition to cultural influences—that is, a lack of trust in alien situations with which they are not familiar—the mothers have strong psychological needs to keep the daughters' babies, to assuage their own guilt, particularly if they too have had children out of wedlock, and/or to provide themselves with another opportunity to prove their adequacy as mothers.

The girls' attitudes and feelings toward their own pregnancies reflect a wide range of responses and defensive reactions. With few exceptions, the girls deny having been forced to engage in the relationship.

The participating girls' role in the family indicates that they are reared to be mothers rather than wives. They are often treated as functional extensions of their own mothers in specific household duties, especially in taking care of younger children. They are expected to assume responsibilities normally carried out by a mother. At the same time, they are denied the compensatory privileges, satisfactions, and recognition of maturity that customarily accompany this role. The subsequent dichotomy in roles poses a dilemma for the girl, resulting in behavior inconsistent with either role. Frequently this catapults her into actions in which she seeks gratification on an adult level, thereby competing directly with her mother. This situation is further complicated when her mother is openly involved in extramarital relationships, especially when these result in pregnancy out of wedlock. Once a girl has had sexual relations, she is regarded as a woman.

General observations indicate that sex mores in this group are inbred and circumscribed. They are the direct result of experiences within the group. As a subculture existing within a larger culture, the group tends to be insulated against ideas and attitudes prevalent in the community about it. Overcrowding and the anonymity of public housing and slum tenements, as well as a lack of constructive and meaningful ties to one another and to the community, contribute to a breakdown or lack of controls, and help to mold the background against which sexual acting-out thrives.

From psychological testing, the following characteristics stand out in participating girls: (a) All girls see their mothers as prohibitive regarding sex, with much checking on their activities. (b) There is considerable denial of sexuality. This is associated with a lack of male identification. There is a tendency to substitute a boy with whom they are or have been involved for a father, which few have had in reality. (c) There is marked denial of being pregnant. (d) There is a tendency to see sexuality as an act of violence. (e) The female is seen as dominant; the male as passive and ineffectual. (f) There are marked feelings of ambivalence toward their mothers and their unborn babies.

CURRENT STATISTICS AND
CHARACTERISTICS OF PARTICIPANTS

From April, 1963, through November, 1964, the project received 201 referrals. Of this number, 60 girls have been accepted into the program. They have ranged in ages from eleven to fifteen, and in school grades from the sixth to the eighth. Over one-half of the participating girls were born in Chicago and are living with a mother or grandmother only. Fifty-six percent have mothers or siblings who have had children out of wedlock. Over one-half of the parents of participating girls were born in the rural South, and received less than an eighth-grade education.

The majority of the girls referred to the program to date have had difficulties in school—repeating one or more grades. In interviews with project staff, they often describe themselves as having few friends, being physically unattractive, untalented, and unskilled.

The overwhelming majority of the girls have expressed a wish to keep their babies. Of the forty-four live births, only one child has been placed for adoption. While cultural and psychological factors serve as a deterrent to placement, the extremely limited resources available for Negro babies augment the difficulties in adoptive planning.

The relationship of the girls with the putative fathers have varied from casual encounters to an intense relationship of long duration. Where possible, an in-person contact has been made with the father. Of the fathers seen so far, few have shown sustaining interest in the girl's well-being or a desire to participate in any planning in her behalf.

Of the girls in the project, 46 have delivered, 37 being full-term births; 7, premature; one a spontaneous abortion; and one a stillbirth. A total of 39 girls have left the project school following their participation; 26 of this group were graduated from the eighth grade, with 24 entering high school. Of the 13 girls who were still in elementary school when they left the project, 12 have returned to regular elementary school.

TENTATIVE CONCLUSIONS

Although no final and definitive evaluation of the program can be made at the present time, the following observations are substantiated by experiences to date:

(1) Contrary to the widely-held view that persons from culturally deprived groups feel no shame and/or anxiety about illegitimate pregnancy, our staff has seen many expressions of such feelings, even though they may be manifested and handled in ways markedly different from those shown by persons from middle-class groups.

(2) The girls and their families served by the project are part of a social fabric in which there is much economic, cultural, educational, and social deprivation. Often these families are in continuous anxiety-producing situations, resulting in despair and hopelessness. They have difficulty in expressing themselves, are suspicious, fearful, and frequently isolated in their social and other contacts. At the same time, they often appear helpless and dependent.

(3) There is every indication that most of the girls are potentially of average intelligence; however, their performance, both intellectual and academic, has been definitely impaired by the obvious cultural deprivations and gaps in their academic preparedness.

(4) With regard to the planning being contemplated for the baby, it has been apparent that the attitude of the girl's mother conditions and influences the girl's decision. Kinship mores and the psychological needs of the participating girl's mother appear to be key factors in their inability to consider adoption. Undoubtedly, their reluctance has been reinforced by a realistic knowledge of the lack of placement resources for Negro babies.

(5) Regularity and promptness of attendance, higher academic achievement, and a total involvement in all school activities have been the most notable aspects of the school program. Especially significant has been the girls' growth in self-discipline and purpose. This growth has been reflected not only in their academic performance, but also in their attitudes and behavior.

(6) In addition to the productive way in which the girls have been able to utilize social work services while on the project, many make constructive and ongoing use of these services after they have returned to regular school.

(7) Locating the class in a neighborhood center, such as the YWCA, has proved especially fortuitous. In addition to the contributions of YWCA staff time to the project's program, the girls are being exposed to a community resource that they and their families may not have utilized previously.

(8) The multiple demands inherent in such a school program underscore the need for having at least two teachers. In addition to professional competence, such qualities as warmth, flexibility, imagination, and maturity are especially desirable traits in teachers, as in all others working with unwed pregnant adolescents.

(9) The comprehensive services necessary for this type of program require the utilization of many disciplines. It is, therefore, fundamental that the staff function as a team, sharing their individual training and skills for the enhancement of the girls' total well-being.

(10) There is significant indication that the group with which this project is concerned is not "untreatable," "poorly motivated," or "impervious to standards of socially acceptable behavior." Rather, this group can be positively involved through collective professional efforts that are flexible, aggressive, and reaching out.

Services, as encompassed in such a program, are immeasurably strengthened by community understanding and active support.

PART III

Psychodynamic Factors
in Sexual Delinquency

In the two chapters presented in this section, the mental life of the sexually-acting-out girl is taken under the microscope, as it were. The stresses and conflicts of intrapsychic life which determine the behavior of such girls are presented in their complexity and in depth. The clinical experiences of the psychoanalyst have permitted both Dr. Herskovitz and Dr. Blos to plumb the unconscious life of such girls in detail. They have provided the reader with an otherwise not accessible approach to the inner dynamics which are operating in the female sexual delinquent. If cultural forces are seen as environmental, the factors presented here can be viewed as the central determinants impinging upon the girls. Both environmental and central factors are stimulated, transmitted, and frustrated in family interaction, as will be shown in Part IV.

CHAPTER 9

A Psychodynamic View
of Sexual Promiscuity

Herbert H. Herskovitz

The predominant expression of delinquency among girls in our society is promiscuous sexual behavior. The sexual behavior of young girls is of great concern to their parents, and the current status of standards and practices of premarital sexual behavior is an issue of great concern for society in general. In professional case conferences conducted in psychiatric and child guidance clinics on adolescent girl delinquents, the chief subject is usually their sexual behavior. Many types of delinquent behavior that are common in boys, such as car-stealing, reckless driving, vandalism, setting of fires, assault, and malicious mischief, are quite rare in girls. Such activities as chronic truancy and running away, though not quite as uncommon in girls, are nevertheless seen more frequently in boys. The use of alcohol and drugs is currently giving us more concern in regard to girls as well as boys. But except for rape, we pay little attention to the boy who is very active sexually.

Now when does a girl's sexual behavior become "delinquent"? I must confess that I am unable to give a precise definition of sexual delinquency. To put the question another way, what does society consider to be nondelinquent sexual behavior? Kissing is not only generally acceptable, but for the most part expected. To say that a girl is "sweet sixteen" and has never been kissed is not, today, a compliment. If all adults agreed that nothing should transpire between a girl and a boy except kissing, would the prohibition be followed? Legal codes forbid any type of sexual behavior outside of marriage; if this code were enforced to the last measure, the great majority of adolescents would be in correctional institutions.

Is a girl promiscuous if she has had sexual relations a number of times with two boys—or must it be three? Or ten? Or is a promiscuous girl one who has had relations one time each, with several boys, or must it be an even dozen? Obviously we cannot make a diagnosis purely on numbers.

To ask why adolescents indulge in sexual pursuits may seem stupid— yet it is not to satisfy physical tensions alone. The other factors involved are many, varied, and complex; they have to do with the individual, the family, and the culture. Interpersonal and intrapsychic elements are both _esent. It is a misconception to believe that adolescence is necessarily a time of extreme turmoil, trouble, and tears. It is, rather, a period of psychological and physiological change and adjustment to these changes. Much depends upon the strength of the personality—of the ego—and this in turn depends upon previous influences, conflicts, defenses, identification, and anxieties, together with family and other relationships.

It is generally believed that sexual desire is satisfied through sexual intercourse more often today than it was a generation ago; yet from time immemorial, each generation has believed that "today's" adolescent is less responsible and sexually more immoral than in previous times. I shall not dwell on this question, but would like to emphasize that for society's preservation there were sexual taboos even before biblical times. Were there not such strong drives in this direction, we would not have to have a commandment against adultery, or the "who is to throw the first stone" philosophy. It is true that adolescents today have much more opportunity to be alone. It is also true, as it has been for a long time, that a girl is expected to be beautiful, popular, socially active, and to dress attractively—which means to be dressed in such a manner as to be sexually seductive. Movies, television, unchaperoned dates and social events, the very common use of the automobile, and many other factors contribute to situations wherein thoughts and feelings about sex are stimulated. However, counterparts existed in times of yore. Both from internal and external stimuli, the adolescent has always had an interest in, and conflict about, matters sexual. It must be remembered that such interest existed in the child long before adolescence. Sex education, regardless of how skilled and sophisticated, cannot prepare the individual for the intense and varied emotions he experiences when the time arises. It is small wonder, therefore, that sexual activity is widespread among adolescents. We must accept this fact whether we condone or condemn it, and in order to help those who come or are brought to us, we must know something of the causes of emotional illness manifested by maladjustive or unwholesome sexual activity.

All who have studied adolescents even superficially are familiar with certain aspects of their behavior as it applies to sex. I refer to such facets of the problem as curiosity, the need for self-expression and assertiveness, defiance and rebellion, a wish to prove adequacy, imitation of adults, the mistaking of "being in love" with mature loving, and so forth. In relation to peers, the adolescent is often caught on the horns of a dilemma. When peers are engaging in sexual activity, the adolescent will feel ashamed if he does not behave similarly; on the other hand, if he does he may experience intense guilt. Ordinarily, however, these problems do not produce the unbearable tension that one associates with promiscuity or other psychopathological sexual behavior.

There are many other external influences that help determine sexual behavior in adolescence. It seems that certain families of certain subcultural groups take delight in having ten-year-old girls behave as though they were older. The girls are taken to beauty parlors, wear lipstick, and are given adult-type dresses to wear to parties for which the girl has a "date."

If this occurs very occasionally, no particular harm may be done. However, when such "pretend" is made a regular practice, it is as though the girl were catapulted into midadolescence before she has had time to mature. She is made to feel—indeed it is demanded of her—that she is to be sexually attractive and feminine before she has had the chance to be a tomboy.

Another practice that leads adolescents into sexual activity, when otherwise it might have been avoided, is the custom of "going steady." More than ever, youngsters today are dating but one person at a time over a relatively long period of time. This is contrary to normal psychological development. Ordinarily, as the adolescent matures he sees many of the opposite sex—or rather, he sees the opposite sex rather than one person, even though he may believe otherwise. Eventually, at a later age, he "sees" but one, or approximately one. But through such frequent intimate association with one person as going steady entails, sexual relations that might not otherwise have occurred take place. If the girl becomes pregnant, a teen-age marriage results. My disagreement with the practice of younger teen-agers' seeing but one person, instead of dating freely, is based on its interference with normal psychosexual maturation, rather than purely on the fact that the practice facilitates early sexual experience. Such teen-age marriages are very seldom successful. In fact, whether the partners had been "going steady" or had known each other but a short time, teen-age marriages too frequently lead not only to unhappiness but to such tensions and pressures within the home that extramarital promiscuity results. At best there is a broken home, whether by divorce or staying together, and the children of these marriages may well develop psychopathology.

Movies and similar media are not the specific cause of promiscuity; other conditions must prevail. However, the behavior of those in the public eye, particularly those in the entertainment media, exerts a very strong influence upon adolescents. They identify with certain personalities and follow their lives and fortunes closely. The idol becomes one to emulate; and when this idol's sexual behavior is publicized, it acts as a powerful suggestion. There are many girls who, in defense of their sexual behavior, say "If it's all right for so-and-so, why isn't it all right for me?" Or, "It didn't hurt her, did it? So why should it hurt me?"

There are many other cultural factors of a national, local, ethnic, or religious nature that affect the adolescent and his behavior; these are more properly the province of the social sciences, and cannot be discussed here. For example, the sexual permissiveness and promiscuity of the parents, which prevails in many homes in the underprivileged, uneducated slum areas as well as in some upper-class homes, may make such casual sexual relations so acceptable that little or no intrapsychic psychopathology is necessary to explain the promiscuous behavior of the daughters. But of the many factors that lead to promiscuity, we must, in the final analysis, look at and into the individual himself. By this I mean that the final outcome of any stress, whether from within or without, depends upon the strength of the ego. We can draw an analogy from physical medicine: the end result of an infection depends upon both the number and strength of the invading bacteria and the ability of the body to resist and overcome the invaders. At any rate, regardless of the degree to which social conditions contribute to its development, we view all unhealthy, antisocial or asocial sexual behavior as a symptom of an illness. The causes of the illness can be diagnosed, and treatment predicated on these causes.

Accordingly, my thesis in this paper is that a promiscuous girl is psychologically maladjusted. In the context of this discussion, I would define any act as a product of mental illness when it is compulsive, repetitive, and stereotyped; an act wherein the individual has little choice but is, instead, driven. Given a particular stimulus, a certain type of situation or combination of situations, the individual will always react in the same manner. He may believe he has a choice, and others may share this belief, but any reasons given are only rationalizations. The true reasons are unconscious, and their roots will be found to go back into early childhood.

Promiscuity contains within itself many of the elements which constitute normal psychosexual development but which, for complicated reasons, have gone awry. Promiscuity is a symptom rather than an illness. As with other types of psychiatric disturbance, the categories usually considered are: adolescent adjustment reaction, neurosis, ego-impairment, and psychosis. Causes for the symptom are frequently similar, the diagnosis being only a rough guide as to the type of treatment indicated, and the prognosis. The term "delinquency" is used in the sense that police or other authorities take notice of the conduct. But our specific area of concern with this problem is in the psychopathological origins of the behavior. For instance, "adjustment reaction of adolescence" means that, because of certain pre-existing conflicts and complexes, the adolescent is having a much rougher time in this maturational stage than would be expected.

But diagnostic categories give little help in understanding the psychodynamics of a particular promiscuous girl. Although we cannot enter here into a full discussion of childhood and personality development, it is important to remember that at birth each individual differs in his capacity for tolerating stimuli, frustration, and anxiety. This is due to a variety of factors, the least of which is probably heredity. The child is born with certain basic needs and instinctual drives which must be satisfied; as a child grows older, their mode of fulfillment changes. The purpose of child-rearing is to channel the drives into socially constructive and acceptable ways, while at the same time affording the individual maximum mental comfort. The child should acquire through the years a capacity to tolerate frustration, to master both inner and outer stimuli, to be able to delay immediate gratification for later rewards, to sublimate, and to develop a conscience and value systems. In promiscuity, as in other types of psychiatric disorders, the individual has not acquired these attributes. To state the matter in other terms, when a harmonious relationship between the ego, id, and superego does not exist, malfunction occurs. This may be in any form from undesirable personality traits to crippling mental illness. In an effort to bring about a more harmonious relationship among the warring factions of the personality, a compromise, in the form of a symptom, is effected. Against basic drives which cannot be expressed, certain wholesome or unwholesome, functional or nonfunctional, healthy or unhealthy defenses are developed, in order for the individual to adapt as best he can to both his internal needs and external environment. In the promiscuous girl, the symptom is maladjustive or unacceptable sexual behavior.

In the following panoramic outline of the psychodynamics involved in promiscuity, I cannot stress sufficiently that the specific factors are not mutually exclusive, and that seemingly contradictory factors may exist side by side. The factors to be presented, while the most common, cannot be described in the order of their importance and frequency, because the possible combinations of such factors are innumerable. It is pointless to speak in terms of frequency. In regard to importance, the psychodynamics of the particular girl we are studying and treating are, at that moment, the most important for us. Also, it must be understood that different symptoms may develop from a similar set of neurotic anxieties, conflicts, and complexes. The reasons for the "choice of neurosis" are not well understood. Yet when we come to treat the promiscuous girl, we try to understand what influences led her to this particular mode of expression instead of resulting, for example, in prim, proper, or prudish behavior.

A basic feminine need is to be wanted, recognized, and above all, loved; a basic feminine anxiety is that these needs will not be met, that she will be deserted, abandoned, rejected, or humiliated. Although men have similar needs, they are not present to the same degree; instead there is more emphasis on the need to be admired for power, strength, and capability. This feminine need and its attendant anxiety originate in the early months of the mother-child relationship, and if not sufficiently resolved, certain personality traits and symptoms develop, among which may be promiscuity in adolescence. Normally a woman is more sensitive to real or imagined hurts than a man. When an anniversary or a birthday is forgotten, when she is not invited to a particular affair or is seemingly ignored in other ways, she may feel slighted; the incident is interpreted as meaning she does not count, is not accepted or recognized. "Hell hath no fury like a woman scorned" applies not only to romantic situations. A promiscuous girl may have an inordinate amount of this normal need to be admired, accepted, loved, and may find fleeting satisfaction of these needs by engaging in sexual relations. I have seen many girls whose only precondition for sexual relations was for the boy to say he loved her. It is as though it does not matter from whom attention comes, just as long as it comes.

Another typical feminine trait, which sometimes is not evident without close study and observation, is the wish to serve, to take care of, to mother, to succor with pain and sacrifice. This is a corollary of the need to be loved and some other phenomena, to be discussed in a moment. A universal fantasy of adolescent girls, often expressed in fairy tales, is that of the maiden who is imprisoned, about to be carried away by a villian, or in some other dangerous situation. Because he loves her, the knight, at great danger to himself, rescues her. In a concurrent fantasy, the knight is the one in great danger, and the maiden saves him without regard to the cost to herself. Some promiscuous girls may be acting out one of these fantasies in order to be "loved" or to satisfy in a distorted manner the wish to serve and suffer.

Conscience, more than fear of external authority, together with the ability to love, makes for those aspects of the civilized person that we value most. Human beings are born with the capacity to develop a conscience. In ordinary usage, conscience is thought of as being conscious and under the control of the individual's will. However, the greatest part of conscience (the superego) operates chiefly on an unconscious level. It contains all our value systems, all that we automatically respond to as being good or bad, right or wrong, acceptable or unacceptable. It helps determine specific thoughts, feelings, and behavior. Among the many manifestations of superego maldevelopment is an exaggerated, neurotic, unconscious sense of guilt. The causes are to be found in the earliest strivings, loves, hates, and fantasies, and are related to all stages of psychosexual development. Later experiences may intensify or lessen this unconscious sense of guilt. At any rate, this phenomenon may be a potent force leading to promiscuity. The need to prove herself unworthy and detestable because of unconscious guilt feelings is prominent in many promiscuous girls. To be promiscuous is self-defeating and self-destructive. Painful tensions are momentarily relieved by the feelings of punishment implicit in the promiscuity.

A frequently used method of allaying guilt feelings is to commit some antisocial act and be punished for it. This is evident in those girls who "permit" themselves to be discovered, so that they may suffer punishment either from parents or legal authorities, or through the scorn and condemnation of the community. It must be remembered that guilt, especially, may be involved in the other potential causes of promiscuity being described.

Freud's concept of the castration complex in girls, and its attendant penis envy, is considered by some to be controversial and unsubstantiated. Aside from this theoretical formulation, it is generally observed that at a certain age girls envy boys and make various attempts to prove that they are equal. The reverse is seldom true. Normally the complex is resolved so that the girl grows up to enjoy being feminine and all that this implies. If the complex is not fully resolved, one of the manifestations may be promiscuity. Possibly the girl behaves in such a manner as to render the boy impotent, as she imagines herself to be, while at the same time acquiring for herself a phallus. Other girls, having accepted the fact that they are feminine, may have deep-seated fears regarding their adequacy. They fear not only that they will not be adequate wives and mothers, but that they will not be able to function sexually. Adequacy in this respect concerns the ability to give the partner satisfaction, rather than concern over not securing satisfaction for oneself. Promiscuity may be an attempt to allay such fears and to prove adequacy.

Defense against unconscious homosexual impulses is another common cause of promiscuity. Its manifestations may be overt or latent. During puberty and early adolescence, homosexual thoughts and experiences are not unusual. These may become quite frightening to the girl. When such fears are conscious, they are not likely to lead to promiscuity because, in addition to her own reality-testing ability, the girl can compare herself with other girls, or be reassured by the interest that boys take in her. She may even indulge in a sexual relationship to prove she is feminine, but she does not usually indulge compulsively. When, however, homosexuality is latent and unconscious, promiscuity may be the most likely method the girl knows of reducing tension and allaying fear.

Another common fear is the experience of sex itself. This has to do not only with the girl's moral code, including earlier remembered or unremembered prohibitions, guilt, and other factors, but also with the conscious and unconscious fear of pain, of being penetrated, of physical injury to, and even destruction of, the genitals. There may be a disgust reaction associated with sex. As a counterphobic measure, either to prove that there really is no danger or to "get it over with," the girl may indulge in sexual relations repeatedly. A counterpart is seen in many children who, knowing they are to be punished, ask that the punishment be meted out immediately, anticipation being too painful.

Confusion in identity and poor object relations are often to be found in the promiscuous girl. Not knowing who she really is, what she is, or what she wishes to be, she slips easily into certain patterns of behavior. She assumes the behavior pattern of others, and is or does what others wish. Or in her search for identity she finds that by having a man, she is a specific person; that is, the male looks at her, wants her, approaches her, touches her, talks to her, so that for the moment she has a specific identity. Those with poor object relationships cannot make friends, and particularly they cannot *be* a friend. They do not understand the individual roles of people; they cannot identify or "tune in." They are unable to commit themselves emotionally to one person. Such a girl, given a particular set of influences impinging on her at a particular phase in her life, may express her poor object relationships in unwholesome sexual behavior.

Promiscuity is frequently found as a symptom of a psychosis or as a defense against an acute psychotic break. Some adolescents, in an attempt to ward off a depression, will indulge wildly in promiscuous sexual behavior. In the history of two adolescent girls who had committed suicide, it was found that their male acquaintances believed that each girl did so because of guilt concerning promiscuity. Actually, the promiscuity was a precursor of the depression that led to suicide. Similarly, many ambulatory or preschizophrenics will be promiscuous, using the sexual contact as the most available means of attempting to hold on to reality. Why the individual chooses promiscuity rather than some other form of action in an attempt to avoid ego disintegration can be explained only by the total of the individual's internal and external experiences since birth.

The intense unconscious wish for the father expressed in an acute resurgence of the oedipal situation is frequently seen in promiscuous girls. This occurs particularly in those girls who are suffering with an adjustment reaction of adolescence, wherein impulses cannot be controlled except by finding another man in place of the father. The complex of these impulses includes the hostile need to retaliate against the father, as well as against the mother, for his having disappointed her by choosing another woman over her. These impulses may not lead to compulsive promiscuity but, rather, to having a few love affairs that include sexual intercourse.

Compulsive promiscuity is seen more often in girls who have not known their father very much or in any close relationship, or whose fathers died or left them at an early age, so that the child grew up with an idealized fantasy of what the real father is; and the search for him by means of intimate contact with men is intensive and misdirected. A universal fantasy that occurs in puberty in both sexes has for its theme the fact that the parents are not the real parents—who, being of royal birth or very wealthy and powerful, will come to claim them. In psychopathological conditions where the parent was missing, either in fact or in spirit, the search for either the father or the mother may entail promiscuity, among other neurotic or antisocial symptoms.

In none of the previous discussion has sexual desire per se been mentioned as an element in promiscuity. Except for one category, nymphomania, sexual needs are not an important factor leading to promiscuity. Ordinarily, sexual needs may be tolerated without sexual action, or may be satisfied through means that do not have the compulsive, driven quality of promiscuity. These means may be through dreams, masturbation, or even premarital relations of a different quality or without sexual intercourse. Nymphomania may be a symptom of a psychosis or a relatively rare neurosis in which, in spite of intense desire, satisfaction cannot be obtained. The causes are as deeply rooted as any that have been described. Also certain promiscuous girls who claim to have strong sexual desires will admit, after they have gained confidence in the therapist and have studied themselves, that the need for sexual satisfaction is secondary.

Many girls are only temporarily promiscuous. After a fling of a few or perhaps several months, they become much better integrated, objective, and realistic. There may be considerable guilt later. Promiscuity, we see then, has both a qualitative and a quantitative element.

It should be noted that the girl who is more chronically promiscuous seldom makes a good marriage or is an adequate mother. As has been indicated, she has difficulty in object relationships, in identity, in addition to all of the other possible factors involved. Unless her problems are to some extent resolved, she would have no concept of mature love and responsibilities. She is more than likely to have extramarital affairs. She finds it impossible to control impulses, just as she did before marriage. Some later become alcoholic as an alternate form of expression of the early fixation on frustrated "oral" needs deriving from problems in the relationship with the mother during the first few years of life. Such a fixation on the earliest unsatisfied wishes may in some cases be one of the predisposing factors setting the scene for later promiscuous behavior.

Adult prostitutes have not been studied very much, certainly not in depth. It is known that they also have extremely poor object relationships, cannot feel deeply about anyone for any length of time. Many are latently homosexual and obviously lacking in basic values regarding human relationships. Their "generosity" is too frequently misdirected and misguided. The degree of the prostitute's maladaption would depend upon her culture, but this would still be a matter of degree only. The adolescent prostitute no doubt has a very similar personality, again with few close ties and little true feeling for people. There has not as yet been sufficient study of this condition, but some of the psychodynamic causes of promiscuity presented here apply to prostitution as well, in addition to other yet-to-be-determined dynamic factors.

I should like to say a word here about the unwed pregnant adolescent. She is not necessarily delinquent or necessarily compulsive in her sexual behavior. The reasons for her becoming pregnant may vary from simple naivete, which is not so frequent, or from being overwhelmed by what she believes to be love, to a wide variety of developmental and unconscious pathological complexes. It may represent an act of rebellious revenge, the giving of a symbolic gift to either parent for a variety of psychopathological reasons, the wish for a toy, or one of many other motivations. The decisive reasons, however, are unconsciously purposive. This is not to say that a promiscuous girl cannot become pregnant. The point is that the pregnancy is not as unconsciously purposive as with certain other girls when they become pregnant. There is one type of adolescent girl, not mentioned previously, whose psychopathology is expressed in sexual behavior but who frequently becomes pregnant. I am referring to the girl who engages in what is known as a "line-up." In this instance, she will have relations with several boys whom she hardly knows and probably will not see again. Such incidences are more apt to occur near army camps and colleges than in the girl's own neighborhood. Such girls may be retarded, psychotic, or at least much more disturbed than the usual promiscuous girl.

No parent or family, unless they be severely disturbed or social deviates, consciously encourages promiscuity in their daughters. However, we frequently find, in the case of the promiscuous girl, that unconscious parental attitudes and family interaction have been a compelling force in producing some type of sexual acting-out. The parents' anxieties, unfulfilled wishes, desire for vicarious outlets, resentment against their own parents or other authority, and many other factors may conspire to have the parent impart in a subtle manner the suggestion to act out sexually. Not so subtle is the situation wherein either or both parents are having extramarital affairs, which they then consciously or unconsciously manage to tell the child about. More overt influences also occur, in situations in which a divorced or widowed parent openly spends the night in the home with a partner. Here there is less need to postulate unconscious psychodynamic conflicts as the basis for the sexual acting-out of the daughters.

Little girls of preschool age are usually quite coquettish. Recently, a child was brought to the child guidance clinic because her mother felt "she has sex on her mind all the time." A few interviews determined that the mother had much anxiety about her own sexual impulses and was projecting these onto the child. (Of course, the psychodynamics are much more complicated than indicated in this description.) One can readily see, however, that if the mother's anxiety was not alleviated, the suggestions given by her to the girl over a long period of time would lead to sexual acting-out. It is not uncommon for prohibitions to have been given so often and so strongly that they are unconsciously assumed by the child to be a command.

It is interesting to study children who have been molested sexually. Those children who go home and complain to their mothers do not give as much cause for concern as those children who say nothing. It is as though they feel too guilty to report the incident or, because of mother's previous attitudes, too fearful of the consequences. The guilty child may unconsciously or consciously know that the affair was not one-sided, i.e., the victim invited the crime. Older girls and adult women often find themselves in similar situations when rape occurs.

A mother who feels confused or unhappy about her role as a woman, sexually inadequate, or sexually unsatisfied may suggest or offer more freedom to her daughter than the girl is capable of managing. Sometimes parents blind themselves to what is going on. The parents of a sixteen-year-old girl did not permit her to go to public dances and otherwise were quite restrictive, with one exception. They encouraged, in fact insisted, that she go out with the son of a friend. The children were in the home alone when the parents were out; they were permitted to spend time in the girl's room, to study together in the girl's bedroom. The parents encouraged the boy to take a hand in the girl's management. They were then devastated when the girl became pregnant. In therapy, the father's passive acquiescence and the mother's unconscious but active encouragement were studied. Both came to recognize that their psychological blindness was due to their own denied drives and wishes.

Intense arguments and even hatred between father and adolescent daughter as a defense against sexual temptation is quite common, and with certain other conditions existing, sexual acting-out may occur. Also, in homes where the girl is frequently accused of sexual misbehavior, or where the child has heard repeatedly that she will end up as a streetwalker, the end result may be as though direct suggestion had been given—another instance of the nonverbal command being obeyed.

Family influence in the production of sexual acting-out is discussed elsewhere in this volume in greater detail, as are the influence of broken homes, poor socioeconomic conditions, cultural deprivation, and other unhealthy situations. Here we can only affirm that in all sexual delinquency the family situation and interaction should be studied. Homes that are merely poor boardinghouses, homes where family members are intensely enmeshed in each others' neurotic needs, and homes where communication is lacking or "messages" are garbled—all are fertile grounds for the development of maladaptive or unwholesome sexual behavior.

CHAPTER 10

Three Typical Constellations
in Female Delinquency

Peter Blos

In this chapter the psychology of the adolescent girl will be compared
with the clinical picture of female delinquency in the hope of transposing
the clinical picture into the conceptual and operational terms of developmental psychology and psychodynamics. By transposing facts into theory
we may formulate a model of female delinquent deviancy, a model that
can serve as a guide in practice as well as a tool in research.

Delinquency is a sociolegal term with ill-defined behavioral and psychological references, and inconsistent connotations as to the age of
the offender. The state of "delinquency" can be compared to the state of
"fever" in the medical field. Neither of these data can point to any specific
cause or disease entity. All that we can conclude from fever is that the
organism is in an abnormal condition; all that we can conclude from
delinquency is that the individual and his environment are in a state of
violent disharmony.

The phenomenon called "delinquency" lies at the intersection of
several disciplines of the behavioral and life sciences: psychology, psychiatry, sociology, history, biology, ecology, and epidemiology. Each of these
disciplines rightfully claims that delinquency can be described in its terms
and can, furthermore, be affected or influenced by its rationale and its
operational theory. There is no implicit rank order among the various
disciplines. However, a rank order pertains to any particular delinquent
case or group of cases. This means, for example, that sometimes in the
psychotherapy of a delinquent the sociological factor might be totally
ignored; this will occur, for example, when therapy attempts to correct
pathological ego mechanisms, such as phobic or projective distortions of
reality. This correction lays the foundation for a more adequate and objective evaluation of the environment, particularly as to its pathogenic influence. Hopefully, the individual will institute, as a consequence of such
insight, a spontaneous protection of the self against the noxious influences
in his environment—or, in other words, he will become able to erect a
stimulus barrier that reduces the impact of noxious environmental influences to such a degree that they can be mastered.

It is a truism to say that each delinquent individual has his own psychology, which in one way or another is intrinsically interlocked with his delinquent behavior. There is more, much more to the phenomenon of delinquency than just that. But nonetheless it stands to reason that delinquent psychic structure and functioning can be studied on the level of the psychology of the individual delinquent. From the study of individual female delinquents, I have arrived at generalizations in terms of typical psychodynamic constellations; these formulations I want to present.

It must first be stated that the cases from which I have made my deductions are restricted to a circumscribed group. Delinquency due to psychotic and "psychopathic" adaptation, or to mental deficiency, are excluded from my considerations. Keeping this restriction as to types of cases in mind, we can discover in delinquent behavior one or several of the following predicaments: (a) a losing battle to overcome a maturational arrest; (b) an unsuccessful effort to resolve a conflict; or (c) an abortive effort to master a trauma through acting-out: in short, a struggle against total regression. This fact alone sets these cases off sharply from the psychotic delinquent. I address myself, then, to that aspect of delinquency that can be looked at as a symptom equivalent (6). This refers to the fact that in delinquency an inner conflict is avoided by experiencing it as a conflict between the self and the outer world. The struggle between psychic institutions is sidestepped by maintaining or instigating a struggle between individual and environment. The aim of this struggle is to change the environment instead of changing the self.

The phenomenology of delinquency shows a distinct difference between male and female. It has been pointed out by Herskovitz, in the preceding chapter, that while the clinical picture of the male shows an infinite variety of delinquent behavior, the girl, in contrast, possesses an extraordinarily limited delinquent repertoire. Her offenses are restricted to sexual acting-out, vagrancy ("running away"), and stealing of the kleptomaniac type. The treatment of the delinquent boy and girl also shows a conspicuous difference. Clinical experience tells us that treatment of the delinquent girl is wrought with the greatest difficulties, and that the therapeutic results are quite discouraging when compared with those for the delinquent boy. Every self-observant therapist is aware of his or her emotional reactions that work against a spontaneous empathy with the delinquent girl. Her behavior—seductive, impulsive, fickle, insincere, vengeful, and capricious—is hard to take, difficult to understand, impossible to predict, and frustrating just when improvement seems within reach. This behavioral description fits the American delinquent girl. In other countries—in Scandinavia, for example—she appears shy, closed-up, or quietly stubborn, but elicits similar reactions of perplexity in the professional helper. In contrast, the boy's aggression, his offenses, or his negativism are usually tolerated by the professional helper with far greater equanimity. In order to understand these clinical facts, we have to consider first some selective aspects of female psychological development.

FEMALE PRE-ADOLESCENCE

I shall start these explorations by discussing pre-adolescence, the first stage of adolescence at the age of about ten to twelve and a half. At this phase of development, delinquency either makes its full-fledged appearance, or it can be observed in its incipient state. In its typical and normal form, this phase of female adolescence can be described as follows: The beginning of pubertal, i.e., sexual, maturation is marked by a quantitative increase of drive energy. This drive increase is initially responded to by a regressive movement toward all those libidinal and aggressive modes of gratification that have served the child well during the early years of her life. For both sexes, pre-adolescence is marked by a strong turn to the active component in relationship, behavior and self-image formation. This process manifests itself in bodily restlessness, play-acting, action fantasy and daydreams, imitative behavior, and intense affecto-motor states. While a regressive pull is operative in boy and girl alike, their reactions are totally different.

For all children, boys and girls, the first love object is the mother. The early period of life, the pregenital and pre-oedipal periods, is for both boy and girl intimately associated with maternal physical care and infantile dependency. However, a regression to the early mother on the adolescent level will affect boy and girl in entirely different ways. Regression to early childhood, to pregenitality and the realm of the active, archaic mother, remains for the boy in consonance with his sex-appropriate development. The same does not hold true for the girl. Regression to the early, active mother, the pre-oedipal mother, stands in fatal opposition to the girl's normal progression toward femininity. The girl's dissolution of passive dependency on the mother is a precondition for this development. Should she regress and surrender to infantile passivity and dependency, then a dangerous rupture in her emotional development will occur. Should she fall back on the first love object of her life, the early mother, and surrender to this regressive pull, then she has forfeited the development toward femininity by settling on a homosexual object choice. Homosexuality, latent or manifest, will be the ultimate outcome of the girl's surrender to the pre-oedipal mother.

This fateful rupture in her progressive development is resisted by the girl in her resolute turn to the opposite sex. Her defense against regression or primal passivity is recognizable in her typical pre-adolescent behavior, which is demonstrably active, stubborn, and resistive to any situation that connotes submissiveness, passivity, or dependency. Of course, we still see at this stage the little girl who desires her mother's protection and guidance. However, the severity of the delinquency is always determined by the strength of fixation on the early mother or, rather, by the degree of ego strength required, but unavailable, for loosening the infantile tie to the early mother. Female pre-adolescence is the stage of the tomboy or of the little woman, rather predatory and aggressive. In both we recognize a defense against regression or, to say it positively, an effort at keeping progressive development in flux (2).

We might now state that the central emotional task of the pre-adolescent girl is successful resistance against the regressive pull to the pre-oedipal mother. The stronger this pull, the more intensive will be the girl's defensive maneuver, or to put it descriptively, the more compulsively does she resort to heterosexual acting-out. Normally, the ego maintains the enormous gains derived from the latency period and does not participate in drive regression. This works against sexual acting-out. This is to say that the ego's relative maturity bends infantile instinctual aims into substitute modes of behavior as well as autoplastic adaptations. This fact prevents the novel conflict of pre-adolescence from deteriorating into a raging conflict between self and environment (3).

Normally, then, in early puberty the normative influence of reason, the acceptance of moral models, the ability of displacement as exemplified in play-acting and fantasy creation—in short, the capacity for delay and inhibition—can be counted on to relegate to the inner life of the normal young girl what the delinquent girl externalizes through acting-out. The study of juvenile diaries illustrates this point with great clarity. If progressive development continues, then a qualitative change of drive will propel the pre-adolescent girl into the feminine position; this occurs during the phase of adolescence proper.

In order to highlight the characteristics of female pre-adolescence, I shall contrast it briefly with the development of the boy. Whereas the girl defends herself against regression, the boy in fact regresses to the pre-genital phases of development. From these sources his behavior draws the richness and variety characteristic of this age. It is well-known that the boy in this phase shuns girls, belittles, boasts, brags, and teases in their presence, only to seek refuge in the company of his own sex. This is typical behavior during the pre-adolescent phase of the boy. What is so striking in the comparative picture is that the pre-adolescent boy appears more childish, while the pre-adolescent girl gives the impression of far greater maturity. Nothing quite similar to the boy's regression can be observed in the pre-adolescent girl. She rarely shows a comparable and extensive drive regression, but, in contrast, she actively turns toward the other sex or to tomboyish pursuits. In short, she hastens to leave the stage of her development at which regressive temptations and wishes threaten the forward movement of her emotional development. The psychological situation, quite different for boy and girl, is responsible for the fact that the girl advances more rapidly in her emotional development as compared with the boy of the same age.

THE FIRST CONSTELLATION

We can now formulate the first typical constellation of female delinquency by pointing to the psychological predicament of the delinquent girl: she has failed in the pre-adolescent developmental task of emotional liberation from the pre-oedipal mother—the active, nurturing, procreating, omnipotent mother. The delinquent girl has succumbed to the regressive pull to the early mother; consequently, we can speak of an abortive pre-adolescence, which in and by itself acts as a foreclosure of progressive development. Manifest delinquency makes its appearance in the defense against regression, in the denial of the intensive craving for the nurturing mother, and in warding off the homosexual surrender. In the attachments of the delinquent girl formed under these auspices, we look in vain for feminine love or personal interest in the sexual partner; in fact, her hostility toward the male is more often than not fierce and vengeful.

We can recognize two components in the heterosexual acting-out: defensive use of the heterosexual object and a substitute gratification of infantile needs, such as body contact and oral-receptive passivity. Dramatization of a sado-masochistic relationship is usually an essential aspect of her transient attachments. The girl's insatiable need for object contact, together with a primitive stimulus hunger, are demonstrated in her frantic and excited sexual involvements. These should be understood in terms of a restitutive formation. She struggles desperately against the ever-present danger of ego loss and an anaclitic depression. We recognize, then, in her behavior: (a) a search for primitive gratification; (b) a defensive aim; and (c) an effort at restitution (1). This thesis of female delinquency postulates a fixation of the girl at the level of early mother-child relationship.

It is not surprising to find within this emotional constellation the wish for a baby—in actuality or in fantasy—as an ever-present theme. The longing for a baby, often a dominant fantasy in running away or in sexual acting-out, is essentially an undoing of a disappointment in the mother or mother substitute, e.g., teacher or therapist. By becoming pregnant, the mother-child unit becomes re-established by proxy. Such mothers can find satisfaction in motherhood only as long as the infant is totally dependent, and turn against the child as soon as independent strivings assert themselves; infantilization of the child is the well-known result.

In the foregoing, I have formulated the paradigmatic condition of one type of female delinquency. Case histories of delinquent girls abound in clinical data that will bear out my theoretical discussion. We are accustomed to finding two recurrent themes in relevant case material: one pertaining to the girl's emotional conflict with the mother and the other pertaining to the problem of homosexuality. Of course, both these themes are easily pushed into the background and out of sight by the glaring fireworks of heterosexual acting-out.

A delinquent fourteen-year-old girl, when asked why she needed ten boy friends at once, answered with a sense of desperation and urgency: "I have to do this; if I didn't have so many boy friends, they would say I am a lesbian." The "they" in this statement is the projection of those instinctual impulses the girl endeavors so vehemently to contradict by her exhibitionistic behavior. A sixteen-year-old girl who is closely attached to a girlfriend denies her homosexual tie by sporting tight, seductive skirts in order to attract the attention of boys. She says of herself: "People must be crazy if they think these skirts are sexy. They call me boy-crazy. Nobody believes me—I don't like to be feminine. It is just that if I weren't feminine, I would look kind of funny. I wish I were a boy. I hate being a girl even if it looks right. I like what boys like. I should think I am a girl, but I don't." In this case the girl's desire to be a boy and to become the love object of her girlfriend is warded off by her provocative sexiness. She pretends to be boy-crazy and, true enough, the environment believes her. Only because she dissimulates to the point of inducing others to share in her defensive operation by accepting her behavior at its face value ("nobody believes me") does her homosexual conflict remain unnoticed.

Another fourteen-year-old girl, who had suffered sexual abuse by her father and brother, is known in the neighborhood to behave like " a tramp and a bum"—i.e., seductive and provocative. After she was in treatment for some time, her rage against her mother burst forth in blame for not having offered her protection against abuse. She vengefully arouses her father's and brother's sexual desires by walking around in scant clothing at home, yet she expects them to turn their sexual abuse against the mother, whom she despises. The girl's heterosexual behavior is a revenge on the mother whose love, nurturing, and protection she craves. Once, finding the girl in a state of undress at home, her mother accusingly yelled at her, "What are you trying to do, rape your brother?" The girl shouted, "No, I am trying to rape you. Why don't you get into bed with me and show me how it is to be loved by a woman?" In paraphrasing this remark, we might word it in the simplicity of its original meaning and say: "Why don't you keep me close to you and let me feel how it is to be loved by a good mother?"

In order to further emphasize the girl's delinquency as a uniquely female syndrome, I shall again contrast it briefly with comparable regressive phenomena in the boy. His fixation on the early, active mother, who nurtures and cares, does not stimulate defensive heterosexual acting-out, as is the case with the girl. While delinquents of both sexes display hostile and aggressive behavior, the boy seems to possess a far greater proclivity for symbolic expression in the process of exercising and establishing his mastery and control over the object world. The direct instinctual (sexual) gratification of the male delinquent who is fixated on the passive-dependent stage of development tends to lead him into homosexuality or into symptomatic behavior such as imposter-like action, use of drugs and liquor, or emotional surrender to a male gang or coterie. The heterosexual drive is either markedly inhibited, or it is encumbered by potency disturbances. The male adolescent whose psychosexual development is arrested on the passive, incorporative, and receptive oral modality searches in vain for a sex-appropriate—i.e., heterosexual—accommodation of his pubertal genital urges and his overwhelming passive-dependent needs. The act of sexual intercourse remains for the orally fixated pubertal boy—for a certain time at least—closely associated with wildly aggressive, destructive, and retaliatory urges. No wonder that we so often find in cases of this kind that castration—fear and wish—dominates the emotional scene. Even though male and female delinquents have an identical drive fixation and ego distortion, the clinical picture of the boy contains little that is analogous to the syndrome of female delinquency.

This schematic presentation has not taken into account one relevant and unique aspect of male puberty. Sexual maturation in and by itself has the tendency to push masculine strivings into the foreground and to throw passive, regressive trends into a temporary eclipse (5). These trends emerge again in full force during late or post-adolescence in both characterological formations and drive propensities. These two tendencies toward gratification and stabilization find expression in vocational choices as well as in the attachment or marriage to either a "powerful" woman or her counterpart, the submissive, undemanding, docile girlfriend or wife.

THE SECOND CONSTELLATION

The second typical constellation of female delinquency refers to the girl who has advanced to the oedipal level but has never achieved the semblance of an oedipal resolution. The hostility against the mother in these cases is not defensive but actual. As the basis of this hate we recognize the girl's accusation of the mother who has all through childhood destroyed for her daughter the magnificence of the oedipal father through belittling, devaluating, ridiculing, emasculating, and generally degrading him. The revenge which the adolescent girl takes on her mother for this fatal deprivation can assume violent proportions. By displacement, she acts out this conflict in relation to people outside the family. Again we observe sexual acting-out. The enmity, rebelliousness, and hostility of the girl toward the oedipal mother is on first sight in such cases hardly distinguishable from the girl's defensive antagonism toward the pre-oedipal mother.

The girl cannot advance in her adolescent psychosexual development without having transcended the oedipal stage and brought it to a settlement during the adolescent period. It is my opinion that it is the rage and hostility against the oedipal mother who has ruined and degraded the oedipal father which propels the girl into oedipal sexual acting-out. Only the girl's positive identification with the mother can protect her against retaliatory sexual relations. The father unloved by the mother appears to the girl in these cases as degraded and devalued. She feels betrayed by the mother; as a young adolescent girl expressed it: "Mother, I hate you for not loving my father." This sounds paradoxical unless we recognize in accusations of this kind the girl's appeal to the mother that she cease to degrade the father or, in other words, that she help the daughter to attain a positive father-image. Obviously, what appears as an actuality in adolescence is in fact a reactivation of the past. Thus the present appears at times distorted, exaggerated, and quasi-delusional. Paraphrasing Diderot's words, "If God did not exist he would have had to be invented," we might say with equal cogency that the father of the positive oedipal period must be created as a transient and inner reality during female adolescence in cases where he never existed in this role before.

If the search for the oedipal father is pursued through transient heterosexual acting-out, various forms of deviant development, including delinquency, will follow. Frequently this type of oedipal re-enactment leads to promiscuity. It seems to me, however, that oedipal re-enactment during puberty leads to fewer severe pathological formations than the defensive pseudo-heterosexuality described in the first constellation. If oedipal acting-out is not persistently retaliatory and vengeful but contains feelings of love and idealization, then it sustains progressive development and constitutes an effort to loosen early object ties for good. Much of this sexual behavior belongs in the realm of adolescent sexual experimentation, and most of it remains hidden from the public eye.

A characteristic of all types of female delinquency should be made explicit at this point. The predominant aspect of the girl's delinquent behavior is essentially a relationship problem; everything else seems to be subordinate to this central theme. The girl normally keeps her major concerns and interests within the scope of relationships. Her interest, often expressed in a contrived disinterest in attire and looks, reflects her wish to be seen and responded to by others. In her delinquency the preponderance of the girl's relationship-centeredness is demonstrated by her behavior. It is obvious in sexual delinquency. Kleptomaniac stealing is understood as an aggressive grab at the "goodness" that the mother has withheld (whatever that might be in a given case). Vagrancy usually follows a catastrophic disappointment, real or imagined, in a relationship. The boy's delinquency, in contrast, has an entirely different structure. The boy's predominant concern lies in the mastery of the object world and of the environment; in the discharge of aggression through destructiveness and vandalism; in the use of inanimate objects, such as cars and weapons, as symbolic body-part representations; and, most important, in the struggle with external, institutionalized authority.

The relationship-centeredness of the delinquent girl appears in every treatment situation and complicates it by its very nature. Without continuously assessing the role and the implicit emotional dangers of the therapeutic relationship, the treatment of the delinquent girl remains a hazardous undertaking. This aspect of treatment deserves emphasis, because the therapist is ceaselessly pushed by the delinquent girl into the most intense, regressed, erotic-aggressive relationship. These affects are often nearly impossible to detect in her look or to decipher from her countenance, because the girl hides her intense feelings behind an expressionless mask. Her violent reaction often comes as a total surprise. Should the girl feel rejected, humiliated, or too closely approached by the therapist, she might run away or get herself pregnant. However, should one ever reach the point in treatment where interpretation can serve to neutralize the sexual and aggressive component in the relationship, then a therapeutic alliance promises to emerge. At this point, then, ego interests of both partners have become—at least partially—identical, replacing the intensity and fickleness of an all-pervasive sado-masochistic tie.

THE THIRD CONSTELLATION

The third constellation that is typical of female delinquency can be formulated as acting-out in the service of the ego (4). As a corollary of the adolescent's emotional disengagement from the family, there appears on the ego level a need for the establishment of a temporal or historical continuity within the ego. This ego continuity can no longer be maintained by proxy, by the simple reliance on the parents' omniscience, a condition which might be paraphrased as follows: "Even if I do not understand or remember or know fully what really happened in the past, my parents do; therefore nothing has been extinguished nor lost, as long as I continue, by word, gesture, or action, the reality of crucial events that took place in the family." Whenever an unassimilated trauma gives rise to ego lacunae or gaps in ego continuity, the child experiences a disturbance in the sense of reality. This will reach a critical impasse during adolescence. In an attempt to restore the sense of reality, the adolescent resorts to acting-out behavior of all kinds, frequently of an asocial or antisocial nature.

Such cases often respond extremely well to a rediscovery of the undistorted past. I am inclined to give this fact a weighty significance by saying that acting-out in the service of re-establishing temporal or historical ego continuity, or, too briefly, in the service of the ego, must be distinguished from those cases of acting-out in which instinctual demands predominate or those in which the re-establishment of a one-ness with the object (merger) is sought through the magic control of the external world.

We are all familiar with cases in which a wilful falsification of reality was perpetrated by the parent, and has resulted in the child's doubt in the reality of his own perception or memory. This might refer to a mother telling her child that her father is dead while he actually lives in a mental hospital, or concealing the reality of illness, death, crime, adoption, or less dramatic events of family life. In such a case, acting-out can well represent an effort of the ego to contradict the parental command, often only gestured and never verbalized, namely, the command not to know. An effort at a rectification of a specific past event through restitutive behavior in the present provides the special content of such acting-out behavior, which indeed can be termed as acting-out in the service of the ego.

In the delinquent boy, such behavior usually appears with greater clarity in terms of the historical component of his restitutive actions. In contrast, in the case of the girl, the picture always becomes blurred by the fact that sexual involvement remains her outstanding symptomatic behavior. This, however, must not deter us from searching for ego-restitutive components in her behavior. A sixteen-year-old diabetic girl enacted the denial of a memory she was unable to integrate into her ego organization. She truanted from school, had sexual relations, and removed herself from parental control; in short, she lived the life of an adult. In doing so, she contradicted by magic gesture a remark by her mother, overheard at an early age, that her diabetic daughter "will not live to grow up." The growing-up time of puberty became the time of likely death. In therapy the suppressed memory was lifted into the light of recognition. The recollection of fact and affect, both traumatic in their consequences, permitted the adolescent period to be freed from doom. The girl had no further need for her restitutive and defensive behavior; consequently sexual acting-out and truancy ceased.

DISCUSSION

I have described thus far three typical constellations of female delinquency. In concentrating on the psychodynamics of the individual delinquent, I have only inferred a pathogenic environment. Of course, in each
case certain personality predilections and family constellations contribute
to the formation of the delinquency and to the maintenance of this state.
Adelaide Johnson (7) has described the dynamics of many of these cases in
terms of the child's acting out the unconscious wishes of the parent. This,
however, can only take place when the emotional separation between
parent and child is pathologically incomplete. In fact, it is the remnant of
the symbiotic tie between mother and child that constitutes a preconditional factor in acting-out. We recognize in the acting-out propensity the
preservation of a continued need for immediate object possession.

We discover in these cases that outer reality has never been relin-
quished as a source of direct satisfaction on the infantile level of need
fulfillment. The observation that to the acting-out girl the other person
involved plays only a small role and that one person is easily exchanged for
another, is one more proof of the primitive psychic organization in which
her acting-out is anchored. We recognize in her acting-out an auto-erotic
use of the outer world, which is always available for immediate gratification. True object relation requires the recognition of a self-interest in the
partner, and can develop only within the boundaries of compromise and
empathy. The acting-out girl, in contrast, turns to the outer world as a
tension-relieving part object. To this Anna Freud (5) alluded by saying
that "the acting out of fantasies . . . is a derivative of phallic masturbation . . . its substitute and representative." The gratifying object is represented by the environment as a continuously available source of satiatory
supplies. The acting-out adolescent uses the external world for self-
aggrandizement and tension reduction, in the same way the child once
used the parent for gratification of his emotional needs.

Whenever we deal with cases of manifest female delinquency, we wish
that this condition could have been recognized earlier, in its latent or
predelinquent state, before the full onslaught of puberty had pushed the
girl into acting-out behavior and before sexual delinquency had thrust
secondary perils upon the already vulnerable personality of the adolescent
girl. Implicit in the theoretical formulations of female delinquency is the
assumption that certain typical preconditions exist before delinquency
becomes manifest. These preconditions can be recognized on the level of
drive pathology and of ego deformations. There always exists a complementary pathology in parental drive and ego organizations. We have recognized the following as preconditional: (*a*) a fixation on the passive, nurturing level of mother-child relationship; or (*b*) an incomplete, negative,
or abortive oedipal phase; or (*c*) the rectification of a distorted past or the
restitutive externalization of a traumatic loss. However, any one of the
preconditions just mentioned will never lead to manifest delinquency without the essential propensity of experiencing an inner tension as a tension
between the self and the environment. In these cases the environment is

treated as if it were a person giving or withholding gratification. The acting-out propensity, or the incapacity to internalize conflict, are the preconditions for manifest delinquency, as it is under discussion here. Extreme ambivalence of the mother-daughter relationship, or to be specific, the sado-masochistic tie between them, seems one further preconditional factor. Early indicators of female delinquency along the lines just mentioned are usually apparent in family, school, and peer behavior, showing the prototypical dynamics of the delinquent girl in the latent state.

In order to illustrate my remarks, I shall refer to an adopted girl of fourteen. She was recognized as being in a pre-delinquent state. More important than the conflict with her parents, especially the mother, was the avoidance of conflict through acting-out. She recreated her adoption. Knowing that she was the offspring of a Jew and a Catholic, without knowing specifically the religion of father or mother, she recreated her natural family situation by "adopting" herself into families of an alien ethnic group. She acted out her search for the good mother in this foreign milieu, to which she felt attracted because it was as strange and unfamiliar as her origin. Her search for the good and lost mother was recognized as an imminent danger for this girl. Her need to act out the mother-child unit predestined her to become an unmarried mother. In order to avert this outcome, the girl was assisted in her suppressed curiosity about her origin, and an active search was initiated in order to establish some facts regarding her descent. When her wish for babies had turned into the caring for babies, the compelling drive toward illegitimacy had passed. Religious and denominational issues became from here on the battleground on which she tried to establish her identity. Instead of enacting in reality a re-projected traumatic episode of her history, she now dealt with the same basic issue on a higher psychological level, namely, on the level on which love objects become replaced by ideational representations. She now wanted to become a nun or a baby nurse in an orphanage. There is no doubt that the shift of psychic functioning from the concrete to the ideational and vocational would have been infinitely more difficult, if not impossible, had sexual acting-out already established itself.

We must never lose sight of the fact—clinically borne out in abundance—that female sexual delinquency is far more profoundly self-destructive and irreversible in its corrosive consequences than is male delinquency. With the aggressive and retaliatory use of her body and her reproductive functions, the delinquent girl deeply violates the protective and caring attributes of her maternal role. This remains a foreboding defect that will harm not only her but her offspring in the future. The ultimate goal in the treatment of the delinquent girl should be her attainment of the capacity to become a good mother. Only then can we break the chain that perpetuates deviant development and maladaption through the generations.

In this paper I have described three forms of female delinquency which, it is true, are not as neatly distinct in practice as they appear in theory. Our start in studying the problem remains always the clinical picture and the case history. However, only a theoretical formulation can reinstate the delinquent picture into the process of personality formation. From a theory of female delinquency, we can expect to recognize it in its latent form. By bringing order into the ocean of clinical data, a theory of female delinquency may pilot us through the treacherous passages we must navigate whenever we undertake the treatment of a delinquent girl.

REFERENCES

1. Blos, P. *Preoedipal factors in the etiology of female delinquency*. Vol. 12. *Psychoanalytic study of the child*. New York: International Univer. Press, 1957.
2. Blos, P. Preadolescent drive organization. *J. Amer. psychoanal. Ass.*, 1958, *4* (1).
3. Blos, P. *On adolescence: A psychoanalytic interpretation*. New York: Free Press, 1962.
4. Blos, P. The concept of acting out in relation to the adolescent process. *J. Amer. Acad. Child Psychiat.*, 1963, *2* (1).
5. Freud, A. *Adolescence*. Vol. 13. *Psychoanalytic study of the child*. New York: International Univer. Press, 1958.
6. Glover, E. Psycho-analysis and criminology: A political survey. *Int. J. Psychoanal.*, 1956, *37*, Parts IV-V.
7. Johnson, M. A. Juvenile delinquency. In S. Arieti (Ed.), *American handbook of psychiatry*. New York: Basic Books, 1959.

PART IV

Family Interactional Factors
in Sexual Delinquency

Family system theory is not only a theory of the reciprocal functions which the family members perform for one another in health, but also a theory of dysfunctions which produce a relationship pathology and a development pathology. In this section, the chapters present interactional explanations of system pathology, expressed through sexual acting-out. Encompassed here are such specific forms of behavior problems of adolescent girls as running away, promiscuity, illegitimate pregnancy, and incest.

These explanations cover father-daughter relationships, mother-daughter relationships, and sibling relationships on various levels of regression and arrest. It makes little difference how fargoing the regression is, or in what phase of early development the primary fixation and arrest has occurred. There is always a lag in the psychological development which creates disharmony between it and the relentless push of physiological maturation. This seems to produce the relationship crisis resulting in sexual acting-out.

Over and beyond explanations of dysfunction in the dyadic relationship between a parent figure and a child, acting-out behavior of adolescent girls will be presented in the broader perspective of triadic systems (i.e., mother-father-daughter relationships) and whole family systems.

CHAPTER 11

The Family and the Female
Delinquent: An Overview

Alfred S. Friedman

Sexual delinquency in adolescent girls is a problem of central concern in our culture and presents society with a complex of economic, medical, legal, religious, moral, and ethical problems. Promiscuous premarital sexual behavior raises questions not only of the moral code and society's interest in controlling the sexual impulse and maintaining the family system; it is also generally recognized as an expression of negative values in human relationships, in which one or both partners have immature and exploitive attitudes toward the other, rather than developing more positive, mature, and loving attitudes. These experiences are not generally considered constructive in preparing the girl involved for a later satisfactory marriage.

There is abundant tragic evidence that sexual delinquency is far more profoundly self-destructive and irreversible in its consequences for a girl than is the delinquency that is seen in boys. As Blos points out, "The sexually delinquent girl violates the caring and protective attributes of her maternal role in a way which will harm her and her offspring for the remainder of her life." Even in ethnic and social-class groups where illegitimacy is not so great a social stigma as it is in white, middle-class groups, the girl, her baby, and her family usually face additional handicaps in achieving economic and family stability, as a result of the pregnancy. We must all agree that it would be well if the predisposing conditions for female sexual delinquency could be recognized and dealt with earlier, in the latent or pre-delinquent state, before the full onslaught of puberty has pushed the girl into acting-out behavior, and before the consequences have brought additional stress to the already vulnerable personality of the adolescent girl. An out-of-wedlock pregnancy affects the future lives not only of the girl, the baby, and the boy who fathers the baby, but of the two families involved, and the future spouses of the boy and the girl. A progression of emotional, mental, social, and economic problems, as well as unstable family conditions, accrue to the second generation from one out-of-wedlock pregnancy.

Promiscuous behavior for many girls reflects a superficiality in human relationships. Sexuality for them is usually an empty gesture; oftentimes personal satisfaction is totally lacking. A vain search for pleasures, escape, fear, a sense of personal inadequacy, and inability to establish an appropriate identity are often determining factors. With an unfulfilled need for affection from her parents, and in her desire to be accepted, the adolescent girl may seek substitute males who, unfortunately, exact a sexual tribute for attention, and she may confuse sexual popularity with bona fide concern and care. Some premarital sexual relationships occur on a more mature, constructive, and satisfactory level than that just described. It should be made clear, therefore, that we are not herein labeling all premarital sexual relationships "promiscuous" or "delinquent."

While the young male delinquent shows a wide variety of behavior, the girl, in contrast, possesses a quite limited delinquent repertoire. By and large, her legally defined offenses consist of sexual acting-out, vagrancy, running away, and stealing of the kleptomaniac type. In 1963, sex offenses constituted the largest single group of complaints against adolescent girls in the Philadelphia courts. More than 25 percent of all the girls who came to the attention of the County Court of Philadelphia were directly charged with sexual misbehavior (1). Many additional conduct difficulties involving sexual waywardness in girls were not so clearly stated. S. Robinson (2) reports from a survey of court practice that girls guilty of sex offenses "are customarily designated as ungovernable or as having deserted their homes." Reports of the United States Children's Bureau, supported by local surveys, indicate that the two most frequent infractions among girls are "ungovernable behavior" and sexual offenses. Although the police are largely responsible for bringing boys to court, it is of special interest that in the case of girls, the petitioners are usually the parents. Many additional cases of sexual promiscuity and sexual delinquency never reach the courts. Some of these are privately handled by psychiatrists, private agencies, psychiatric out-patient clinics, private correctional schools, and the like. Block and Flynn (3) report that commitment or referral to agencies and institutions for sexual behavior is far more frequent for girls than for boys.

At Sleighton Farm School for Girls, a state-supported institution near Philadelphia, a survey revealed that 32 percent of the 190 girls had been admitted primarily for sexual promiscuity, and that 76 percent of all the girls had some history of sexual delinquency, ranging from contacts with only one boy to the relatively few more serious cases with as many as fifty different men and boys. Only three of the girls had been known to engage in prostitution. One girl, on the other hand, had had sex relations with only one boy and claimed that they loved each other and wanted to get married. Her parents disapproved of the marriage and preferred that she be institutionalized. In such a case, there is a question whether the institutionalization of the girl is not more for the purpose of solving the parents' problem than of solving the girl's problem. Virtually no parental counseling or family group treatment had been attempted with these cases.

High schools have reported that the sexual behavior of some of their female students is an increasingly acute problem. For example, the existence of a non-virgin club was revealed, through a clinic, in a suburban school district of the Philadelphia metropolitan area. The girls underwent "initiation rites" in which they lost their virginity, with the assistance of several high school boys and some servicemen from a nearby army installation. The girls were required to undergo this initiation in the presence of other girls who were already members. Some of these girls were daughters of prominent citizens in the community. In some gangs, the peer culture even requires homosexual contacts between girls for membership status, and these are bragged about.

One might speculate that the relative lack of discussion of this problem in the literature on delinquency, compared with the voluminous treatment of delinquent behavior of young males, is partially due to its taboo and socially embarrassing aspects. It is also more difficult to define clearly, or for society to agree on, the degree of sexual contact, or the type and amount of sexual behavior, which is to be classified as delinquent. However, our society as a whole may be somewhat more ambivalent about its desire to terminate sexually promiscuous behavior in young girls than it is about its desire to terminate the destructive behavior of delinquent boys, directed against property and other persons.

In contrast to other forms of delinquency, this particular problem has received relatively little systematic study and evaluation. As far as we can find, there are virtually no adequately controlled studies of the problem or of its treatment in the literature. For example, we do not know whether there is the same incidence of sexual promiscuity in Negro girls as there is in white girls of the same socioeconomic class. We know that there are more unwed mothers among Negro girls than among white girls, when the socioeconomic class variable is not controlled; but we do not know how much of this results directly from the historical effects of the slavery system on Negro family structure, how much results from poor socioeconomic conditions in the present, and how much relates to specific differences in cultural attitudes and family psychodynamics. We do not know how much of Negro family instability and illegitimacy is due to current conditions of Negro socioeconomic inequality, and how much of current Negro inequality is, conversely, the result of illegitimacy and unstable family structure.

The Negro family constellation that currently accompanies illegitimacy, in the setting of the northern urban slum communities, needs to be studied. All speculation aside, it is not really known whether the values, standards, and life aspirations of young Negro girls, or their attitudes toward premarital sex relations, are significantly different from those of young white girls of the same educational and socioeconomic status. Are the self-perceptions of young unwed Negro mothers, in regard to their unwed status, the same as those of young unwed white mothers?

The ability to form relationships with boys and attractiveness to boys are determining factors in the development of self-identity and sex-role differentiation of adolescent girls, and in their peer-group status. Butman (4) considers a number of areas crucial in affecting the adolescent's approach to heterosexual relationships, interactions with the opposite sex, and attendant sexual behavior. Among them are: (*a*) motivations and orientations to cross-sex relations, such as "fun morality," "puritanism," etc., and the degree of dependence on cross-sex relations to satisfy affiliative status needs; (*b*) opportunities for sexual behavior and the control structures determining whether sexual behavior occurs, including external restrictions and internalization of standards and restrictions regarding sex; (*c*) information and attitudes regarding sexual behavior conveyed by significant others and by social and religious authorities, including the nature, depth, and openness of sex education and information available to the adolescent.

There is a clear need for development of further systematic approaches to the prevention and treatment of sexual delinquency in girls, as well as for controlled studies to evaluate the effectiveness of various forms of treatment.

Although all delinquency is a manifestation of disregard for, or rebellion against, authority in one form or another, there are indications that sexual delinquency among girls reflects more serious personality disturbance. It indicates the breakdown of parental control and an acute disturbance in the parent-adolescent relationship. It has been noted that delinquent girls generally appear to be more seriously disturbed than do delinquent boys. Many such cases are referred for psychiatric study and treatment. Monachesi and Hathaway's findings (5) with the Minnesota Multiphasic Personality Inventory support the view that delinquency in females is a manifestation of personality difficulty, rather than only a demonstration of subculture standards or group norms.

Some authors have speculated that certain factors of cultural change in the United States may be contributing to increased sexual acting-out and illegitimate pregnancies: the prevalence of a pattern of maternal dominance in American homes, the disappearance of the European and Victorian autocratic-leader type of father in the home, and the higher divorce rate. These factors result in the absence of a strong father figure, both as an identification model and as a love object in the lives of American girls. Much has been written about the serious implications of the absence of a strong father figure for the American boy, particularly the Negro boy, and how this has contributed to juvenile delinquency. The need of the girl for a strong father is almost as important. Dame et al. (6) have speculated that this lack has resulted in a delay in the resolution of the oedipal problem for these girls. The wish for a father was neither sufficiently satisfied nor was there an adequate opportunity to learn to control or delay it. The oedipal relationship was so lacking, or existed so exclusively in fantasy, that there was no possibility of working it through. This predisposition of a yearning for a father, combined with anger at the mother for chasing the father away or for emasculating him, is seen as precipitating the girl's sexual acting-out. Her negative dependency on her mother may be transferred to a rebellious, aggressive, or delinquent boy, who acts out the aggression she has suppressed in herself.

In addition to the family constellations characterized by passive, weak, or absent fathers, we found in our own study and treatment of families of sexually-acting-out girls a type of father-daughter relationship that appears, at least on the surface, to be quite different: the father's seductive, incestuously-toned behavior toward the girl, accompanied by a restrictive attitude toward her. He is threatened by the onset of her puberty, projects his sexual guilt onto her, and becomes angry and restrictive. He accuses her of sexual misbehavior with boys and thereby justifies his restrictiveness. The girl, disappointed at being pushed away by her father, flouts his authority and seeks outside sexual objects. Although this constellation is quite different from the first one described above, they both have in common the lack of a substantial father-daughter relationship based on trust, warmth, and affection.

To summarize our observations on the group of families we treated: Most of the fathers were seen as passive, under-achieving, dependent, needy, and wanting their wives to assume mother roles for them. Further, the fathers were seen as seductive to their daughters, caught up in the daughters' unresolved oedipal feelings, and going out of their way to seek attention from their daughters. In our family therapy work, we have seen many adolescent daughters pushed to the brink of promiscuous sexual behavior by the continuous detailed, provocative, and suspicious questioning and dire warnings of their fathers. One of the fathers would check the speedometer and the amount of gas in his daughter's car before and after she went out on a date. He would then interrogate her in detail regarding her whereabouts of the night before, until he reduced her to tears and anger. She sometimes reacted to the repeated accusations with the attitude, "If I have the name, I might as well have the game." The father did not realize that his obsessive concern was an unwitting provocation to sexual acting-out, in that he impressed on the girl the picture he had of her misbehaving sexually.

Another father was obsessively preoccupied with his attractive daughter's relationship with boys. He continuously made suggestive remarks about what his daughter must be doing with these boys, in a manner that indicated that he was jealous of the boys, but also that he was excited by the fantasy of their sexual behavior with his daughter. He would say to her, "Well, you know what boys want. If you don't give it to them, they're not going to be interested in you." The daughter, in one session, told of a fantasy she had of getting her own apartment and earning money by having men come over. She said she had thought about it, but of course she would never do it. The father then said, "Oh yes, this is something to think about." While he may have intended this to be mildly sarcastic, it was not really clear whether he wanted her to be promiscuous or not.

The mothers as well as the fathers were unduly suspicious of the daughters' dating activities. Nearly all the mothers had excessive emotional investment in their daughters—while, simultaneously, they saw the daughters as very much unlike themselves. Concomitantly, the mothers' own neediness, while not superficially apparent, was revealed in their struggle with their daughters over who should be the parent: about half of the mothers were trying to make their daughters take over some significant aspects of their own mothering role. Since both parents are weak, the entire family becomes emotionally needy and puts pressure on an older daughter to assume the mother role.

One might speculate whether there is some connection between the increased incidence of sexual acting-out in girls of the current generation and the relative clinical rarity today of the classic picture of hysterical neurosis described by Freud. That reaction was characterized by guilt and contained both the hidden wish and the punishment. The modern female is less prone to guilt over sex. She may also be less likely to derive masochistic gratification from submitting sexually in fantasy, whether consciously or unconsciously, to a male. She has been more accustomed to submitting to her mother than to her passive father.

Giffin, Johnson, and Litin (7) describe a subtle form of parental seduction, or inappropriate sexual temptation of children, which occurs under the guise of parental love and tenderness. "It confronts the child with an ambivalent, genital passion which he or she cannot understand or begin to integrate. The child becomes unconsciously aware of and absorbs the parent's hostile, guilty, shameful feelings, and experiences genital frustration, confusion, fear of detection and anxiety. In cases of perversion, we always see the overstressing, usually by the mother, of at least one aspect of polymorphous sexual proclivities of the young child, such as to lead to unusual selective hypertrophy." Thus the parent is consciously or, more often, unconsciously permissive and inconsistent in stimulation of the small child. The parent later achieves an unconscious vicarious gratification of his own inadequately repressed instinctual needs through the child's acting-out. For example, inordinate curiosity regarding an adolescent daughter's experiences on dates with boys carries with it implied sanction; overly stimulating family discussions about sex may constitute unwitting approval; and the parent's warnings and accusations about sexual behavior, coupled with the parent's intense curiosity and excitement, may result in blocking the child's natural development of an adequate conscience and standard of behavior. Szurek (8) observes that "if the discipline of the parent is administered with guilt, it permits the child to act out and to subtly blackmail the parent until the particular issue is befogged with irrelevant bickerings."

Blos has pointed out that Johnson and Szurek's (9) dynamic formulation of sexual delinquency, in terms of the child's acting out the unconscious wishes of the parent, can only take place when the emotional separation between parent and child is pathologically incomplete. In fact, he considered the continuation of the symbiotic tie between the mother and the child, and the continued need for immediate object possession, as the precondition for sexual acting-out. Blos presents in psychoanalytic terms a comprehensive psychodynamic formulation of female sexual delinquency, of which he describes three "typical constellations." He sees the sexual acting-out as a defense against regression to the intense attachment to the pre-oedipal mother, which results from a failure in the pre-adolescent task of emotional liberation from her.

Some cases develop into a compulsive form of promiscuity (10). Because she is so filled with her earliest unsatisfied wishes and so disappointed in her relationship with her parents, the girl, according to this formulation, is fearful of committing herself to a new love relationship. She may, depending on other factors, either avoid all heterosexual contact or, still having insatiable desires, develop a partial depersonalization in the area of sex, splitting off the experience and sensations of the physical sexual contact from her emotional object relationships, which permits promiscuous sexual behavior.

Kaufman, Peck, and Taguiri (11) found that incest could not be explained in terms of the personalities of the father or daughter alone. Rather, both parents were involved in a pattern of unconscious stimulation and permission of the incestual behavior, the mother from the unconscious desire to place the daughter in a maternal role. The girl reacts to this desire of the mother's by developing a pseudo-maturity and by seeking gratification from the relationship with the father. The parents do not provide the girl with adequate controls or adequate assistance in reality-testing and superego-formation.

Robey (see Chapter 12) noted quite a similar pattern in young girls who run away from home and act out sexually with one or more boys. Robey did not see quite the depth of pathology in the families of the runaway girls that Kaufman et al. reported for the incest cases. Robey speculated that it is because of the girl's strength that, when she is given the choice of taking over the mother's role or running away, she chooses the latter as a method of fighting off the incestuous wishes unconsciously shared by all members of the family. The immediate or superficial conflict from which the girl runs away is usually between herself and her father, although there often appears to be an equally important underlying conflict with the mother.

It is obviously not sufficient to postulate that the incest threat within a family is the immediate precipitant to a girl's running away and acting out sexually. After all, every family must develop controls for incestuous impulses and feelings. We do not yet know the differences in the intensity of the incest threat, nor in the ways of defending against it, between delinquent, schizophrenic, and "normal" families. This could be a subject for future research.

Ernst et al. (12), of the San Francisco Department of Public Health, studied 139 "habitually promiscuous" women by psychiatric interview and history, and classified them according to "motivation" into the following four groups:

Actively-conflicted group. Promiscuity is an expression of intrapsychic neurotic conflict (55 percent of the white females and 28 percent of the Negro females studied).

Dependent group. Promiscuity is an expression of dependency and immaturity causing relatively little concern, since responsibility for behavior is placed on the sexual partners (14 percent of the white females and 28 percent of the Negro females studied).

Maladapted group. Promiscuity is part of an unstable character formation, with lack of responsibility and social restraint but no evidence of internal conflict (22 percent of the white females and 16 percent of the Negro females studied).

Nonconflictual group. Promiscuity appears to be a means of satisfying sexual desires primarily, with no conflicts revealed within the self or with the social group (3 percent of the white females and 20 percent of the Negro females studied).

In summary, some of the family dynamics that are considered contributory to female sexual delinquency are: primary emotional deprivation and an unfulfilled need for closeness and tenderness in the girl; longing for a missing father; rejection by the father; excessive strictness by the father; overstimulation or seduction; overpermissiveness and inconsistent parental controls; hostility, provocation, suspicion, and accusation by parents; confusion over sexual identity, resulting from inappropriate role relationships in the parental marriage; a defense against regression to the infantile relationship with a nurturing mother; a defense against homosexual threat; a flight from incest threat within the family; a tendency to fulfill a parent's dire prediction; identification with a pregnant mother, sister, or friend, or with a promiscuous mother; and combinations of the above factors.

While there is not complete agreement, there are a number of consistent elements of family dynamics that recur frequently in the descriptions of the observers reviewed above.

TEEN-AGE ILLEGITIMATE PREGNANCY

Teen-age illegitimacy, or the problem of the pregnant unmarried girl, is an increasing social problem that requires special attention. During the twenty-two-year period from 1938 to 1959, the national illegitimacy rate for fifteen- to nineteen-year-old girls almost doubled. The total number of unmarried mothers during the single year of 1963 was 259,000. It has been speculated that, including unreported cases, somewhere between a half million and a million unmarried girls were pregnant last year, and that 200,000 illegal abortions were performed, constituting in a sense a social emergency for our national community.

Elizabeth Herzog of the U.S. Children's Bureau (see Chapter 7) has pointed out that these figures do not necessarily represent a sudden crisis or a teen-age revolution in sex mores, but are symptoms of a chronic problem. She calls for coordinated planning of long-term, comprehensive basic services.

High school and college teachers today are faced increasingly with the problem of the presence of pregnant single girls in their classrooms. On the other hand, the absence of these girls from their courses, and in some cases their eventual dropping out, also pose problems to be solved. In Chicago, Visotsky (see Chapter 8) reports that less than 30 percent of the lower socioeconomic class girls excluded from elementary school because of pregnancy returned after the enforced absence; and that the termination of schooling for the other 70 percent had serious consequences for their future lives.

In addition to the need for facilities, there is a need for developing a more adequate rationale for the treatment of this problem. The problem is multiply-determined, and therefore requires a broad approach in understanding and treatment. There is evidence (13) that subcultural, religious, and educational values, differential intrafamilial relationships, differential peer experiences related to dating and heterosexual contacts, as well as the personality dynamics of the individual girl, are all involved both in the occurrence of illegitimate pregnancy and in the girl's subsequent decision to keep or surrender the infant.

Butman (4) conducted a controlled research comparison of girls who dropped out of school because of illegitimate pregnancies with other girls of similar background in the same schools. She found that the following factors differentiated the girls who became pregnant: (a) a low self-image, reflected in a low estimate of their own competence in meeting performance expectations; (b) inadequate and inaccurate sex information obtained from personal experience, boyfriends, or books; (c) perception of boys as more definitely expecting sex relations; (d) orientation to marriage as an immediate goal; and (e) psychological involvement in, and commitment to, a relationship with a boy.

Young (14) found that 48 out of 100 unmarried mothers she studied had dominating and rejecting mothers, and 20 of those who had fathers had dominating and rejecting fathers; the girl's relation to the dominant parent "was a battleground on which a struggle was fought, and the baby was an integral part of that strugle." She also had the impression that all of the girls were neurotic, unhappy, and had poor interpersonal relations; only a few of them made constructive use of their native ability in work, and none had genuinely cared for, or been happy with, the father of her baby. The tendency to self-punishment and self-destruction was found to be a deeply ingrained and powerful force in these girls.

Vincent (15), in a controlled study of pregnant unmarried girls, found a large subgroup who had either been rejected or had withdrawn from their parents to a considerable degree. The only major difference he found between these pregnant girls and similar nonpregnant girls who had also been rejected or had withdrawn from their parents was that the girls who had not become pregnant were able to identify with a teacher or another adult in the community, from whom they learned and internalized traditional middle-class sex mores. The pregnant unmarried girls were guided almost exclusively by the permissive sex mores of a small peer group, upon whose acceptance they were dependent in the absence of positive meaningful relationships with a parent, a teacher, a minister, or another adult friend.

In our own work with lower-class families in which a girl gets pregnant, we have seen some, but not all, of the attitudes reported by Visotsky occurring in white as well as Negro families. (See Chapter 8.) A key differential factor appears to be the more established responsibility of the father in the middle-class families, whether white or Negro, and the greater expectations from him, and correspondingly from young peer males, for authority, control, and satisfactions other than sex.

The girl brought up in a rather strict middle-class home who becomes an unmarried mother may tend to be, on the average, emotionally sicker than the girl in the same situation who comes from a more permissive lower-class home. The circumstances of illegitimate pregnancy in middle-class white families typically bring additional stress to already highly conflictual family relationships. The girl may withdraw further from family ties and from outside friendships. She often hides the fact of her pregnancy from one parent, and sometimes from both. The family feels that the girl should "hide" from the community until the pregnancy is terminated. The home, instead of being considered as a haven during this period of stress, is experienced as a place of exile; the pregnant unmarried daughter is expected to exist in oblivion. It is clear that there is an acute need for counseling with the whole family in regard to their attitude and role in this problem. It is also clear that when the girl comes to an agency for help, she can be encouraged more often than occurs in current practice to face the problem openly with her parents and family, rather than to hide it in shame. Loesch and Greenberg (16) conclude that the majority of unwed mothers today, re-enter the world after the pregnancy with little emotional or internal change, remaining still in conflict with their family and capable only of dependent or hostile, chaotic relationships with men.

Most psychoanalytic studies emphasize the unconscious "purpose" of the act of becoming pregnant. Although the girl does not plan consciously and intentionally to bear an out-of-wedlock child, she does act in such a way that this becomes the almost inevitable result. She often continues to behave as though she were not pregnant after it has happened. The act of insemination is described by Young as a dissociated episode in the lives of the girls: "They conceive without knowing it, and as it were from no one; they bear and deliver as easily as the most fortunate of their married sisters, but they relinquish the newborn child to their mothers" as a gift they hope will be accepted. Characteristically, the mother is ambivalent about accepting the gift. The girl's strong unconscious need to become pregnant is motivated by the need for a love object she never had. The longing for a baby is a dominant unconscious fantasy in the sexual acting-out, although the girl may consciously believe she does not want to get pregnant. This longing for a baby may be considered to represent the unconscious wish to have a child with the mother, and is essentially an undoing of a disappointment in the mother; the mother-child unit thus becomes re-established by proxy. Greenberg, Loesch, and Lakin (17) found that pregnancies frequently appear to occur after the loss of an important love object by the girl—the death of a parent or separation from a boyfriend, a significant relative, a valued job, and so on. The emotional state during pregnancy is often dominated consciously, also, by the girl's conflict over the coming loss of her future infant.

OBSERVATIONS FROM TREATMENT OF FAMILIES WITH SEXUALLY DELINQUENT GIRLS

We have conducted family therapy in the special demonstration and training project at Philadelphia Psychiatric Center, with a group of families with sexually-acting-out adolescent girls. We have also conducted family therapy with a group of families with adolescent schizophrenic daughters or sons. These two experiences have afforded us an opportunity to develop some impressions regarding the differences and similarities between these two types of families. Since our therapeutic contact with the "delinquent families" has been of shorter duration and perhaps less depth than with the "schizophrenic families," our impressions listed below must be considered as only tentative hypotheses, which deserve more careful and controlled evaluation:

(1) We do not see in the sexually delinquent families the intense and overwhelming degree of pathological dyadic relationship and symbiosis between the mother and child that we see in the schizophrenic family. The schizophrenic child has less capacity to break out of the symbiosis and to form real or intimate relationships with peers on the outside. The delinquent can also perhaps relate somewhat more simultaneously to both mother and father in a triadic relationship, at least in a tentative way, than can the schizophrenic. If there is more of a real marriage between the parents in the acting-out family and a less complete emotional divorce, then it follows that there will be less freeing of the generational lines, and that a less intense and pervasive symbiotic bind will develop between the mother and daughter. It appears that the fathers of the sexually-acting-out girls are able to give their daughters something that the fathers of schizophrenics are not able to. Perhaps the key difference is that the former treat their daughters more as though they were real people.

(2) The parental marriages in both types of families can be characterized by intense conflict. Nevertheless, there seems to be more hope in the marriages of the acting-out families, in that they are still struggling to work out their differences with each other, whereas the parents of the schizophrenics seem more resigned to their schism and to their hostile recriminations. Prior to marriage, the parents of the acting-out families appear to have had some degree of satisfying relatedness to the community, but their marriage and the appearance of children were sometimes regarded as unhappy interruptions of those earlier rewarding experiences.

(3) The acting-out families are livelier and more mobile, less predictable and repetitive, less stereotyped, and not as frightened by sex. However, in some of our delinquent families where the girl's sexual promiscuity was not very extreme, the instability in the family organization was not particularly marked. The schizophrenic families often appear more funereal and "dead," and sex is often a forbidden, frightening thing to them. In addition to the feeling of an underlying reservoir of loss, mourning, and

resignation, some of the schizophrenic families are just plain boring, as a result of their massive denial, repression, superficiality, and rigidity. This is consistent with the finding of Meyers and Roberts (18) that their female schizophrenic patients, regardless of class status, were sexually inhibited, whereas their female neurotic patients were sexually "hyperactive, which represented a rebellion against a strictness and control of parents." We agreed thus with the finding of the Stabenau et al. study (19) that the schizophrenic child was more "inactive." At one level, the parents wanted the child to be inactive, conforming, and suppressed. However, at another level in some of these "dead" families, the schizophrenic child represented the life or the "id" of the family that the parents needed for their own pleasure.

(4) Part of the reason for the above difference is that the fathers in the acting-out families have more and somewhat livelier relationships in the outside world than the fathers in the schizophrenic families. They are generally more worldly, more interesting to talk to, have a wider range of interests, interact more spontaneously in the treatment, are not as withdrawn, vague, and concealing. The family system is thus more open, and more people are allowed to interact, not only with the father, but with all family members. Because they have more to do with the outside world, the acting-out families may not have the excessively important and influential "peripheral persons" that many schizophrenic families have and depend on. These latter families form pathological dyadic relationships with such significant peripheral persons.

(5) The fathers of acting-out daughters tend to be more overtly aggressive, spontaneous, and labile in affect expression, with temper outbursts and rages, than the fathers of schizophrenics, many of whom we have described as "cardboard" fathers. The former can become punitive, authoritarian, restrictive, and critical toward their daughters. This overt behavior may cover feelings of inferiority and underlying passive-dependent wishes toward their wives and daughters, but nevertheless the overt behavior may be aggressive. We did not find as much difference in regard to the assertiveness and the aggression of the mothers in the two groups, as we did in regard to the fathers.

(6) The delinquent girl—not having had the shared past of a crippling symbiotic relationship with her mother and not having been arrested at the level of the submissive, inert child, as is the schizophrenic girl—finds her status with her father too much that of a peer or rival with her mother for her to remain comfortably at home. Consequently her rebelling and acting-out outside of the family, in an aggressive sexual fashion, serves to shore up the incest taboo.

The oedipal involvement of the daughter with the father has a more real quality here and does not appear in a pseudo or fantasy fashion, as it does between the schizophrenic girl and her father. In the acting-out families, the parents have less delay in impulse gratification. They are more prone to have conscious fantasies of acting-out sexually. While the parents of the schizophrenics may not admit these fantasies into consciousness, the family acts as if, should they wait long enough, sex and other pleasures will be delivered within the family unit. One does not have to look out-side; in fact, it is taboo to look outside—the reverse of what is considered normal.

The incest threat is probably reacted to differently in the two types of families, and we do not know the combination of subtle factors that causes the delinquent girl or boy to run away from the incest threat in the family and to act out—while the schizophrenic remains stuck at home and preoccupied consciously or unconsciously with his incest fantasies.

(7) The roles of "badness" and "madness" may be distributed according to different patterns in the two types of families. The "good sibling" of the delinquent child, who is unrealistically idealized by his parents, may be analogous to the "well sibling" in the family of the schizophrenic. Accordingly, the "good sibling" deserves special study and should be made a part of the family's therapeutic commitment.

(8) In the schizophrenic case, the family, particularly the mother, tends to dwell on symptomatology and helping the sick or problem child. It may be that the presence of symptoms seals the symbiosis, and as long as symptoms can be talked about the symbiosis is fortified. In the acting-out families, there may be less of a need to continue the disturbing behavior over a long period of time or to continue talking about it in treatment sessions. We notice that the acting-out frequently stops shortly after family treatment begins. To the extent that the acting-out is a bid for attention and results from the child's doubting the parents' interest in her, the family's coming to treatment might make the acting-out less necessary.

(9) We postulate that the family image in the schizophrenic families is distorted or defective. The family image in the delinquent family may also be distorted to some extent, but more specifically there may be a deficit, the absence of an adequate family image, a lack in development of a consciousness among the family members of being an integrated family unit. Each member of the family finds himself at a particular level of arrested development and immaturity, beyond which the family cannot foster growth.

REFERENCES

1. Brown, T. (Ed.), *50th annual report of County Court of Philadelphia*. Philadelphia: Dept. of Statistics & Research, 1963.
2. Robinson, S. *Delinquency: its nature and control*. New York: Holt, 1960.
3. Block, H. A., & Flynn, F. T. *Delinquency: the juvenile offender*. New York: Random House, 1956.
4. Butman, J. W. Summary, conclusions, and implications. In *The social, psychological, and behavioral world of the teen-age girl*. Final report to the Department of Health, Education and Welfare, Social Security Administration, Grant #028, and to the McGregor Foundation, Detroit, Mich., June, 1965.
5. Monachesi, E. D., & Hathaway, S. R. *Analyzing and predicting juvenile delinquency*. Minneapolis: Univer. Minnesota Press, 1953.
6. Dame, N. G., et al. Conflict in marriage following premarital pregnancy. Paper presented at 42nd Annual Meeting, Amer. Orthopsychiat. Assoc., March, 1965.
7. Giffin, M., Johnson, A., & Litin, E. The transmission of superego defects in the family. In *The Family*. New York: Free Press, 1960.
8. Szurek, S. Some impressions from clinical experience with delinquents. In K. Eissler (Ed.), *Searchlights on delinquency*. New York: International Univer. Press, 1949.

9. Johnson, A., & Szurek, S. The genesis of anti-social acting out in children and adults. *Psychoanal. Quart.*, 1952, *21* 322–343.
10. Bychowski, G. Object relationships in women. *J. Amer. psychoanal. Ass.*, 1961, 9.
11. Kaufman, I., Peck, A., & Taguiri, C. The family constellation and overt incestuous relations between father and daughter. *Amer. J. Orthopsychiat.*, 1954, *24*, 266.
12. Ernst, C., et al. *An experiment in the psychiatric treatment of promiscuous girls.* San Francisco: Dept. Public Health, 1945.
13. Jones, W. C., Meyer, H. J., & Borgotta, E. F. Social and psychological factors in status decisions of unmarried mothers. *Marriage & Fam. Living*, 1962, *24*(3).
14. Young, L. R. Personality patterns in unmarried mothers. In: *Understanding the psychology of the unmarried mother.* New York: Fam. Serv. Ass. Amer., 1947.
15. Vincent, C. E. *Unmarried mothers.* New York: Free Press, 1961.
16. Loesch, J. G., & Greenberg, N. H. Some specific areas of conflict observed during pregnancy: A comparative study of married and unmarried pregnant women. *Amer. J. Orthopsychiat.*, 1962, *32*.
17. Greenberg, N. H. J., Loesch, J., & Lakin, M. Life situations associated with onset of pregnancy. *Psychomat. Med.*, 1959, *21*, 296.
18. Meyers, J. K., & Roberts, B. H. *Family and class dynamics in mental illness.* New York: Wiley, 1959.
19. Stabenau, J. R., Tupin, J., Werner, M., & Pollin, W. A comparative study of families of schizophrenics, delinquents, and normals. *Psychiatry*, 1965, *28* (1).

CHAPTER 12

The Runaway Girl

Ames Robey

Juvenile delinquency has been of concern to mental health personnel since the turn of the century. Attention has been focused mainly on the boy, however, and it is only more recently that the acting-out behavior of the girl has come under intense scrutiny.

With reference to juvenile delinquency, acting-out may be defined as a repetitive attempt, through actions, to solve areas of conflict in defiance of authority. One of the most frequent forms of acting-out in the adolescent girl is running away. Although a common symptom in both boys and girls, in the girl it usually represents a far greater level of pathology. Review of the records from several courts indicates that running away may constitute over half their case load of adolescent girls. Considering other behavior such as stubbornness, disobedience, or sexual promiscuity, where running away may also be part of the pattern, the incidence is even higher. Further, there are ample indications that running away is in reality even more frequent than reported by the courts. This is presumably due to the fact that running away is far too often treated extremely lightly by the parents, or by the police when it is called to their attention, and court complaints are not made. It is usually dealt with by a "talking to," and no investigation as to the cause of the girl's actions is made. Unless the girl becomes unmanageable or her behavior repetitive, this situation rarely reaches the attention of the professional mental health worker. However, it should be strongly emphasized that, in the adolescent girl, running away, far from being a childish escapade, is almost invariably indicative of extensive and severe individual and family pathology.

It must be recognized that running away from home can result from a wide variety of intolerable home situations, and that no one cause will be seen consistently. However, in a large proportion of cases, there is considerable indication that the girl runs away from home to ward off the unconscious threat of an incestuous relationship with her father, the fear of the resultant dissolution of the family, and the concurrent depression.

The study on which this chapter is based (1) was carried on in the Massachusetts Court Clinics. The Division of Legal Medicine of the Department of Mental Health of Massachusetts maintains thirteen such mental health units in courts throughout the state. Their purpose is to help the judge understand individual cases, make diagnoses, offer recommendations on dispositions, and treat offenders placed on probation. They have also been active in conducting research in various aspects of the psychodynamics of offenders. Clinics in two courts were involved in the study. The first of these serves an essentially suburban area of approximately 150,000. Using the classification of Hollingshead and Redlich (2), the families seen in this district are predominantly from Classes 2 and 3 (upper middle and middle class), with some families in Class 4 (lower-middle class). The second court covers a population of some 60,000 in an economically deprived area of the city of Boston where the families are mainly from Classes 4 and 5 (lower-middle and lower class). Records from the first of these courts indicate that approximately 55 percent of their case load of adolescent girls were charged with running away. In the second court, this charge appears in only about 25 percent of the cases. Despite this recorded lower level in the economically deprived area, however, it becomes clear that the incidence was as high, if not higher; but the referral rate by parents to the police, and by the police to the courts, was considerably lower. While not specifically included in the study, a review of cases from both courts with charges such as stubborn child, lewd and lascivious cohabitation, or unauthorized use of a motor vehicle, revealed that the girls had really been running away from home.

For purposes of this discussion running away is defined (as it was for the study) as leaving home without permission for at least overnight, with the stated intent to run away. The study was restricted to girls who were living either with both parents or with one parent and a stepparent.

It should be noted, when discussing cases evaluated by court clinics, that a great deal of preselection has occurred by the time the case is referred. The parents will not inform the police until they feel they can no longer handle the problem. It is also clear that the police themselves prefer not to bring a girl into court unless her attitude is particularly stubborn or her behavior repetitive. After a court appearance, the case is usually referred to the court clinic, unless the girl's behavior is so uncontrollable that commitment to the Division of Youth Service is considered necessary.

Upon referral of a case to the clinic, arrangements are made for the psychiatrist to see both the girl and her parents as soon as possible. While some parents are reluctant to have any contact with the clinic, the court is, of course, able to provide considerable motivation for them not only to participate in the diagnostic evaluation but also to engage actively in treatment where it seems indicated. Where possible, all cases are seen at least three times in diagnostic evaluation, although many fathers, despite pressure from the court, refuse to come to the clinic after the first interview.

Evaluation of these families discloses a remarkably consistent pattern of family interaction. Typically this pattern includes a disturbed marital relationship between the parents, very poor control by the parents over their own impulses, equal inability of the parents to control the girl's impulses, an orally deprived mother-child relationship that shows a lack of any real maternal warmth, and subtle, usually unconscious pressure by the mother on the girl to take over the maternal role. It appears that the girl usually accepts this role prior to puberty. Within the bounds of her intelligence, she responds by becoming a competent and apparently almost hypermature individual, in terms of taking on many maternal responsibilities. An equilibrium is established and usually maintained until the appearance of adolescent secondary sexual characteristics and libidinal drives. At this point, the girl becomes involved in a bitter rebellion that culminates in her running away. With the beginning of her dating and associated behavior, the father tends to become quite restrictive, suspicious, and accusatory about imagined sexual activities on the part of his daughter. Very often the father's accusations antedate any such behavior by several weeks or even months. At least superficially, the girl, when she finally runs away from home, does so to escape the conflict with her father. What becomes clear only on closer inspection is the role that the disturbed mother-daughter relationship plays in this conflict and the need for the mother to find a maternal figure herself, which she solves by forcing the daughter into this role.

In their paper on incest, Kaufman, Peck, and Taguiri (3) noted not only the strong dependent wishes of both parents and their search for a mother figure, but also the mother's pressure on the girl to assume the maternal role. The girl reacted by developing a pseudomaturity, and in the absence of effective controls, her search for oral gratification led to an overt incestuous relationship with her father. In our experience with runaway girls, there is a striking similarity to the family interrelationships noted by Kaufman and his collaborators although an equivalent level of pathology is not seen. In over one hundred and sixty cases of runaway girls that fit the pattern described above, there were only five cases of alleged incest. In may be because of the girl's strengths that when she is given the choice of taking over the mother's role, including the sexual role, or running away, she chooses the latter as a method of controlling her incestuous wishes, which are unquestionably shared by not only her father, but also her mother.

The following two case examples illustrate the complex dynamics commonly seen in the runaway girl and her family:

THE CASE OF GAIL

Gail T. first ran away with another girl for several days, a few months before she was brought into court. No action was taken on her return. Although she had been dating for three years, she suddenly began to go out with a much older boy—she was just fifteen at the time and he was almost twenty; he drank a great deal and was well known to the police. Mr. T. tried his best to break up the relationship; but Gail continued it by lying about where she was going, and she finally came to her parents saying she was pregnant. The father became panic-stricken, and although the mother tried to get him to calm down, he insisted on rushing Gail to the Florence Crittenton Home the same day. There the parents were advised to let Gail marry if she were pregnant, and to seek counseling later. Gail wore the boy's ring for a few weeks but soon wrote another boy that her parents were forcing her to marry someone she did not love. The father discovered the letter, became furious, and finally extracted an admission from her that she was not pregnant and had not had sexual relations. Mr. T. then became extremely restrictive and in a few weeks Gail ran away again. After four days she was apprehended and brought into court, and then referred to the clinic.

In the first interview, the parents were seen together. Mr. T. described Gail as a completely uncontrollable girl who was dating too much and running around with a crowd of which her parents disapproved. He tended to be particularly suspicious of her sexual activities and used this to rationalize his extreme restrictiveness. Mrs. T., however, had sabotaged his efforts to restrain Gail. In the interview the parents began fighting over this, the father finally threatening divorce if the girl were not controlled. He did not come in for interviews after than, preferring to sit in the car outside.

Gail was an extremely pretty, but quite angry girl, who appeared older than her stated age. Initially she refused to talk at all, except to complain bitterly about how unreasonable her father was.

Gail was the oldest by eight years of three children, and was described by Mrs. T. as being like "a little mother" when she was younger. An extremely close relationship with her father existed until the girl began dating at the age of twelve, at which time Mr. T. began to be suspicious about her sexual activities, and many fights arose over this. The mother had long forced the girl to take an adult role in caring for her two younger siblings, and apparently allowed and encouraged her to wear makeup and appear older than she was.

On the surface, the relationship between the parents seemed very good. Mr. T. earned an adequate income as a high school teacher, and Mrs. T. appeared to be the devoted, busy housewife. In therapy, however, the mother brought out her contempt for her husband's refusal to take any responsibility, and admitted that she had avoided sexual contact whenever possible for many years. She denied extramarital affairs on the part of her husband or herself. She said she felt "caught in the middle" between her husband and the girl, feeling that Mr. T. was somewhat correct in his attempts to control Gail, but still wanting her daughter to have the "fun I never had."

Gail and Mrs. T. were seen in treatment for fourteen months, during which the girl's running away stopped and her marks came from failing up to honor-roll level. She dated less indiscriminately, and finally began going with a boy much closer to her own age. Some initial evaluation of this relationship showed it to have a number of pathological elements—but in comparison with her previous relationships, it seemed relatively healthy.

When Gail's initial probation came to a close, the court, despite the urging of the clinic staff, was reluctant to continue her under any further probation or supervision. Both she and her parents stated that they would continue to attend the clinic, but none of them showed up for the next appointment. It was not until a few weeks later, after Gail had falsified her birth certificate and run away to New Hampshire to marry her boyfriend, that the parents returned for assistance. At first they were strongly motivated to obtain an annulment, but were cautioned against this because Gail would be eighteen within a few months and would be able to marry without their permission. It was felt that an annulment would probably achieve nothing but increased bitterness. No more was heard from Gail for approximately a year; then she called, stating that she was intending to leave her husband because he was beating her and taking no responsibility financially or at home. She also suspected him of some extramarital sexual relationships. She was contemplating divorce, and in a first interview this was discussed with her. She stated that she could now really see much of what had been discussed during therapy prior to her marriage. She reached no decision by the end of the first interview, and just prior to a second appointment a week later she called to say that she had "made up" with her husband and that she saw no need to come back.

THE CASE OF ANN

Ann G. was almost fifteen when first arraigned in juvenile court. She had run away after her mother had found her in bed with a boy whom she had been forbidden to see. She was referred to the clinic by the probation officer; during the diagnostic period she ran away again. She had in her purse a letter to her boyfriend, which her mother had discovered and shown to Mr. G. when he returned home from work at one o'clock in the morning. On reading it, Mr. G. became furious, pulled Ann out of bed, and slapped her several times, then said he would take the matter up further in the morning. Mrs. G., evidently sensing that Ann would run away again, tried to sit up in the girl's room all night but fell asleep after a few minutes. When she awoke, Ann was gone. When picked up by the police, Ann, fearing her father's reaction, refused to return home, and was placed at the Division of Youth Service Detention Center. Again appearing in court, she promised there would be no further trouble, and was returned to her parents. There was some improvement during the next few months, while she and her mother were being seen in treatment; but after her boyfriend attempted suicide and was hospitalized, the situation deteriorated rapidly. Ann was placed at the House of the Good Shepherd, and seemed to adjust well for several months, until her boyfriend appeared at the door one day with a pistol and demanded her release. This incident led to Ann's placement with her paternal grandmother, and she was again seen at the clinic once a week.

The patient was the first of two siblings, having a younger brother toward whom she evinced both intense jealousy and guilt. She was often left in charge of him; at one of these times, when she was eight and her brother eighteen months, he fell down the stairs and was badly bruised. Both mother and daughter mentioned the incident during the diagnostic period, and the patient felt that her mother still blamed her for the accident. Mr. G. was a steadily employed waiter who slept late in the morning and whose job kept him away from home in the afternoon and evening. As the contacts with the clinic continued, he became difficult to reach and showed considerable resistance when he did come in. He apparently had had a very close relationship with Ann until she reached puberty, at which time he became rather strict about her activities. However, his concern over her alleged poor control seemed superficial. An earlier marriage of Mr. G.'s had lasted only a few months, and he did not bother with a divorce until after he began living with Ann's mother. Mrs. G., an extremely anxious, thin, depressed woman, went into considerable detail in presenting her own history of extensive deprivation: her father was a severe alcoholic, her mother spent most of her life in a mental hospital, and she was brought up by her grandmother. While she tended to see herself as a very inadequate mother and in severe need of help with her own problems, there was considerable anger just under the surface, and she was obviously the dominant force in the family. Despite an external appearance of a nice home and family situation, the marital relationship was very poor; Mrs. G. was contemptuous of her husband and denied him sexual relations; he frequently beat her, drank heavily, and indulged in numerous extramarital affairs with her knowledge.

Ann herself was a colicky infant, and at the age of three months, when Mr. G. went into the service, Ann and her mother had gone to live with the paternal grandmother, who took over the child's care. When mother moved to another city three years later, Ann adjusted poorly, became sick, and was sent back to her grandmother's to live until she was almost eight years old. She did quite well in school until the age of thirteen, when her marks began to slip. When she first came to the clinic, she was failing several subjects, despite an IQ of over 120.

While Ann's mother had allowed her to begin dating at around thirteen, both parents and the girl insisted that the trouble had begun only over her most recent boyfriend, whom the clinic knew to be depressed, emotionally unstable, and easily manipulated. It became clear during therapy that this boy had gotten into bed with her—the precipitating event for her initial court appearance—at her request, but had not had intercourse with her. The patient admitted that she had set up the situation and, when her mother walked in, had said, "What do you think of me now, Mother dear?" It is interesting that the mother had not left the girl alone at night for many months, and this time had warned her that she would be back early and not to call her boyfriend.

Ann was a tall, slender, attractive girl who appeared several years older than her stated age and was obviously very intelligent. Initially she was sullen and angry, but soon became talkative and quite seductive. After six months, treatment was discontinued at Ann's insistence, although the mother continued coming to the clinic. Ann resumed treatment several months later at her own request, and at that time began to use therapy in a much more mature manner. She returned to high school and, despite some minor difficulties, did very well. Following the end of probation, the girl did not come in regularly any more, but her mother continued to come and showed a marked improvement in her relationship with her daughter as well as with her husband. Ann began dating a man five years older than herself, and our most recent information came from the local newspaper, in which there were simultaneous announcements of her graduation and her marriage.

DISCUSSION

In these two typical case histories, as well as in many others, the families may appear relatively normal. However, while the fathers usually do well at work, at activities other than their job—particularly around the home—they tend to be extremely passive and to withdraw from family responsibilities. They show poor control over their aggressive and sexual instincts, and many of them are given to violent outbursts of temper and wife-beating, usually when drinking. In many cases they also indulge in extramarital activities. The mothers are frequently better educated than their husbands, occasionally older, and clearly dominant in the marital relationship. However, they almost invariably show a significant level of underlying depression, and with only a little encouragement they will verbalize their rather intense feelings of rejection by their own mothers and often give a history of having run away themselves. In addition to this depression there is a feeling of inadequacy as mothers, and many of them can see how they have turned to their daughters for assistance in carrying the responsibilities of the household. Although they usually appear seductive toward their husbands, a history of long-term unsatisfactory sexual adjustment is seen.

The depression that plays such a prominent part in the mother's basic character adversely affects the relationship with her daughter. The mother, incapable of providing her daughter with sufficient warmth and affection, instead offers material incentives to force the girl into a position of gradually increasing responsibility and assumption of the maternal role, even from a very young age. In addition to rejecting her husband sexually, the mother also encourages a warm, close, and highly eroticized father-daughter relationship from which all three can derive considerable satisfaction.[1] The family appears to stabilize fairly well during the daughter's latency with the girl appearing, at least superficially, to be a rather hypermature individual who is extremely competent in managing the home and caring for her siblings as well as for her mother. With only material rewards for her efforts to meet the mother's demands, she turns to the father in her need for love; from an early age she learns to use seductiveness to gain her ends. Like her mother, she sees men as objects to be manipulated and controlled, primarily to satisfy primitive needs for oral gratification. The father himself, during the girl's latency, also tends to foster this strong, eroticized relationship with his daughter and derives considerable support from her. His drinking, which is so frequently a prominent problem at the time the girl actually runs away, is considerably less severe during this earlier period.

---

[1] It is possible that this relationship is fostered as early as birth through the choice of a name. Frequently the girl is given a feminine form of her father's name: e.g., Joseph–Josephine, Glen–Glenda, Alexander–Alexandra, etc. Even where the given name is not strikingly similar, the nickname is sometimes almost identical.

The family balance is disturbed by the onset of the girl's physical maturation. Both parents react to the girl's pubescence and the appearance of secondary sexual characteristics. The mother tends to push her daughter into premature dating and sexual sophistication, in an attempt to work out her own poorly resolved oedipal conflicts. She allows the use of lipstick, padded bras, nylon stockings, high heels, and other dress and behavior that are inappropriate to the age level. At the same time, the mother not only rejects her husband even further, but continues to foster the very close relationship between him and the daughter. With neither parent showing any real ability to establish effective controls, the fear of overt incest comes uncomfortably close to consciousness for both the father and the daughter, and the relationship that once provided each with considerable satisfaction now becomes extremely threatening.

As a defense against his own feelings, the father reacts with a rather accusatory, angry, and restrictive attitude. He projects his own sexual wishes and feelings onto the girl and then accuses her of sexual misbehavior, thereby justifying his extreme restrictiveness. These accusations may precede any actual misbehavior on the part of the girl by a considerable period of time. The girl responds to her father's attitude with anger and rebellion. She flouts his authority and turns to her mother for support and even encouragement, which the mother subtly gives. When the girl seeks other men to serve as objects of her unresolved oedipal feelings, her own underlying feelings of worthlessness push her to a choice of boys who are themselves degraded or emotionally disturbed. The mother now finds herself very much on the horns of a dilemma, wanting unconsciously to continue supporting her daughter's behavior, but being fully aware of the realistic dangers of a relationship between her daughter and this type of boy. Her tendency is to do nothing. The father, however, on seeing these boys, feels even more justified in imposing further restrictions. The girl becomes more rebellious and begins lying more extensively about her activities. Frequent and violent fights break out between the parents as to methods of control, and with increasing tension in the home, the girl begins to fear that she will be the cause of the family's dissolution. At this point, she sees no alternative to running away.

While fairly common, this situation is so slow in its development that it may go completely unnoticed by the casual observer. Certainly, when individuals outside the family are called in for advice, they would be extremely unlikely to object to the father's wish to protect his daughter from an emotionally disturbed, poorly educated, delinquent boy. On the other hand, the girl can hardly be blamed for showing some rebellion against a large number of rather rigid restrictions on her activities, particularly when many of them seem unjustified. Indeed, she can point, as can the mother, to the encouragement that our contemporary society gives to early dating and sexual maturity. Earlier in the development of this pattern, it was not unreasonable, either, for the mother to expect help from her daughter with the household duties and the care of the younger children. However, when these reality factors are considered in the more pathological setting of long-term oral deprivation and misdirected and inadequate controls, the tendency for the girl to run away becomes not only comprehensible but almost predictable.

Without treatment, the girls tend to leave school at the earliest opportunity, usually at the age of sixteen, and frequently continue to run away, although once having left school the majority of them find such jobs as hairdressers or waitresses; the former providing contact with the sought-after mother, the latter providing contact predominantly with men. Occasionally these girls become involved in prostitution. The most frequent outcome, however, is an early marriage, usually before the legal age of consent, with the girl contriving to get married either by falsifying her age or by becoming pregnant. While many of these marriages show considerable instability and end in divorce, some of them continue long enough to foster a repetition of the runaway pattern in the next generation.

If the more socially acceptable ways of resolving the home situation by marriage or employment are not available to the girl, and her running away continues, court intervention often becomes necessary. The court, following a hearing and a brief trial period of probation, in which the girl promptly runs away again, frequently finds the only solution available is to place the girl in a foster home or institution. Such settings, unless combined with treatment, are usually inadequate to control the girl's behavior. Almost inevitably she will again attempt to run away, flout authority despite disciplinary action, and in an institutional setting may even show signs of considerable homosexual activity or fairly acute depression with suicidal gestures. Several institutions throughout the United States have now become more aware of the dynamics and needs of the runaway girl, and have been able to set up programs that are carefully tailored to take these into consideration. However, when the girl does show improvement, the court or parole board will usually return her to her home. Such action almost invariably results in a rapid reactivation of the previous situation, and the running away begins again. It appears that a few weeks or even months of symptomatic improvement are not sufficient to warrant termination of any program that brought about the improvement.

Even with treatment, the prognosis for successful adult adjustment must remain guarded. In the absence of the controls the court may bring to bear, treatment may be almost impossible, because of the difficulty of enforcing attendance. Even when a very strong patient-therapist relationship can be achieved, it may not be enough to foster continued treatment. Invaluable and perhaps even essential in this connection is the availability of a female probation officer who can provide the warmth and controls not supplied by the mother.

It should be emphasized that successful treatment of the girl necessarily includes simultaneous treatment of the mother, where the major goal is improvement in their relationship and a lessening of the mother's demands upon her daughter. This can be effected quite rapidly in many cases by direct interpretation to the mother of the girl's underlying dynamics. However, such direct interpretation, in fairly simple terms, should be attempted only after careful evaluation not only of the mother's capacity to understand, but also of the therapist's ability to present it in a clear and nonthreatening way. The mother's need for dependency usually becomes largely transferred to the therapist, and she may attempt to control the situation by becoming somewhat seductive. This may be minimized by emphasizing her maturity, her role as a mother, and her concern over her daughter. This course is primarily responsible for reducing her demands on the girl. It has been interesting to note that in some of our cases, even after the daughter no longer came for therapy, the mother continued to use the clinic for occasional support and guidance. In such situations, the girl's improved behavior tended to continue.

While occasionally the mother may be seen by a social worker, usually both the mother and the daughter are seen by the same therapist. From a technical standpoint, interview arrangements are of considerable significance. In the initial interview, both the mother and the girl are seen together for a few moments. After introductions and explanations of the procedure, the girl should be reassured, in the mother's presence, that nothing she says will be reported back to either parent unless she so requests or unless she is present at the time. Both she and the mother should be told, however, that at the therapist's discretion anything the parents say might be told to the girl. The girl can then be excused to wait in the hall while a history is taken from the mother. After half the allotted time, the girl can be seen alone, and no further conversation held with the mother except to confirm the next appointment.

When first seen, the girl is usually hostile and uncommunicative. After an initial standoff period, however, she gradually begins to talk more freely; as she does, her own depression becomes quite apparent. In an attempt not only to control the treatment situation but also to help ward off her depression, she tends to utilize previously successful defenses by becoming quite seductive with the therapist. This behavior requires interpretation for control; also, warm but pointed remarks concerning her behavior and clothing, along with tacit assurance that seduction is not necessary to continue the relationship, can frequently be very useful. It is at this point in treatment that the most rapid and striking improvement will often be noted. It is not unusual, at the end of an interview in which the girl's seductive behavior has been brought up, to have her leave still somewhat angry, bitter, depressed, and threatening to run away—only to appear a week later, behaving not only as though there were no problems in her life, but as if there never had been any.

The maintenance of this degree of improvement is completely dependent upon the continuing therapeutic relationship with both mother and daughter. Too often, with improvement the girl's probation is terminated, despite warnings to the court. Even though the girl promises to continue coming to the clinic, she frequently misses her appointments after court controls have been removed, either directly refusing to come or offering a variety of excuses, which her parents are usually willing to support. If the mother also fails to come in, this break in treatment usually results in a fairly prompt deterioration of the home situation. In our experience, although few treated cases ended in severe difficulty with the courts, the usual outcome was an early and impulsive marriage, and the strong possibility that the situation would repeat itself in the next generation.

It is interesting that the fathers are seldom willing to come regularly to the clinic; indeed, the majority actively refuse to have anything to do with the treatment process. Experience has shown that their participation is not necessary for improvement of the home situation, however. The father rationalizes his resistance to treatment in a number of ways and with a variety of excuses, and it becomes clear that awareness of the dynamics is just under the surface. This is shown by the extremely active sabotage of treatment that occurs if the mother reports back what is said in her interviews. For this reason, it is appropriate to caution her about discussing treatment with her husband.

Much more could be said in reference to the treatment process. It is felt, however, that due to the enormous variation in patients, as well as in therapists, the major emphasis should be placed on the dynamics and on the observed fact that treatment is difficult and complicated, and must be continued far beyond the time that either the girl or the referring agency feels necessary.

The prognosis for a successful adult adjustment must remain guarded, but despite these difficulties, it is felt that treatment is eminently worthwhile. Without treatment, the long-term results are almost always undesirable; whereas with treatment, striking improvement can often be achieved.

REFERENCES

1. Robey, A., Rosewald, R. J., Snell, J. E., & Lee, R. E. The runaway girl: A reaction to family stress. *Amer. J. Orthopsychiat.*, 1964, *34*, 4.
2. Hollingshead, A. B., & Redlich, F. D. *Social class and mental illness: A community study.* New York: Wiley, 1958.
3. Kaufman, I., Peck, A., & Taguiri, C. The family constellation and overt incestuous relations between father and daughter. *Amer. J. Orthopsychiat.*, 1954, *24*, 266.

CHAPTER 13

Variations on a Theme of Incest

Lora Heims Tessman and Irving Kaufman

Incest may occur either in fact or in fantasy, with very different consequences for the psychological development of the individual. Throughout history and in various cultures, incestuous fantasies have been acted out symbolically or actually. For example, as Freud (4) pointed out, it is a custom among a number of tribes for a ceremonial act of intercourse or defloration of the bride to be accomplished by one of the elder men of the tribe, often the priest, and at times the father of the bride. However, in our culture the normative pattern is that incest is not acted out in reality. Instead, one of the normal developmental tasks for the adolescent is the resolution of incestuous wishes to a sufficient degree to allow redirection of instinctual energy to new channels of ego and libidinal development.

Unconscious incest wishes appear to exist in all individuals. Normally, their sublimation may be a powerful impetus for enriching ego development in adolescence. The role of incest fantasies in the psychopathology of the neuroses is condensed in the concept of the oedipus complex first described by Freud (5). Whether it is acted out in reality, becomes a fantasy, or is part of the characterologic development is related to environmental influences on the child.

This paper focuses on the relationship among various themes of incest between fathers and daughters, family patterns, and personality development. The girls described and some of their parents were treated from one to five years in clinic and private-practice settings. We distinguish four types of girls who have difficulty in resolving their incestuous wishes. They are:

Girls who have had overt incest experience. This group includes those girls who have had actual sexual relations with their father or stepfather.

Girls who are "unchosen" for incest. This group includes girls who witnessed or were aware of sex relations or sex play between their father and a sister, or their own age-mates, but who were not chosen by the father as a sexual object.

Girls for whom incest is prohibited by one parent. In this group, strong stimuli for incest are present but it is prohibited by one parent. In some families the prohibition comes from the father, in others from the mother.

Girls with stimulated incest fantasy. These girls' fathers stimulated or shared incestuous fantasies, but did not engage in overt sexual acting-out with the daughter. Included in this group, for example, would be a girl whose father slept in her bed until her menarche, but without direct sexual contact; also a girl whose parents had stopped having sexual relations when the girl was ten, and whose father had long, nightly "talks" with her on her bed during her puberty and adolescence. The stimulation, in other cases, may be more subtle but equally effective.

We briefly review some relevant aspects of normal adolescent development before discussing the above four clinical groups. As a prerequisite to evolving her own identity and commitment to her future sexual role, the pubescent girl normally goes through a series of developmental phases in her struggle to divest herself of the attachment to her infantile love object. As Helene Deutsch (2), Peter Blos (1), Selma Fraiberg (3), and others have pointed out, the pubescent girl experiences a strong regressive pull toward the pre-oedipal relationship to the mother. She may express this ambivalent tie through such contradictory behavior as indignantly complaining that her mother treats her too much like a baby and does not let her stay out nights, at the same time demonstrating her regression by her unkempt appearance or sloppy care of her room, so that her mother has to pay attention to her as though she were a little child.

Some girls may defend against the dependent tie to the mother by a frantic turn toward heterosexuality, sometimes in actuality but more often in conversations with girlfriends. The fantasies about boys during this "boy-crazy" period of puberty are in part a defense against regression, but also in part preparatory for the girl's future sexual role. However, if during this period sexual relations actually occur, the experience may have a disruptive influence on the ego of the girl if she is not yet emotionally ready to give up her identity as a little girl and move on to the role of the woman.

Blos (1) stated that during the course of adolescence there normally is a genuine turn toward heterosexuality and a final renunciation of the incestuous love object. Annie Katan (6) has called this process "object removal" (implying that it is a more permanent shift of psychic energy than displacement). This may be so even though during this time, as Helene Deutsch (2) has stated, "the girl represses conscious realization of the direct instinctual claim for a much longer time and in a much more successful manner than the boy. This claim often manifests itself indirectly in her intensified love yearnings and the erotic orientation of her fantasies—in brief, the endowment of her inner life with those emotional qualities that we recognize as the psychically feminine." For both boys and girls, the ego utilizes libidinal energy at this stage to reorganize the pre-oedipal and oedipal wishes. In this process they enrich their inner experiences in such familiar adolescent ways as intellectualization, creativity, self-discovery, and the establishment of new ego interests around a philosophy of life or political or social issues. Frequently for the girl the fantasies also have a quality of psychic "nest-feathering" for her future libidinal life.

The emergence of the normal phases summarized above can be profoundly influenced or distorted by the following: the family pattern of object relations and identification as experienced by the girl; the proclivity toward a particular pattern of tension discharge, e.g., aim-inhibited in contrast to acting-out; and the developmental level of the girl's libidinal aims compared to her chronological age. Thus an overt heterosexual relationship will mean something different to the adolescent fixated at a pre-oedipal level than to a girl who is emotionally also in adolescence. When the sexual relationship is to a parent while the girl still needs parenting, it becomes even more complicated. In the first two clinical groups that we describe, sexual activity occurs in the context of pre-adolescent and pre-oedipal drive organization. In the last group, in contrast, the girls were struggling to extricate themselves from particularly intense oedipal conflicts and felt compelled to renounce their sexual aims along with their wished-for incestuous object. These girls were unable to accomplish the "object removal" of which Katan (6) speaks.

Although the mother provides the girl with the example of what it is like to be a woman, father's reaction to both mother and daughter shows her what she has to look forward to in womanhood. In childhood the impetus for oedipal inhibitions and guilt arises from the need to maintain the relationship to the mother, and finally to identify with her. However, the girl also needs the approval and acceptance of her femininity in appropriate ways by her father. An outright rebuff of oedipal yearnings by the father appears to be associated with the kind of devaluation of femininity that may later take the form of despair about her self-worth as a woman.

The relationship between the physical act of incest and subsequent ego development is a complex one. Since overt incest in the cases we have observed appears to occur within a specific type of family, it is difficult to evaluate the effect of the sexual act independently from the family's influence on the personality of the girl. We recognize the possibility that incest may occur in other personality types and other cultures, and have potentially different consequences.

The emotional significance of incest and the associated development of fantasies within the four groups was related to prior family experience and the maturity of psychological development at the time of incest. For example, the incestuous sexual relationship is perceived by the "overt incest" group primarily in terms of an exchange in warmth and nurturance between father and daughter. For the group of "rejected incest objects," it is seen in sado-masochistic terms; a gratification which is first displayed and then sadistically withheld by the father. The sadistic component of the fantasy associated with incest for these girls is not in the sexual act per se, but in the fact that its occurrence with someone else left the girl feeling acutely deprived. Thus for the first two groups, (types 1 and 2), characterized by pregenital fixations, the phallus is seen as a powerful instrument used, according to the father's whim, as either an instrument of torture or a horn of plenty. In contrast, the fantasies about incest for the group with the "stimulated incest fantasy" have a typically forbidden and hysterical form, as the wished-for but feared sexual intrusion. These fantasies are associated with forbidden excitement, guilt, and rivalrously hostile wishes toward the mother.

TYPE 1. GIRLS WHO HAVE HAD OVERT INCEST EXPERIENCE

This group is comprised of girls who have experienced overt sexual relations and/or intensive sex play with their fathers or stepfathers. Their parents generally demonstrate an impulse-ridden character disorder and a particular type of family pathology (7). Overt incest appears to occur when both parents unconsciously agree that it should happen. The father who overtly acts out incest with a child, rather than being sexually involved with an adult, appears to wish to be a child himself. The mother who unconsciously fosters the incest is also seeking mothering, and is threatened by the adult sexual relationship to a husband. The daughter was often prematurely pushed into a mothering role, including the incestuous relationship with her father. The mothers handled their own anxieties about loss and desertion by acting this out in relation to their children, whom they exposed to periods of neglect or multiple foster-home placements. Interspersed were periods during which the children were overindulged. Impulse controls tended to be inconsistent, predicated on the momentary mood of the parents. Many of these children witnessed their parents physically abusing each other or them. The primary pattern of attempted tension discharge in these families centered around impulsive behavior such as aggression, sexual acting-out, or alcoholism. Like the mother, the father tended to see the girl as the nurturant mother in the household, turning to her for care and comfort. The pseudo-maturity often appeared early. In childhood some of these girls had been precocious in certain areas of ego development, such as motility and apparent independence.

The girl who has experienced incest with her father tends to see herself as the adult in the family and feels responsible for providing the mother and father with care. Because the girl was aware of complying with the parents' unconscious wishes, which included having an incestuous relationship, she did not experience guilt about the act itself. However, the girl did express depression and remorse when exposure of the incest relationship resulted in separation or object loss—e.g., if the father was sent to prison or the girl was sent away. Family disruption rather than incest seemed to be the trauma. Following family disruption, the sudden onset of learning problems, somatic symptoms, or depression led to the girl's being brought for psychotherapy.

The acting-out seems to interfere with the ego process of sublimating the incest fantasy. After incest is terminated and followed by the trauma of family disruption, the girl frequently turns to homosexuality. While the homosexuality includes some reaction to the above emotional traumas associated with incest, the more basic needs are at the level of early mother-child relationships. In some instances promiscuity alternated with homosexuality.

Case Example:

Lou Ann's childhood consisted of periods of extreme deprivation and desertions, alternating with occasional indulgence. Her family was characterized by impulsive behavior and repetitive acting-out of their problems about loss. The parents separated when Lou Ann was three. Her mother moved in with the paternal grandmother, expressing her own need for a mother. Lou Ann was sent to the father and his new wife, with whom she remained until she was seven. The father's new wife was promiscuous, locking Lou Ann in a closet while she entertained men. Years later, Lou Ann remembered the noises in the room, her own hunger, and her fear of crying out lest she get punished. At age seven she was returned to her mother, now alcoholic and married to a seafaring man who only returned home occasionally. Between the ages of eight and twelve Lou Ann became highly competent in the care of her mother and siblings. She did much of the housework and cooking. In order to buy milk for the younger children, she took charge of the finances, at times hiding money from her mother, who she knew would spend it on drink. The mother, on occasion, bought great quantities of cake and candy; at other times there was famine. The mother said she wanted another baby to keep her from being lonely, and at times played with the children's dolls. Lou Ann's own father moved downstairs with his mother after the failure of a third marriage. When he began making passes at Lou Ann, her mother went on a weekend trip with the younger children, leaving the father and Lou Ann alone. Lou Ann felt sorry for her father, who, like herself, was always being deserted. Sex relations between them began that weekend. The mother found out about the ongoing relationship after some months and became enraged, threatening to castrate or kill the father with a kitchen knife. Simultaneously she made Lou Ann promise to give her "the little rascal," should she be pregnant by the father. When pregnancy tests proved negative, the mother said to the social worker, "I know I'm not supposed to let her see I'm disappointed."

The treatment of this group of patients is long-term and difficult. They tend to have an impulse-ridden character disorder, a fear of object relations, a need to act out, and a tendency to flee from all contacts, including treatment itself. However, their oral dependency can be of some help if the treatment is geared toward establishing an object relationship that is acceptant and initially noncritical. Because of the family disruption and disorganization, there tends to be an underlying depressive core which ultimately requires resolution (8, 9, 10, 11).

TYPE 2. GIRLS WHO ARE "UNCHOSEN" FOR INCEST

The girls in this group witnessed or were aware of overt sex relations between a sister or playmate and the father, but were not themselves chosen as a sexual object by him. They come from the same types of families described for the overt incest group; these girls, however, have a different role in the family interaction. They have experienced the intense frustration of dependency needs by the mother that we see in the overt incest cases, but are less often pushed into the precocious pseudo-adult role of mothering the family. However, in some families the mother's difficulty in nurturing extends to all the children, and the push toward adulthood is as great for these girls as for those in the previous group.

A crucial trauma for the girl unchosen for incest seems to be the repeated experience of premature stimulation of the sexual drive, under the excruciating conditions of watching or knowing about sexual activity between two people with whom she is highly involved, while being herself excluded. The girl not only finds herself without a love object in the situation, but in addition is apt to become the target of hostility from the father. For example, one father threatened to kill his daughter if she told her mother what she had seen him doing to her sister. Another father constantly devalued his daughter's brains and appearance, in contrast to her sister. In this traumatic situation, an enormous quantity of aggression is apparently mobilized by the ego against the deserting and rejecting object. However, we find that in these girls the direction of the aggression is quickly reversed and turned against the self in the form of severe self-devaluation, depression, or suicidal tendencies.

These girls, like the overt incest cases, remain fixated at the pre-oedipal level, despite their often having transferred intense wishes for gratification from the mother to the father. Because the girl perceives the father's love object as more similar to herself (in age, etc.) than to her mother, she has difficulty in developing the usual oedipal conflict in which the father is renounced as a love object for the sake of evolving an identification with the mother. When first seen for psychotherapy, these girls may be involved in active fighting with, and rejection of, the father and sexuality in general. However, these verbalizations may be deceptive, because the girl does not renounce the aim of winning the father away from her rivals. This aim may eventually take the form of attempting to make the father jealous, as he made her jealous, by sexual acting-out or becoming pregnant, and then confronting the father with this evidence of her unfaithfulness to him.

During adolescence, ego development in these girls is impoverished. Defenses are mobilized to ward off the underlying depression that further constricts the ego. The traumas of overstimulation without gratification and the loss of the love object are frequently acted out with the self in the active rather than the passive role. Such girls become the stimulators and do not gratify others. Two aspects of adolescent feminine development—intellectualization and fantasy development—are missing in these girls, because they lack the libidinal energy, derived from aim-inhibited sexuality, which normally can be utilized for such development.

In addition, the girl has difficulty in the necessary disengagement from infantile love objects in adolescence. While she may act precociously independent from her parents, giving evidence of displacing her libidinal aims from them to others on a behavioral level (e.g., in sexual acting-out), she does not achieve "object removal." Instead, she retains her infantile sexual aims toward the incestuous object.

The girl feels socially isolated from her peers, who may be at the stage of acting "silly" and being preoccupied with their daydreams about boys. The girl unchosen for incest indicates that she feels years older than her peers, and may evince a cynicism which, while it simulates the normal cynicism of late adolescence, stems from different sources.

Psychotherapy, as with girls in the first group, is long-term, often punctuated with periods of acting-out, somatization, depression, and regression. However, unlike the first group of girls, who are apt to establish a clinging relationship to the therapist, the girls unchosen for incest relate cautiously and are often hypersensitive to any possible narcissistic injury in the transference situation, e.g., a missed appointment because of the therapist's vacation. We find that during the early stages of therapy the traumatically stimulated incestuous wishes may lead to sexual acting-out and verbalized wishes for hostile revenge on the father.

Self-destructive wishes as an aspect of depression tend to make their appearance early in therapy. This is related both to the loss of the mother's care and to the turning on the self of the aggression, inadequately differentiated from sexual tension, which is experienced in the father-child relationship. During therapy the girl acts out the theme of having her needs stimulated and then being abandoned at the height of tension. The girl indicates an inability to tolerate the resultant aggression toward the object, and is left with the alternatives of withdrawing from the relationship, acting-out as an illusionary means of maintaining the relationship, or turning the aggression onto the self. Sometimes a clarification of this pattern with the girl facilitates the emergence of the affective components of the depression—e.g., sadness—while reducing the need for defensive action sufficiently so that the traumatized ego may begin to integrate its experiences.

Case Example:

Roberta, an attractive Negro girl of fifteen, saw herself as the "black sheep" in a family that might have passed for white, were it not for her own dark coloring. The family placed great emphasis on cultural interests, social respectability, and status. Robert, the father, for whom Roberta was named, was a professional man who dressed elegantly, spoke precisely, and constantly criticized his children's manners and elocution. Beneath the veneer of respectability to the public, impulsive behavior was pervasive at home.

Both parents had severely deprived childhoods and had lacked stable parenting. The father's mother had died when he was two, and he had been brought up by a series of relatives. The mother's mother had committed suicide when she was an infant, and she was alternately cared for by two maternal aunts. When she was fifteen, she had her first daughter, illegitimately. She then married an alcoholic, physically abusive man whom she divorced. Her second marriage was to Robert, by whom she had two daughters and a son.

It had been the father's habit throughout the marriage to bring young mistresses to the house. In addition, when Roberta was twelve, the father had frequent sex relations with the older daughter, Francine, which Roberta sometimes witnessed. Roberta was told angrily that she should stay out of the way. This reminded her of earlier times when she felt her father was ashamed of her dark color and kept her out of the way when visitors came to the house. The incestuous relationship was terminated when Francine refused one day and the father hit her, breaking her jaw. Francine quit high school and moved out of the house. The father was arrested, but the mother withdrew charges after he became ill.

Roberta described her father as always criticizing her conduct and speech; then, with vehement affect, she said he was a hypocrite for whom she had no respect and nothing in common, who had only sex on his mind and could not understand that she was not interested in such things. She added, significantly, "No matter what he says, I am not going to commit suicide." Although Roberta was overtly sullen and disdainful toward her father, she was still very much involved with him and preoccupied with her image of herself as discarded by him. One day she reported having a "violent dream." She dreamed that the "Creature from the Black Lagoon" was coming and would kill her family. "I knew some people he had killed already, and I was going to save my family. We had thrown a party and the creature came unasked. I was supposed to kill it, so I tied it up and took a rolling pin and hit it on the head. Then I put it on the shelf—but instead of being dead, it looked like in a prison, and it watched everything while on the shelf. I tried to get rid of it, but I couldn't." Her associations revealed that the "Creature from the Black Lagoon" was a fused image of her father and herself, or her "black" aggression. She protected the family from the danger at a party, which symbolized sexual activity, by keeping the creature immobilized "on the shelf" watching, much as she had been shelved by the father during his sexual encounters. She incorporated this pattern and turned it against herself, wishing to get rid of "the creature." Throughout the early stages of treatment she was preoccupied with suicide.

Repeatedly in Roberta's and her father's interaction, there was a re-creation of a promise that stimulated her hopes and then went unfulfilled. Roberta eventually married a white boy by whom she had become pregnant. It was only at this point that she and her father had a reconciliation, centered around the incestuous wishes. She stated that for the first time she felt close to him when he took her to buy maternity clothes and an outfit for the new baby.

TYPE 3. GIRLS FOR WHOM INCEST IS PROHIBITED
BY ONE PARENT

Incest prohibited by one parent appears to occur in two subtypes. Some of the fathers are like the fathers in groups 1 and 2, who seek out a daughter as a sexual object. Many of these fathers, especially when drunk, approach their daughters sexually. However, the wife will notice and interrupt such behavior by taking over and not permitting anything further. These girls tend to identify with their mothers and become strong and aggressive; they choose passive ineffectual men for boyfriends and ultimately husbands.

In the second subtype, the mothers in many ways are like the mothers in types 1 and 2. They tend to be infantile, and have unresolved dependency needs. The fathers in this group tend to take over the parental role in the family, and do not get involved in sexual acting-out. In some cases they treat their daughters as masculine-type buddies with whom they engage in fishing, carpentry, etc. Other fathers of this group become hostile and sadistic to their daughters. The effect of this type of family pathology on the daughter is to complicate and make impossible a resolution of the oedipus complex. Instead, we find that these girls have severe characterologic problems. They tend to be masculine in their orientation, dress, and manner. However, unlike the girls in groups 1 and 2, they rarely demonstrate overt homosexuality.

Treatment of this group of girls is complicated by the fact that verbal interaction is least acceptable to them. They are often action-oriented, finding it easier to change a tire than discuss emotions. It is often necessary at first to relate to them through activities such as driving or going for a walk, as one does with delinquent boys. Hostility is used as a defense against affect, and the therapist has to be careful not to be drawn into a hostile interaction. The aim of treatment is to establish an object relationship within which these girls can trust the therapist. Many of these girls are quite lonely because they feel so different. Their object hunger often keeps them in treatment, even though their anxiety and hostility also make it difficult for them. Once an object relationship is established, one can begin to help these girls evolve a different concept of masculine and feminine roles, and help them deal with their confused identifications. They tend to resist affect, and can sometimes react first to an intellectual, logical approach, even though the goal of treatment is to help them deal with their feelings about being deprived, different, and angry.

Case Example:

Edwina was a fourteen-year-old girl who was brought for treatment because she was functioning poorly in school. Despite adequate intelligence she was failing, and had poor relations with her peers. She came in wearing blue jeans and a leather jacket. Her answers to questions were monosyllabic, and she was very angry, sullen, and resentful. Mother was a passive, ineffectual woman who continually turned over the care of the other children to her daughter, and would run to her own mother. The father, who believed everyone should be independent and self-reliant, was very critical of mother. However, he displaced his hostility onto the daughter; and if she did not prepare the meal or clean the house, he would beat her. At other times he took her fishing or got involved with her in woodworking, repairing the car, or tending the vegetable garden. Although father and daughter spent many hours alone together while mother was away, they did not engage in any overt sexual behavior. Instead, the daughter became masculinized as a buddy of the father, and in their own way they encouraged the mother's withdrawal from the family.

This type of girl has difficulty in evolving a feminine identity and tends to become an embittered, hostile person, identifying with the aggressive, angry father.

TYPE 4. GIRLS WITH STIMULATED INCEST FANTASY

In this group, incest is not acted out overtly, but is a shared fantasy between the daughter and her father. The fantasy is not entirely unconscious, but is given some verbalized and token expression. Included in this group, for example, is a girl whose divorced father shared her bed when she visited him on weekends, but who did not engage in overt sexual activity with her. In this group the parents' own disturbances were more often centered around neurotic, particularly oedipal, conflicts, and were not manifested through any gross acting-out patterns. In two of the cases, the father had had a psychotic depression. The girls in this group showed primarily neurotic disturbances, occasionally with some borderline features. Phobic and conversion symptoms were particularly prominent, serving as a defense against the incestuous wishes. For example, one girl, phobic of rats and snakes, dreamed that her father was putting a long silver snake into her drawer. In some girls, a rich adolescent fantasy and affect life, revolving around various solutions to thinly disguised incestuous wishes, was given expression in painting and writing. In these respects, these girls are clinically in marked contrast to the three groups previously discussed.

Characteristically, the girl had experienced a prolonged dependence on the mother, who was apt to be gratifying and permissive with the girl, resenting her demands but being unable to set adequate limits. The mother was apt to repress her own anger, and feared frustrating the daughter lest she damage her. Similarly, although the mother resented the girl's oedipal attachment to the father, her own guilt about oedipal wishes did not allow her to interfere.

For the girl the prolonged childhood reliance on the mother's protection and gratification appears to have a twofold effect. Because the girl both controls the mother and makes the mother give to her as a helpless child, infantile omnipotent wishes coincide with a sense of helplessness. In spite of the apparent air of permissiveness, the incest taboo is strongly operant and associated with guilt at the oedipal level. When the girl enters the oedipal stage of development, her relationship to the mother suffers an abrupt and frightening change. The girl has been accustomed to handling inner temptation by using the external controls of the mother as an alter ego. Aggression toward the mother associated with her oedipal conflict now makes this way of operating unfeasible. Instead, the girl may become phobic of those situations that symbolize either doing, or being punished for, forbidden things.

In adolescence the girl appears to be struggling with the re-emergence of earlier oedipal conflicts, complicated by more than the usual residual dependence on the mother. Hysterical, phobic, or obsessive-compulsive features may be most prominent clinically. Repression or displacement of the incestuous wishes may occur, but the emergence of these wishes is ever imminent. Some girls can use an active fantasy life in a sublimated way, as an aid in the ego-integrative process. The girls in the stimulated incest fantasy group tend to be able to tolerate considerable tension, to form enduring and meaningful relationships, and to function without gross pathology in other areas of their life.

With this group the more usual psychotherapy techniques are applicable. However, early in treatment the ability to make the necessary displacement from the incestuous object is still so tenuous that any insight into these wishes would be intolerable. Hence, the conflicts must be dealt with in ego rather than impulse terms in the therapy situation. Some of these girls are afraid to see a male therapist, but willingly enter treatment with a woman. Initially, they tend to use their female therapist as they did their mother, demanding protection and attention, and wanting to be told exactly what to do in every situation. Although the girl needs strong support toward utilizing her capacities for ego mastery, it is important that she learn that she cannot control the therapist through her demands, as she did her mother. If she could do so, it would symbolize to her the frightening situation of being in the role of the oedipal winner, and yet the loser, because she is deprived of an adult woman with whom she could identify.

Case Example:

Sarah came for therapy at age twelve and a half after she had not eaten for five days and had also developed a fear of school. She had refused to be examined by the family doctor, a man, but was willing to talk with a woman therapist. The acute symptoms had followed a week's visit to her divorced father. Her parents had been divorced when Sarah was six, after the father had had a psychotic depression for which he was briefly hospitalized. The father reported that Sarah was the only one in the family who had shown him affection at that time, and that it was she who kept him from killing himself. After the divorce, Sarah visited him every other weekend, and at these times he had slept with her, until she was twelve. Father had moved back to occupying the downstairs of his own mother's house after the divorce. Prior to Sarah's outbreak of symptoms, he had suddenly decided to move out of his mother's house and now had an apartment of his own. He celebrated this act of independence from his mother by buying and eating, for the first time in his life, a whole pound of bacon, which would have been strictly taboo in his mother's kosher household. The bacon made him sick and he vomited it, losing his appetite thereafter. In the next few days he repeatedly tried to gag himself, to vomit further. He told Sarah at this time that now that he was living alone he could marry a widow he knew, but that he really had a better time with Sarah. It was clear that for Sarah the taboo act of eating the bacon stood for other taboo things one might do away from mother. Sarah described how, as her parents were not on speaking terms, father would let her out of the car a block away and she would "sneak into the house like a criminal." Characteristically, after visits to father, Sarah would accuse her mother of not loving her because she would not take her out to dinner, as father did. She would follow mother around, demanding more attention or complaining of various aches and pains. She would play with girls who came to her house, but was afraid to go to their houses lest she meet boys or big dogs on the street.

During the first interview, it was possible to point out to Sarah that she seemed to be punishing herself for her split loyalties to father and mother by suffering like the father and losing her appetite. She had complained that mother was mean to her by not buying her dinner. Now she was doing this to herself by not eating. The therapist told her they would talk about why she thought she did not deserve food, so that she would not have to be so cruel to herself. The various sexual and pregnancy fantasies underlying the eating disturbance were intentionally not touched on in this initial interview. Sarah went home and ate.

During the year of treatment that followed, a history of childhood phobias and repetitive nightmares emerged. Sarah had repeatedly dreamed of a man climbing in her window and carrying her away in his sack, attached to a big stick. Particularly in situations that represented a forbidden temptation, she had had fantasies that some harm would come to her mother, who would leave her or die. She clung to mother throughout childhood, demanding reassurance about being loved. After some time in treatment, when she was close to fourteen, she began attending church socials in spite of the presence of boys, but was always ready for retreat. For example, she excitedly looked forward to a hayride, but managed to fall off the hay, causing the whole group to turn around and bring her home bruised, in accordance with her fantasy of being the disgraced and fallen woman.

CONCLUSIONS

The resolution of the oedipus complex, though never complete in the girl, prepares for her heterosexual love, and therefore is crucial to her later capacity to enjoy being a woman. Unconscious incestuous wishes are not only normal for the girl, but a powerful impetus for progressive ego development in adolescence. The enrichment of inner psychic life, fantasy, caring about social and ethical issues, and the evolution of an ego identity, all draw on the well of libidinal energy associated with the girl's relationship to her father, in addition to the identification with the mother. However, this process can miscarry for a variety of reasons, some of which have been exemplified by the four groups discussed in this presentation.

Either the acting out of incest or the painful rebuff of oedipal yearnings can disrupt the progressive ego function of incest as a fantasy, eventually renounced in accordance with reality. Disturbances arise not because of the physical act of incest in itself, but rather because of the emotional significance of the experience in terms of the girl's identity and sense of worth.

REFERENCES

1. Blos, P. *On adolescence: A psychoanalytic interpretation.* Glencoe, Ill.: Free Press, 1962.
2. Deutsch, H. *The psychology of women: A psychoanalytic interpretation.* New York: Grune & Stratton, 1944.
3. Fraiberg, S. Some considerations in the introduction to therapy in puberty. Vol. 10. *Psychoanalytic study of the child.* New York: International Univer. Press, 1955.
4. Freud, S. Contributions to the psychology of love. *The taboo of virginity.* Vol. IV. *Collected papers.* London: Hogarth Press, 1918. (1950)
5. Freud, S. *The interpretation of dreams.* London: Hogarth Press, 1900.
6. Katan, A. The role of displacement in agoraphobia. *Int. J. Psychoanal.*, 1951, *32*, 41–50
7. Kaufman, I., Peck, A. L., & Tagiuri, C. K. *Amer. J. Orthopsychiat.* 1954, *24*, 266–279.
8. Kaufman, I., & Heims, L. The body image of the juvenile delinquent. *Amer. J. Orthopsychiat.*, 1958. *28*, 146–159.
9. Kaufman, I., Makkay, E. S., & Zilback, J. The impact of adolescence on girls with delinquent character formation. *Amer. J. Orthopsychiat.*, 1959, *29*, 130–143.
10. Kaufman, I. Stages in the treatment of the juvenile delinquent. *Proceedings of the Third World Congress of Psychiatry.* Toronto: Univer. of Toronto Press, 1961.
11. Kaufman, I., Makkay, E. S., & Zilback, J. The defensive aspects of impulsivity. *Bull. Menninger Clin.*, 1963, *27*, 24–32.

CHAPTER 14

Sexual Promiscuity: A Case History

Charles J. Kallick

This paper will describe some important psychological and familial forces operating in a twenty-three-year-old woman whose major neurotic symptom is that of sexual promiscuity. The information presented here will necessarily be selective in order to focus on the main topic, but it will also attempt to describe a general view of the dynamics of the patient's family life and personality structure.

The material regarding this patient was compiled from an intensive psychiatric evaluation, including psychological testing, plus information that emerged in the course of four years of intensive (three or four times a week), psychoanalytically-oriented psychotherapy. Although the patient entered into treatment with the emergence of generalized peculiarities of thought and behavior, a principal area of her disturbed functioning had to do with her promiscuous sexual activities. It was at the insistence of a boyfriend that she kept an appointment with a local psychiatrist, who subsequently suggested that she withdraw from college and enter a nearby psychiatric hospital for evaluation and treatment.

Joan, who was then twenty, arrived at the hospital dressed like a twelve-year-old. Her clothes were not tattered, but they did look like hand-me-downs, put on with little taste or desire to flatter her appearance. She was bright, vivacious, talkative, and clearly psychologically minded, but it soon became apparent that her accurate observations about herself were highly intellectualized. It was difficult to understand what she really *felt* and what she was trying to communicate to me. As she once said when discussing this problem, "It's like throwing out a handful of jelly beans to see which ones you'll pick up"; the implication was that she would wait to see what I was interested in and then would supply or withhold pertinent information, depending on her whim. Despite this, she was very sincere in her desire to end her disturbed pattern of behavior and to be free of the severe depression that plagued her periodically. It was during these depressions that she was closest to psychosis. The degree of isolation and loneliness was so profound that she felt alienated from everything and could have only murderous and otherwise gruesome fantasies.

The patient is the second of six children, having a brother one year her senior, three younger sisters, and a younger brother. When she was four months of age, her father entered the army, and the family moved close to his army base. At the age of four she moved with her family back to their home in a large, metropolitan area of the Southwest, where her father set up his general surgical practice. He is apparently well thought of and has developed a rather successful private practice.

From descriptions of her mother's past and present behavior, it seems clear that she, the older of two children, has been a terribly disturbed person all of her married life, and most of her teenage and college years as well. Joyfully drowning kittens, having periodic losses of a sense of time, exhibiting grossly disorganized functioning at home, having no friends, being preoccupied with rapes and mutilations as reported in the local press, dressing in ragged clothes, and frequently walking around the house as if in a daze without responding to comments from others—these are the patient's memories of her mother. She sees her mother as a broken woman who, although a graduate of a first-rate women's college, has done nothing with her life, and is completely dominated by her husband. " I was nothing until I married your father" is a theme that both parents frequently and proudly enunciate. One of the patient's most impassioned comments about herself during her first week of treatment was that she did not want to grow up to be like her mother.

Joan's father is the oldest of three sons. His reason for wanting six children (an idea he fixed on even before he married) was that he did not want to subjugate and dominate his children the way his father did. His two brothers are so unstable that neither holds a job, and he supports both of them with an air of martyrdom and a sense of superiority. He seems to be quite insensitive to his children's needs and most of his interest in them is expressed in lectures about sex, money, and the need to suffer. He apparently sees himself as the family savior. Not only does he feel that he saved his wife, but he has said that he can be the patient's psychiatrist if she has any problems; without really realizing it, he apparently offered himself as a substitute mother for her. He seemed terrribly domineering in his control of the family. The patient reported that he would frequently be held up at the hospital until nine or ten o'clock at night and no one, not even the youngest children, could eat until he came home—"so that the family could be together." She also reported that her father proudly told some friends that his children were so devoted to him that if he asked them to hold out their hands so that he could cut them off, they would be glad to do so.

"It was because he had seen so much real suffering during the day" that he seemed unsympathetic to his children's complaints about a dance they were not invited to or problems with boyfriends that they wanted to discuss. On occasion he illustrated his stories with slides of a sixteen-year-old girl in the terminal stages of inoperable breast cancer. Although he encouraged Joan to tell him all her problems, he quickly topped her complaints or problems with his own preoccupations about suffering. This pattern of his rejecting her reaching out to him and being insensitive to her needs persists to the present. He will write her a long letter asking for certain information, and she will reply with that information. His subsequent letter is as though he never received an answer to the first one. Nothing she ever did was complimented or satisfactory (so she feels)—"I never expected any different, after all you are my daughter," she recalls his saying.

He frequently sermonized about "playing with fire" (meaning flirting with boys); the virtue of doing things *because* you do not like them or *because* they hurt was frequently extolled, as he was lying next to her in bed late at night. Almost nightly he would return from his evening office hours or the hospital and enter the patient's room, lie next to her in bed, and tell her how he loved her best of anybody in the world, that he knew her better than she knew herself, and that next to *his* mother he felt closest to her. This behavior continued, she said, until she left for college.

His treatment of the entire family sounds as though he considered them narcissistic extensions of himself, and he apparently had little regard for how they were reacting to him or what their own needs and sensitivities were. This one was to be a musician, that one a writer, and so on. For the patient he reserved the position of fulfilling his mother's role, which also meant that she was heir to his intense affectionate longing for her. He automatically expected her to attend the same college that his mother attended, which, incidentally, was the one of which his wife was also a graduate. If one considers father's behavior like that of the favorite child who was attempting to annihilate all competition for mother's exclusive attention, one can see it operating not only with his younger brothers, but with his own children, and possibly with any prospective suitors that his oldest daughter might have. Not only is he competing with them for his daughter's attention, but he is also outdoing his own father, who was successfully able to dominate only three children whereas the patient's father was able to do it with six.

Joan's older brother is extremely disturbed. He failed several times at college, has no friends, and spends all of his time in the family home. So far as the patient knows, the parents refuse to seek psychiatric help for him and regard her therapy as something of a lark. The other siblings seem fairly stable by virtue of their allegiance to one another. They seem to have formed their own little association within the family and have very little to do with the parents. They have somewhat isolated themselves from any deep personal involvement with the patient and her older brother, too.

The parents describe Joan's childhood and adolescence as "normal." They saw her as a happy-go-lucky, extroverted child who did very well in school and was rather active in their local church. It was not until her senior year in high school (when she met her first lover) that they considered her behavior abnormal. She pulled away from her family and friends, and devoted herself completely to her boyfriend. Her behavior does sound very disturbed at that point, but it also appears that she was disturbed for many years prior to this period. She remembers her childhood as a very unhappy time when she felt friendless and awkward, personally and socially. She had to wear her brother's clothes, even his underwear, and had little idea how to make friends. She spent many hours reading by herself, which was to some extent an attempt to deal with her extreme loneliness.

Her whole approach to forming a relationship with others has been to put herself completely in their service, to worship them, and to devote herself to her idea of their wishes. This behavior sometimes took extreme forms; one can see it as a continuation of the involvement she has with her father, which itself appears to be the product of a lack of mothering, extreme loneliness, and a distorted attempt to overcome and satisfy that longing. It also represents her view of her mother's relationship with her father. Her repeated notions have been that her father's domineering attitude subjugated and "destroyed" her mother.

With such a background it does not seem at all coincidental that the patient's first strong heterosexual attachment of adolescence was formed under the guise of saving a poor, lost, rejected Hungarian refugee who came to the United States during the 1956 uprising in his country. She functioned beautifully in organizing clothing drives at school and even received a special citation for that work. She also devoted herself to "saving" her bitter and cynical foreigner—while having intercourse with him; she sacrificed and suffered for him—while getting pregnant by him. In essence, she seemed to be trying to establish a relationship that was motivated primarily by drives to fulfill a deep sense of longing and loneliness, a relationship with a member of the opposite sex and with whom she could achieve intimacy on a physical as well as on a higher humanitarian level.

It seemed that she was trying to satisfy those needs within the framework of her father's contradictory and conflicting communications to her. His presence in her bed must have stimulated her sexual fantasies, yet he said that she should avoid those very things that his behavior stimulated. These night meetings also provided a major vehicle for her to attempt to satisfy her sense of loneliness and separateness. This situation is encountered repeatedly in her history, especially in her present relationship with her father and in her involvement with other men. It is always a question of superficially professed devotion to the man—the therapist included—while the real desire is to find a mother, or motherhood as in the case with her pregnancy and fantasies of wanting to be pregnant. During her therapy she frequently experienced intense feelings of warmth and tenderness about breast-feeding her infant girl; and she identified to an excessive degree with projected feelings that she attributed to the newborn, all of which were along the lines of an ecstatic sense of comfort and protection, especially after the baby's feeding.

Following her graduation from high school, the patient went to college for one year, where she had many friends and did fairly well in her studies. She took a vacation the summer following her freshman year, and when she found out that she was pregnant, she stayed away until she delivered her full-term baby girl the following winter. Although she had wanted to return home during this pregnancy, her parents—primarily her father—would have none of that. She returned to school that September to begin her sophomore year.

As mentioned above, Joan had always developed very possessive attachments to people, and at school she began to idolize one of the senior girls. She slept on the floor of this girl's room just to be near her, hoping to bask in the reflected glory of her popularity and scholastic achievements. Her sense of herself was that she was nothing, that she had nothing of value to offer, and that the only way to achieve self-respect and dignity was to be close to someone who she felt had achieved this state. She developed a personality style that was based on humiliating herself and making the other person "everything," again a caricature of the male-female relationship in her family—a sort of desire to fuse with another person. Since that one episode her other attachments have been less extreme and have occurred only with boys.

At the hospital she again had many friends and developed attachments to boys similar to her involvement with her father and with the girlfriend at college. She wanted them to possess her totally and in so doing to let her possess them. She felt impelled to become sexually involved, and it was primarily through this contact that she felt she would establish a permanent bond. This seemed related to her idea that the only reason her father was interested in such a disturbed person as her mother was the sexual contact he had with her. She has subsequently had the notion that it was sex, especially orgasm, that made her mother lose her mind. Also, sex is a physical experience, and physical experience is something that she feels more certain of—feelings and memories of people do not last very long for her. This is probably related more to her borderline functioning than to anything else. She can see a reaction in her partner: he is nice to her, says pleasant things to her while they are in such an intimate position, momentarily it makes her feel good, although once they have intercourse, these feelings are quickly dispelled.

Needless to say the act of intercourse itself was never very pleasurable, and she never had orgasm. During the sexual act she occasionally would feel humiliated, frequently had vivid fantasies of being mutilated, and felt as though she were being used and violated. It was as though all the good feelings inside of her were drained out. I think this relates primarily to the tremendous repression of all pleasurable elements in her experience that regularly takes place, in addition to her disappointment in finding her sense of isolation and loneliness still present. At another level, it seems almost a necessity that she not feel gratified lest she interpret it as a consummation of her infantile sexual wishes, the emergence of which initially sent her into treatment. One might speculate that in so gratifying herself, she might carry out what she had wanted to do while lying next to her father in bed. As a second line of defense she distorts what should otherwise be pleasurable into a sense of pain, suffering, and martyrdom. This kind of defense has in it representatives of her father; as she is trying to get him out of the picture, she maintains some remnants of him. She has, therefore, been forced into accepting a way of dealing with her sexual drives in accordance with what father preached and what she observed in her mother: suffering, martyrdom, and self-sacrifice. There are many other examples of how her father, in her memory at least, intruded himself into the patient's life (and she has kept him there), with the result that he effected a form of brainwashing. After long lectures following some misbehavior, she came away thinking her father was absolutely right and that she was absolutely wrong. She frequently wished for a spanking rather than for such lectures.

During the initial period of her therapy, she ventilated a great deal of her feeling about the memory of her mother's sadistic behavior and grossly disorganized functioning. She also experienced much emotion as she recalled her pregnancy and delivery, and frequently had dreams about that episode, experiencing great maternal warmth and fantasies of no longer being lonely. In some of her dreams her identification alternated between being the mother and being the infant, and she felt an exquisite sense of protection, warmth, and satisfaction.

The transference seemed to be long in developing. At first it seemed indiscernible, and she even said she saw me as "the brown chair," since I was sitting in a brown leather chair. She saw not me, but the furniture. Gradually, her feelings developed into a desire to possess me and to be possessed by me. She even developed a fantasy that I was the center of her life and that everything she did focused on me. The intensity of her ambivalence and the nightmarish degree of helplessness that she experienced are best described in her own words: "I feel that my life is hanging by a thread and that you are holding the other end and might let go anytime you want." Even though the superficial aspects of the transference seemed to echo the relationship she had with her father, the kind of feeling that she conveyed at times in the therapy seemed more related to mothering than to anything else. Her desire to feel a sense of dignity, a right to seek and feel pleasure within appropriate bounds, a sense of being protected from herself and others, and the knowledge (frequently uncertain for her) that there is always one person whose love will be consistent—all appeared to refer to the maternal elements that have been missing in her actual relationships.

An especially good example of how Joan dealt with these various internal forces is illustrated in the following incident:

The patient came to therapy one day and told me that her employer had invited her to accompany him on a business trip to one of their out-of-town offices. She blandly agreed and did not begin to think about it until she came into therapy that day. To some extent this was a flattering invitation, but she had had similar experiences with him before and knew that it was also a sexual overture. She discussed this matter as though she had come to a very definite conclusion and was informing me of it. She was clear about not wanting to go. She said that now that she thought about it, she felt insulted and knew that there was going to be some sexual advance. Besides whatever else was involved, she did not want, because of her boss's difficulties with his wife, to contribute to their having even further problems.

A few days later she forgot completely about her previous position and told me of agreeing to go on this business trip because of some mild pressure he exerted. She said she felt upset because she thought I would be angry with her, and treated the whole thing as though she felt it were *my* desire that she not go. She had projected her own sense of restriction onto me and thereby allowed herself to feel no inner conflict about making way for possible satisfaction of a deeper need. What she did was to convert a potential inner conflict into an external one, between her and me rather than between two conflicting impulses. That was something she could more easily get around. I interpreted this to her, and she responded by indicating that her feelings about such things do not really feel as though they are part of her, but that they are someone else's attitudes, possibly her father's. I disagreed with her about this last point and told her that I thought she was doing to me what she had been doing with her mother, that is, not allowing us to be part of her life in any substantial sense. The patient was actively avoiding this confrontation and resolution, and it became clear that her psychical struggle to dodge the influence of her superego (which represents a precipitate of her impressions of early parental values) was effected primarily by ignoring it or projecting it onto someone else. Her handling of this incident typifies the way this pattern was reflected in her daily behavior. She numbed herself to the influence of her superego and avoided getting into situations where she had to take a strong, decisive stand; so doing would imply that she was holding firm to certain values. Instead, she gave the impression that she was open for anyone's influence: whomever she happened to be close to at the moment was the one whose values she adopted.

Upon her discharge from the hospital (after one and a half years), the patient moved away from her family, and has been successfully working as a secretary. At first, she tended to be involved with fringe elements—the motorcycle crowd, the outcasts, the troubled ones. She felt that she did not know where she fit into the world. Once, during her initial weeks of therapy, she had seemed terribly disturbed (to a psychotic degree), and had described her feeling as being like a "pebble in a well-oiled machine." With a fringe group she apparently felt more at home.

From what I have indicated so far, one can see that this girl adopted a way of life that is marginal, mixed up, and with outcast friends whose values are themselves confused and somewhat unacceptable to society at large. The external life that she has constructed for herself is an exact representation of her internal life: a general lack of discrimination and values that are hidden, disorganized, confused, and neither very acceptable nor adaptable to dealing with life effectively. Another way of describing this behavior is to consider it as a temporary adjustment based on the establishment of a negative identity; that is, an identity based primarily on values that are opposite to those of the culture. As difficult and maladaptive as it seems to an outside observer, it is for her an important and necessary way of life because without it she is lost. It is as though a negative identity is better than none at all. One can easily see, therefore, that a major element of her early life has emerged during recent years as a cornerstone for the establishment of her sense of herself. She thinks of herself as an open wound, vulnerable, and easily violated; something to be possessed, sexually insulted, and otherwise hurt. This is the very position in which she now finds herself in society.

The dictionary definition of "promiscuity" implies an indiscriminate mingling; a heterogeneous mixture of persons, standards, or morals. In this case all three seem to be involved: people, standards, and morals. "Promiscuous" most aptly describes this girl as a person, not just her psychological symptoms. She is an indiscriminate mixture of standards and morals, and mixes indiscriminately with all sorts of people. Promiscuity also is a psychological symptom. For this patient it is a searching for gratification that ends not just in frustration but in a repeatedly masochistic and self-degrading humiliating condition.

Only recently have there been any signs that some inner values do exist, to the extent that they constitute an important force in the patient's choice of friends and in her decisions about which boys she will be intimate with sexually. Previously, promiscuity did not involve her having sexual relations with many boys in a given period of time; rather, she would latch onto a boy and exaggerate her devotion to him and very quickly get involved in a sexual situation over which she seemed to exercise no control whatever. Now she is occasionally able to feel insulted and say "no" when it is appropriate. However, there are still many occasions when her values exist only in thought, and she feels helpless in defending herself against others' desires to exploit her sexually. She feels that she just has to give in, that to say "no" would be to chase away a person who at that moment represents her lifeline, her entire connection to existence. I suspect this embodies some of the important positive though distorted elements of her relationship with her father. He did appear when her mother did not; he did notice her and pay attention to her, even if it was in a possessive and sadistic way. However, this was preferable to being totally ignored.

At present one of the major forces at work in the therapy is the emergence of strong positive feelings about her mother. To some extent we might assume that this formed a part of her motivation to become pregnant—that is, to create a better mother than the one that existed for her.

PART V

Family Therapy Applications

If we see family relationship disturbances as the cause of developmental pathology such as sexual acting-out in adolescent girls, the family interaction in its habitat—the family home—becomes the focus of diagnostic observation and therapeutic intervention. This is not only strategy, it also represents a philosophy of mental health. By seeing the family members interact with one another, and by approaching them as equally committed to the disturbance-producing interaction, we free the designated "sick" or problem member of the family from the odium and loneliness of pathology. Similarly, we claim from the presumably "healthy" family members the commitment to remedial effort in therapeutic interaction, as well as in their usual daily interaction with other family members.

In our specific approach we also change the nature of the family therapist as an individual to that of a team of two counselors or two therapists. We thereby change the interventive interaction from one confined to the relationship between counselor and client to one which can also be interaction between counselor and counselor, and between counseling team and family.

In order to overcome such constellations as family communication breakdown, family stress, destructive and exploitative family patterns of interaction, various forms of intervention are recommended in the following chapters. These include communication enhancement through interpretation, changing the family system through active and empathic participation in family interaction, demonstration of problem-solving, confrontation, promotion of insight, and superego demand.

It is our belief that ultimately the strategy of therapeutic intervention will be determined by the perceptual propensities of the therapist, and that the various approaches presented here represent a range of opportunities from which the practitioner may choose. These various therapeutic techniques are neither mutually exclusive nor contradictory. The reader will notice that the papers by Minuchin and Rabinowitz, although reporting on work with the same patient group, present different perceptions of the nature of family communication and different approaches to therapy. They represent various sets of attending to, and dealing with, the same phenomena of family arrest and family impairment. The differing conceptualizations and techniques of family therapy must necessarily depend to some extent on the different personality tendencies of the particular therapist. While all of the treatment approaches discussed in this section refer to the total-family or conjoint family therapy approach, they nevertheless do not agree completely in regard to details of technique. We therefore do not present here a completely integrated and consistent formula for treatment, nor one specific or unique recommended method of treatment. Rather, we expect the reader to sample from the variety of approaches.

CHAPTER 15

The Family Constellation
from the Standpoint
of Various Siblings

Robert MacGregor

In families that present more than one member as patients, there tends
to be a taking of turns. When the first patient is drawn out of the family's
defensive system, another family member takes on this function. Our basic
thesis is that much psychiatric illness can be viewed as an arrest in development of a family unit. Unable to deal with change, the family as a unit
becomes defensive, and collusion to maintain the status quo displaces
healthy interaction with one another and with the environment. Family
members interact in ways that require each to go on repetitively performing his function or role in the system, thus expressing only an immature
aspect of his stalemated growth. The particular aspect of immaturity
expressed is determined in part by that member's developmental level at
the time of arrest and partly by the function already performed by others.

This chapter[1] is a response to an interesting challenge by Drs. Pollak
and Friedman to study our family diagnostic system by replacing the
example of the male nominal patient with a case of the same type having a
female nominal patient. We found what one might expect—namely, that
girls are different from boys. For example, our systematic prediction was
that when the adolescent nominal patient—that is, the family member for
whom help was first sought—is withdrawn from the system, as by hospi-
talization, a sibling becomes identified by family and self as a patient.
However, when we looked at cases where adolescent daughters were the
original patients, we found that quite as regularly it is the father who next
becomes ill; when the daughter is schizophrenic, the father first becomes
psychotic and then meets an accidental death.

[1] This study is supported in part by Mental Health Project Grant OM-988. Earlier
papers in the development of this thesis were presented at the American Psychiatric
Association Regional Conference on Family Structure, Dynamics, and Therapy;
Galveston, Texas; February, 1965; and at the American Psychological Association
Convention; Philadelphia, Pennsylvania; September, 1963.

We have categorized families by the arrest in development of the nominal patient as:

Type A. Families presenting infantile functioning in adolescence—nominal patient, the schizophrenic.
Type B. Families presenting childish functioning in adolescence—nominal patient, the autocrat.
Type C. Families presenting juvenile functioning in adolescence—nominal patient, the intimidated youth.
Type D. Families presenting pre-adolescent functioning in adolescence—nominal patient, the rebel (1).
Type E. Families presenting adolescent rebellion in young adulthood—nominal patient, the emancipator.

Type E differs from the theoretical norm—adolescent functioning in adolescence—in that there is a felt need to struggle for freedom and to push toward emancipation, resulting in a transition that is less smooth than optimal. This push for precocious adult functioning does not necessarily imply readiness to accept responsibility for the seemingly desired emancipation. We have not previously described Type E patients in the literature, because they do not come to us as identified patients.

This view from within the family was obtained by use of procedures from Multiple Impact Therapy (MIT), which include intake, two days of multiple interaction procedures, and then follow-up. The intake is a brief version of the later procedures: a team-and-family planning session, at which time family interaction patterns are elicited for diagnosis. This is followed, after a week or so, by two days' therapeutic work: an initial team-family conference, followed by a series of individual interviews and joint interviews that involve two or more patients with one or more therapists. "Overlapping interviews" is a term for a particular innovation used throughout, where a therapist leaves one interview and joins in an ongoing session with another member of the family. At that point, both therapists make some summary before the family members concerned. Throughout these procedures there are scheduled team conferences, some of which include consultants.

The therapeutic and diagnostic contacts with the family are recessed on the second or third day with a final team-family conference. During this final conference, the basic family problems may be discussed in terms of specific recurring patterns, noticed during the preceding days, as they relate to behavior and situations that can be anticipated on the family's return home. Subsequent to this two-day MIT procedure, most families were discharged or referred back to resources in their communities. Some families, however, were continued and seen in repeated two-day MIT sessions at our center, sometimes extending over a span of one or more years.

Carolyn Pettis Novak, now a happy housewife, wrote "Dear Abby" letters to the author for a year after her family's two-year work with the MIT team. "A teen-age prostitute, with her family making the bookings" (in the opinion of the referring social agency), seventeen-year-old Carrie, when first seen by the Youth Development Project, was a slender, emaciated girl, potentially pretty, who could easily have passed for thirteen or fourteen years of age. The reason she gave for her promiscuity was that sexual relations were a way of getting rid of boys she did not like. It was also clear that the mother was excessively fascinated with the daughter's genital activity. The referring social worker felt that the mother would take her from one specialist to another until she found one who would perform a hysterectomy. Mr. Pettis's part at this point was to do a kind of desperate but harsh screening of the boys who came to date Carrie. They often turned out not to be the ones with whom she spent the evening. Though sexual activity had indeed been frequent, there was no evidence of gainful employment in this respect.

Mrs. Pettis complained that her daughter was trying to free herself of all parental controls with the intent of getting married and leaving home as soon as possible. A closer look at the evidence showed that all the girl's efforts labeled "rebellious" had succeeded in winning her more supervision and a closer relationship to her mother than her younger sister Polly had. At fifteen Carrie had been transferred from public school to a private correctional boarding school, as a result of her lurid stories about her sexual experiences, and from there to working around home with her mother.

The mother's projects included not only control of her daughters but sponsorship of her husband. When these two girls were young, the father had been hospitalized for depression. This had been precipitated by the marriage of the oldest daughter, Millie, who had been a very close companion of the father. The mother had withdrawn, hurt by the father's favoring of daughter over wife; the father, unable to relate to Millie's advancing womanhood, seemed to abandon Millie to become preoccupied with his business failures. Millie married to escape an uncomfortable situation.

Since that time, Carolyn seemed to grow more and more like her father, with the curious lack of overt respect for him that typifies the "Cordelia role." The mother went to beauty college during her husband's period of relative incapacity. As the father's effectiveness returned, the family moved to a nearby metropolitan area for him to complete his engineering training. There the mother went to work as a beauty operator, and shortly afterward Carrie was sent to the correctional school.

At the time of referral, two years later, the father had invested his inheritance in an expensive house, and seemed to be trying to bribe the younger daughters to stay home with promises to recondition the swimming pool. As a result of the mother's efforts to free her husband of any family duties, he was able to present quite a prosperous "country squire" appearance to the community. In fact, he had really lost touch with the life experiences of his wife and two younger daughters. He was impractical in family matters, in part because his very executive wife prevented decisions—or indeed the data to make decisions—from coming to his attention. He was on a pedestal, but his wife promoted a family secret that father was really weak.

The daughters externalized the family values in contrasting ways. Older sister Millie tended to show the fun-loving side of father. They reared and rode horses together. She was more able than mother or the younger sisters to express direct affection for him. The nominal patient, Carrie, expressed her father's freedom from responsibility and his quarrel with the mother's controlling ways. The younger sister, Polly—intimidated by the impression that when grown up she should be able to argue her parents down—expressed the family values on social conformity, to the detriment of her own individuality. Each in her own way was a specialist at relating to different aspects of her parents, with a minimum of rivalry. Each had worked out a way not to interfere with the specialty by which her sisters exploited the limited emotional supplies of a family where none felt he had much to give.

According to our conception of family functioning, the Pettis family showed an arrest in development. Each performed a part in a closed system that required each of the others to persist in a role. Each found a level of developmental arrest beyond which the family could not foster growth.

Now we come to problems in forming systematic theory. It seems to be recognized that no two children in a family have the same environment. Indeed, we have just described a family in which the family diagnosis is Type D, when rebel Carrie is our focal point, and Type C if we start with conscientious, intimidated Polly. We call older sister's situation Type E, since her struggle had been toward emancipation.

In our schema, the father in this family—Type D, presenting a rebel as the nominal patient—is kept remote on a pedestal as a figurehead at the instigation of the mother, who really runs the home. From this pseudo-prestigeful position, with its lack of understanding contact with the child, the father is not able to deal with his children as a parent. For want of authoritative structuring from father regarding the appropriate differences and barriers between the generations, girls become provocative toward him and move toward panic, and boys insult their mothers. Children generalize such experiences and develop a fear of adult responsibilities that necessitates rebellion against developmental demands. In his rebellion, the child seeks to prolong the privileges of youth. His rebellion says, "Think of me as a teen-ager." The rebellion provokes more adult supervision and withdrawal of the very privileges for which the adolescent seems to campaign.

In forming a concept of the immature aspects of family functioning, we have taken four immature reactions—aggression, passive-aggression, passive-dependency, and emotional instability—to define the area within which the family members relate to each other in repetitive and reciprocal ways. These terms seem similar to the Kassenbaum, Couch, and Slater (2) fusion factors—"impulsivity versus intellectual control" and "social withdrawal versus social participation"—used to describe the general area between major dimensions of personality. In diagramming apparently similar areas from our study, we expressed them as quadrants of a circle representing clinically determined ways in which family members interact

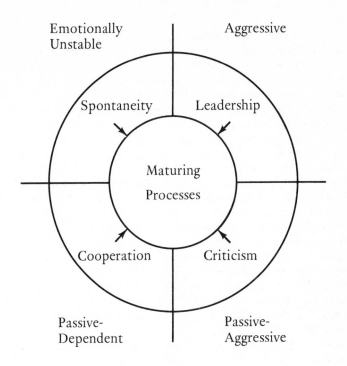

Figure 1
FAMILY CONSTELLATION CHART[2]

with each other. (See Figure 1.) The four quadrants represent immature reactions; their relatively healthy counterparts are indicated as moving toward the center circle of healthy interaction and growth. The correspondence between the quadrants determined from personality traits within the individual (in the schema developed by Kassenbaum et al.) and our quadrants determined by the patterns of relationship among family members, is compelling.

In our Type D family of rebel Carrie, an adolescent arrested at the pre-adolescent level of development, the mother operates within the family in the aggressive mode and the father in the passive-aggressive mode. Outside the family, to society, the parents do not show this reversal of conventional marital and parental roles. The aggressive functioning of the wife within the home is expressed in family leadership. The husband's privileged position "on the pedestal" is her creation, and in time of trouble she acts as though he were hers to destroy. The passive-aggressive function-

[2] From *Multiple impact therapy with families*, by MacGregor, Ritchie, Serrano, & Schuster. Copyright 1964, by McGraw-Hill, Inc. Used with permission of McGraw-Hill Book Company.

ing of the husband is expressed in his way of criticizing his wife and children as though they were equal to each other before him. Our nominal patient, the rebel, operates in an emotionally unstable mode; the younger sibling remains passive-dependent; and the healthier family member, the older sister, shows more role-flexibility, manifesting both conformity and spontaneity—the extremes of which are labeled passive-dependency and emotional instability, respectively.

Now seen from the standpoint of Polly, the intimidated youth, the family constellation is Type C, presenting juvenile functioning in the adolescent. Polly was predicted to become an identified patient should Carrie leave home. When Carrie first left for the correctional school, Polly was only eleven and responded by being a little more dutiful and fearful toward her mother. We would expect her to produce symptoms of stress when family members turn toward her for the kind of functions previously performed by Carrie. In sick families, we notice that young people externalize problems in such a way as to precipitate crises which signal distress. Young people whose development is arrested at the juvenile level are quite neurotic; boys particularly, when they are presented as nominal patients, express themselves through symptoms such as school phobia, gastrointestinal distress, or tics and habits that come to the attention of school authorities.

From Polly's standpoint, her father appears to be aggressive. His facade of adequacy that society sees, together with her sister's defiant acting-out, intimidates Polly. She feels that she could never measure up to the standards she presumes to exist for feminine adequacy. The mother casts too unclear an image, in that she seems to do what she does in the father's name, and so her strength intimidates rather than attracts as a model. The father, while he looks glamorous, is distant, and can only be reached by such overadequate-appearing fanfare as her sister produced. At another level of awareness, Polly is a party to the collusion to protect her father's weakness and, in Erickson's (3) terms, does not take initiative because she would be moving out from her mother's benevolent protectorate. Allied with her mother, she can enjoy some of the advantages of the "well" sibling. This is the way Polly was perceived—a delightful child who was no threat to anyone. Had she been a boy, this opportunity to win security by externalizing what the family favored would have been denied, because the very adequacy displayed in the role would have been a competitive threat to her father. This is a guilt-producing experience that keeps initiative in check in the boy arrested on the juvenile level, and leaves only symptom-formation as a way of expression. Thus the younger sister fared better than do younger brothers in Type D families.

Thus we see that in the Pettis family, several constellations prevail. Certainly the relationship in which the older sister, Millie, knew her father was different from that in which Carrie knew him. Mrs. Pettis said bitterly that her husband liked horses first, his oldest daughter next, and then she and the rest of the family came last. When, after Millie's marriage, the father turned to Carolyn, who had no background of close association with him but had been much more possessively controlled by the mother, this middle daughter began a pattern of rebellion that was provocative toward her father but insured a more active supervising interference from her mother. Mr. Pettis treated his wife and Carolyn as rival petitioners before him; the importance of both to him involved adult sexuality and the ability to stand up to him. This family constellation intimidated Polly, the youngest daughter, so that we see in the two younger sisters two different levels of developmental arrest. Thus there are three different family constellations seen from the standpoint of each of the three daughters: Type E for Millie, Type D for Carolyn, and Type C for Polly.

The Type B constellation is rare with daughters. However, in the Waters family—much like the Pettis family in composition—the father seemed to be a blatant chanticleer who took his little daughter Laura with him to work at an all-night restaurant, where he felt his part in the family business was to socialize with the customers. The mother, meanwhile, drab and dutiful, put her principal effort into the efficiency of their second restaurant and occasionally came over to the all-night restaurant to work in the kitchen. She held her husband's efforts in mild contempt and based her security on her ability to "show up" any of the employees by being better at their work. The father was sexually impotent during this period and seemed to belittle his wife's efforts by claiming that her severity with the "help" and unfriendly attitude toward customers was driving them away. The father indulged Laura, encouraging her flirtatiousness with the customers until she began to show signs of physical maturity—at which point he more or less dropped his attentions toward her. He replaced her with the nominal patient, Cindy, ten years younger, who the mother claimed had been spoiled by her grandparents when she was a baby. Older sister Laura then got the full force of mother's efforts to prove that no one in the family business was as efficient as she. Feeling abandoned by her father, Laura consummated an unhappy marriage to get away, only to be hospitalized after her first childbirth with a postpartum psychosis.

Just as Laura had no close relationship with her mother, Cindy had no background of symbiotic relationship with her father. When he tried to use her as he had used her older sister, she became increasingly mistrustful and manipulative. This is the more pre-oedipal constellation of the childish functioning in adolescence.

Freedom from this arrest at the childish level was eventually reached when the father took a more realistic interest in his wife. This freed his wife from having to prove herself through work and thereby allowed her to recapture with Cindy some of the real rewards of a mother-daughter relationship.

It may seem that in this paper we have identified the family category according to the child's condition, but these family categories are differentiated by quite a number of family attributes. In a family which had presented childish functioning in an adolescent, Type B, we were able to observe at follow-up an instance where the rehabilitation process had been interrupted, and a new arrest appeared in the same patient at the pre-adolescent level. Not only did our patient become a full-fledged rebel, but the rest of the conditions for the Type D family were met. To mention a few, the family had become more socially involved in the community. The lad changed from "oblivous to authority" to "fascinated by authority." No longer a "loner," he had become active in delinquent gang leadership. The pre-oedipal sex role in relation to peers and parents had been replaced with some enduring, even though showy, relationships with the opposite sex. The mother's efforts had turned into a real project, where she sponsored her husband right up onto the "pedestal," from whence he in turn seemed to deal with wife and son as equal petitioners before him. Son's rebellious behavior became more an expression of infantile omni-potence and mother's contempt for her husband. The boy sought out the juvenile authorities because he seemed to prefer their reassuring restraint to father's vague expectation that, because the boy had a job, he could conduct himself like a man.

The rebel in the Type D family rebels to accentuate the boundaries between generations and to diffuse his identity into the teen-age group. The younger brother meanwhile had moved from his extremely passive-dependent way of getting the family to do things for him to the "well" sibling role, from which position he externalized the family's middle-class values by being a good student and athletic team member. In this case, though the nominal patient changed roles, he externalized the family pathology at two different levels of arrested development.

In families of schizophrenic youth, we have noticed that when the schizophrenic adolescent is taken from the family unit, a "well" sibling who has no history of a symbiotic relationship with a parent may also become a patient, with an illness manifesting arrest at a pre-adolescent level of development. From the standpoint of this formerly "well" sibling, the family diagnosis is Type D.

This was the case in the family of Harold Mullins, a schizophrenic youth, and his younger brother Jerry. From Harold's viewpoint his was a Type A family; from Jerry's, a Type D family. Mr. Mullins contributed to his own exclusion from the close relationship between Harold and his mother by frequent hunting jaunts. Sometimes he hunted alone, some-times with cronies from his hill-country past, and sometimes he took Jerry along. By sharing his father's exclusion, Jerry seemed more like a crony than a son. Like his father, Jerry had a superficially genial manner, but he needed the approval of others more than his schizoid father did. He preferred to be as much as possible like the rest of the gang, rather than show individuality.

When Harold, while becoming more manifestly schizophrenic, prom-ised his mother he would go to college and "become great," Jerry, who was really a better student, offered to go to a local trade school instead of college, so he could bring in the kind of money that would help his mother realize the dreams she shared with Harold for the future. But when Harold went to the hospital, Jerry became alcoholic and rebellious. He seemed discouraged and ready to give up on his own future, because others would know of "insanity in the family." He carried to extremes the sort of acting out that the rest of the gang only talked about. The change was intensified when Harold, having improved, was discharged from the hospital and went into the military service. The mother turned toward Jerry, who had indeed worked to win her attentions. But without the shared past of a symbiotic relationship, Jerry's status with his mother was too much that of a peer or a father for comfort. Rebellion served to shore up the incest taboo.

Two family constellations prevail here. With Harold as a focal point, this is a Type A family. Harold and his mother alternately function in aggressive and passive-dependent ways. Mr. Mullins is an expert in the passive-aggressive mode. The functions associated with emotional instability are really the only ones open to brother Jerry.

From Jerry's standpoint, however, father provides some leadership, and the family seems organized to free the father from ordinary duties. Thus, a son is able to identify father's role as aggressive. Mother is seen as the one who keeps father, despite his known weakness, in an ignominious position of leadership by her passive-aggressive means. Her criticism is made especially hostile and bitter by her husband's neglect. Harold is perceived by brother Jerry as the passive-dependent one who had forfeited his rights of seniority in exchange for prolonged privileges of infancy. Here we have the picture of two siblings, both seriously disturbed but manifesting different levels of developmental arrest, who both became identified patients in turn.

COMMENT

The similarities to the domain of personality study, on which converging agreement is impressive, deserve comment. Schaefer (4), and more recently Lorr and McNair (5), have each surveyed a number of large-scale factor analyses and ordered them by Guttman's circumplex to arrive at quadrants that have a striking resemblance to those in our Family Constellation Chart (Figure 1). But the difference is important. The traits factored in the studies cited represent the individual's attitudes or dispositions to relate in certain ways. Our quadrants represent achieved ways of interacting among family members. The whole family can be located in the various positions described on the chart. These two approaches may complement each other, as do content versus process, role sought versus role achieved, saying versus doing, or perhaps material versus form. (Actually, the incumbents in some of our quadrants were ill-suited as individuals for the function demanded by the role and showed correspondingly poor mental health.)

What I have presented here suggests that families do not "achieve" patient status all at once. Gradually, their functioning grinds to a halt, forcing one of their members to externalize the trouble—and then another, and another in turn, if the chosen member's distress draws him away from his function in the family. The psychiatric illness discussed here is best understood as an aspect of unhealthy family interaction.

REFERENCES

1. MacGregor, R., Ritchie, A., Serrano, A., et al. *Multiple impact therapy with families*. New York: McGraw-Hill, 1964.
2. Kassenbaum, G. G., Couch, A. J., & Slater, P. E. The factorial dimensions of the MMPI. *J. consult. Psychol.*, 1959, *23*, 226–236.
3. Erikson, E. H. Identity and the life cycle. *Psychol. Issues*, 1959, *1*, Monogr. 1.
4. Schaefer, E. S. Converging conceptual models for maternal behavior and for child behavior. In J. C. Glidewell (Ed.), *Parental attitudes and child behavior*. Springfield, Ill.: Charles C Thomas, 1961.
5. Lorr, M., & McNair, D. M. An interpersonal behavior circle. *J. abnorm. soc. Psychol*, 1963, *67*, 68–75.

CHAPTER 16

Family Structure, Family Language, and the Puzzled Therapist

Salvador Minuchin

This is a report on work in family therapy with families of delinquents in the low socioeconomic group, initiated by the Wiltwyck School and carried on at the Philadelphia Child Guidance Clinic.[1] This research was oriented toward exploring some of the dynamic characteristics of these families and testing treatment techniques designed to change those characteristics considered significant in the development of the delinquent child.

Often characterized by such picturesque labels as "hard-core" and "unreachable," these families have proven in our experience to be not much harder to reach than the middle-class families we encounter in our private practice—but that is hard enough! Our experience has shown that after the therapist has established contact with the family—and this is usually the most difficult period—the family *will* cooperate in treatment. Further, the possibilities for bringing about structural changes with our short-term family therapy have been encouraging.

This paper will encompass more than our specific work with these families. In our efforts to develop effective techniques for working with families of this type, we began to look anew at the meaning and effectiveness of therapeutic intervention and to focus on two aspects of the family—family language and family structure. We think our observations are relevant to the field of family therapy in general.

As a springboard for presenting these observations, let me first give a summary description of some of the interactional patterns of these families (1): Our subjects are psychologically impoverished, rather than complex; their areas of experience are limited; family themes are very few, with emphasis on aggression, helplessness, abandonment, and nurturance. Role organization around family themes is narrow and stereotyped, and family members adhere rigidly to their expectations and labels of other members.

Interactions center on the here and now. Interchanges reach a high peak of emotional charge and level off equally as fast, leaving the therapist

[1] National Institute of Mental Health Grant No. OM 745 (R1) MHPG (1).

wondering about the appropriateness of affect. This mercurial change in mood parallels Redl's observation on what he calls "the acute rate of emotional evaporation" in juvenile delinquents (2). Equally characteristic is the shift from absolute disengagement of family members—each one functioning in an isolated orbit or isolated subgroup—to intense impingement on each other, whereby every act by one family member seems to carry relevance to every other member. Here again we are impressed by the lack of middle ground and of gradual transitions. The interaction in these families is usually gross in quality, and the underlying patterns become quite predictable; this tended to draw our attention to the structure, and to the possibility of intervention designed to change family structural arrangements.

Communication in these families is characterized by an unusual amount of disconnected and disruptive monologue. The meandering thread running through their communication seems to be available to the family members; the therapist, however, gropes unsuccessfully for a meaningful sequence onto which he can graft a therapeutic insight. Communication also tends to be a chaotic network of jammed messages, and it was the therapist's discomfort as he tried to make himself heard over the background noise that focused our attention on the importance of family language.

FAMILY LANGUAGE

Family language comprises the significant themes around which the family interaction becomes organized, the phrases and words with more or less private meanings that the family uses, usually in relation to significant themes, and the style and organization of communication. Other workers (3) have pointed out the significance of family themes and the importance of multilevel messages in working with families (4). I wanted to focus on the understanding of relationship messages in these families and the use of them for grasping underlying structures.

Let us note first that any communication between people carries at least two messages: a content message and, at another level, a message that defines the nature of the interrelatedness between the participants. The congruency and nexus of these two levels of message will vary with the nature of the task at hand, the people involved, the degree of intimacy, and the like. In certain situations, the content level achieves a predominance that makes it autonomous or independent of the nature of the personal interaction. On other occasions, the defining of interrelatedness between people outweighs the meaning of the content messages. This latter type of communication is exemplified by certain interactions between young children and parents, and by communications that are charged with strong emotional content. The description of Bateson et al. (5) of schizophrenogenic families, where members continuously define the ways in which they are *not* responding or impinging on each other, is another instance in which the meaning of the content is merely a carrier of the "me-you" message. In "primitive" families, such as the ones we treated, the implicit messages defining the ways in which "me-you" are connected become central, but are obscured by a background noise of content messages that are used merely as carriers.

The therapist, responding to the "meaning" of the messages, experiences bewilderment and feels not only frustrated, but helpless (6, 7). Content seems to jump from one member to another, from subject to subject, and the accommodation of the family to this disruptive "unpatterned" pattern proves too much for the therapist. In his attempt to establish contact and to prove his usefulness, he can jump with the family from one subject to another, or become disengaged and wait for an opportunity when the family members interact in patterns that are more familiar to him. At times the therapist makes an interpretation along certain lines but finds that it is integrated into the meaningful themes of the family in a way quite different from his original intention as the sender. If it is true that the content messages in our families are mere carriers of the significant and emotionally-charged implicit messages of interpersonal connectedness, then emphasis on content or its symbolic meaning will blind us to the more meaningful dialogue that is being carried. By paying attention to the basic ways in which "me-you" are relating, we come to the exploration of a limited number of rather global themes. These themes are central, dynamic, and idiosyncratic for each family, and demand that each family member assume a position in relation to them. When therapeutic intervention becomes focused on these themes, the nature of the "me-you" interaction becomes explicit, and members of the family seem to make more sense to the therapist.

The "me-you" language that these families use is the language of unseparated people, where the significance of "objects" is seldom treated as something independent of selves. Communication, whether about food, money, an ashtray, a bed, or a person, is treated by them mostly as a vehicle through which to act out ways of trying to define a "me" dealing with a "you." People uncertain of self boundaries, unclear about their impingement on other people and their effectiveness in tasks, need continuous use of other people for definition of self. This characteristic of language in such families, along with the tendency to use words very concretely, makes verbal modalities very unreliable as a therapeutic tool. The therapist becomes heavily dependent, then, upon intervention to modify structure.

Giving attention to the relationship messages is the royal road to understanding structural arrangement in the family. "Me-you" messages become an important part of a system of clues that the therapist can use to enter into the family structure.

FAMILY STRUCTURE

We will not address ourselves here to the ways a family develops its particular structure. Let us just accept, with most students of small-group behavior, the thesis that in any long association between people there will develop a regulation of behavior, a structural organization of the group

with role distribution and possible subgroup coalitions, and a group culture that sanctions and directs many of the intragroup transactions as well
as the ones with the outer world.

Structure is expressed in action. In the family, structure is observed
through interactional patterns. The members define themselves in interaction. When a mother sends a verbal or nonverbal message to a child, she is
defining who she is in relation to him and who he is in relation to her.
Family structure grows and expresses itself through this transactional definition of selves. Recurrent transaction establishes a system of how, when,
and through whom to relate; this system crystallizes in roles as the
habitual becomes the norm.

As therapists, we are in contact with a family when some of their
interactional patterns bring pain. It would seem logical, then, that once we
have identified the nosologic stimulus and demonstrated how it induces
pain, we would have a green light for structural changes. We are all well
aware of the difficulties of this task, even with the best-motivated family.
Haley points out two factors that inhibit family change: (a) "the compli-
cation which develops in a self-corrective system when one element
behaves differently," and (b) "the fact that when the therapist becomes
included in the family system, he will be dealt with at the level in which
family members are struggling with each other, the level of who is going to
govern the behavior of whom" (6).

We will address ourselves here to the induction of the therapist into
the family interactional system and to the possibilities and advantages
inherent in a focused intervention that challenges family structure. We
postulate that the task of the family therapist is to enter into the family
system and modify the family structure, and that his interventions should
be oriented systematically toward this goal. We are well aware of the
difficulties of this task due to the rigidity of family structure and its
resistance to modification.

THERAPEUTIC PROCEDURE AND ITS PITFALLS

In the initial contacts with a patient family, it is possible to assess the
particular type of structural arrangement that characterizes the family,
from observation of the patterned transactions among its members. One
looks for the lines of power and leadership, the subgrouping and alliances
with their shifts around different significant themes, the labeling of the
members and their assignment to particular roles, the fluidity of these
labels when there is a change in family composition or in family themes,
and the ways in which language is used to support this structural balance.

The therapist becomes aware of the enabling and disabling characteristics of the family and draws his blueprint of therapeutic strategy to
challenge the handicapping nature of present balance and to help the
family toward goals syntonic with his concept of mental health. Too often
the therapist elaborates on family dynamics as a system separate from
himself, hoping to effect change in the family without getting involved in
the neurotic demands the family presents.

On the other hand, the family coming for therapy has its own view of the problems that affect it and of the ways in which it needs to be corrected. The family demands from the therapist that he produce change without upsetting familiar ways of transacting; he must change them within their familiar pathways of dealing with each other. The family says, in essence, that change should follow the direction and organization they are already in. Since the family's problem is precisely a problem of structure, the family is, in fact, saying, "Change us without changing us."

The family has, then, its way of presenting itself, its way of saying "this is who we are, and this is where and how we suffer." It also makes an implicit "demand," manifested through the patterned transaction among its members, about the therapist's modality of intervention. Let us consider the following examples:

The L——family presents its problem as a conflict between the older boy and the father, and demands that the therapist should follow the lines of "helping mother to help father to help the boy with father." In this family, where it is therapeutically indicated that we must shrink mother's function, the family demands that "change should go through mother."

In the S——family, with a depressive, alcoholic, dependent mother, the family presents its problem as "the problem is the boys"; the line of therapy "demanded" is the "help the boys to help mother" so that she will not feel helpless.

In the G——family, similarly, the mother, as a family spokesman, presents the problem as "the boy," and the therapy "demanded" is to "change the children so I can become a powerful mother."

The R——family presents the problem as "mother is not assertive," and the direction of therapy that is "demanded" is to "change her, help husband and children to continue nurturing her." In this case, the family not only dictates the course that change must take, but the means through which it should take place.

These families structure the pathways of change in ways that cannot happen: they demand, in effect, that the therapist must not challenge their usual way of interacting but must follow the habitual channels of transaction. The therapist is often pulled into these transactional pathways; while he may send interpretations that are correct in content, he may be responding unwittingly to the structural demands of the family and addressing himself to the family members in such a way as to fortify and crystallize the present structural arrangement.

Some examples will clarify the meaning of this concept. In the W——family, a brittle, suicidal mother presents the family problem: "Yes, the problem is my helplessness." The line of therapy she implicitly "demands" is: "In order to change me, help my mother to support and sustain my helplessness." This family seen at intake was composed of a mother, a grandmother, and two children. The grandmother had taken the executive role in the family, and she immediately communicated to the therapist that her daughter had been ill and needed to be treated in a special way. Both intake psychiatrists responded through the session by interpreting to the grandmother the pathologic component of her control of her daughter, and the fact that her "concern" handicapped the daughter in her ability to mother her acting-out children. While the interpretations dealt with family pathology and family structure, both therapists directed their communication to the grandmother and, in effect, assumed a role similar to the grandmother's. By attacking the grandmother's pathology, they presented themselves to the family as the protectors of the mother; by addressing themselves predominantly to the grandmother and not to the mother, they accepted and reinforced the grandmother's centrality and power, and supported the mother's dependency on her.

In the A——family, of the Jewish middle class, the problem is presented, through a dominating and highly verbal wife, in terms of the husband's depression and silence; the therapy demanded is a "change in the husband in order to increase marital harmony."

The therapist interprets to the husband that his silence is the only way he can defend himself and take revenge on his controlling wife, and he suggests that the husband should not let her organize his thinking. The co-therapist felt that this interpretation, though correct, was heard by Mr. A—— as a demand for change similar to the demand his wife sends. This therapist then directed his attention to the wife, pointing out the maneuver by which the wife prompted the husband's silence. During the rest of the hour, both therapists talked with the wife while the husband became more peripheral. In both instances, while the therapists' verbal interpretations pointed adequately to family dynamics, the formal organization of pathways kept reinforcing family pathology.

The ways in which a therapist is pulled into the family system and supports a structure that he verbally challenges are multiple. Therapists as people have been trained to pay attention to content, and tend to respond more to the "meaning" of a communication than to formal characteristics of the message. A therapist will talk with the most verbal member of a family without "recognizing" that at this moment he is making this person central, or he may interpret the behavior of the "weaker" member of the family to a more central member and, by eliciting the help of this stronger member or challenging his behavior, the therapist can unwittingly render the less even lesser. The therapeutic problem, then, is how to enter into the family system in order to challenge it while avoiding the power of the system to induct the therapist into the interactive patterns that maintain current homeostasis.

WAYS OF CHALLENGING FAMILY STRUCTURE

Accepting the fact that the "participant observer" is one who participates and later observes his participation, we will acknowledge that certain blindness overcomes the therapist at moments of "interacting proximity" with the family. (A similar observation has been made by Shaffer et al., 7.) Nonetheless, there are a number of maneuvers that the therapist can engage in, in order to challenge the family structure:

(1) The therapist can challenge the family structure by concretely modifying the direction of transactional pathways. He may turn to or address the silent member; he may actively interrupt pathways ("Stop telling her to take over"); he may center on initiating talk from father to son in order to circumvent a regularized father-to-mother-to-son interaction.

(2) The therapist may also challenge the structure by changing the participants in an interaction or the role of the members participating. For example, in a family that scapegoated the oldest son, the therapist asked the child to leave the session, pointing out before he left that during the session with the family all the communication was related to him, thereby limiting the interaction of the parents as spouses and people. When the child left, the therapist demanded participation of the couple only as spouses.

In our work with delinquent families, we use the three-stage session in order to allow the shifting of members to different roles. In the first stage, all the family is seen together, and interaction is between parents and progeny; in the second stage, generational subgroups meet separately, the interaction being between spouses and between siblings; in the third stage, the family is again seen together. Our technique is related to the Multiple Impact Therapy used by MacGregor, in which the family members are subjected to continuous shifting of roles and unexpected pairing with other members (8).

(3) The therapist may challenge structure by changing or increasing the family themes. The families may present a differently structured profile when they deal with different themes. Our type of family has a paucity of themes beyond aggressiveness. The therapist can open or make available new themes by making reference to positive experiences or by questioning or looking for what is "good" or "nice" in this family. He can interrupt or close a family theme, or re-label some unfamiliar experience to permit exploration of new themes. For instance, when a woman presents a mothering experience with her children, showing only her dry sense of duty, the therapist can re-interpret and explore the interaction in terms of what it shows of sensitivity to her children's needs. These instances of re-labeling familiar experiences serve to orient her toward new areas, new definitions of self and child. The need to search for new areas of experience is extremely significant, due to our families' restricted action-prone ways of relation.

We have been exploring another way of maximizing the effects of challenging family structure, and we will just refer to this point briefly here, since it will be dealt with in another paper. This technique consists of systematic interventions of co-therapists who observe the sessions from beyond a mirror and come into the session to point out unobserved material, to redirect a session, or simply to reinforce a message by the therapist that requires the volume of two voices.

Let me emphasize in conclusion that in order to develop and communicate my view, I have talked only about the formal aspect of intervention—dismissing, as it were, other essential aspects of therapeutic intervention. I would like to emphasize that this is only an artifact of my presentation. An effective attack on family structure, as I have described it in this paper, can obviously be made only by a therapist who also has keen understanding of individual and family dynamics, and whose intervention has content that is relevant and meaningful in terms of these dynamics.

REFERENCES

1. Minuchin, S., Auerswald, E., King, C. H., & Rabinowitz, C. The study and treatment of families who produce multiple acting-out boys. *Amer. J. Orthopsychiat.*, 1964, *34* (1), 125–133.
2. Redl, F. Management of acting-out patients in analytic practice. Paper read at Harry Stack Sullivan Soc., December, 1963.
3. Hess, R. *Family worlds.* Chicago: Univer. Chicago Press, 1959.
4. Jackson, D. D., Riskin, J., & Satir, V. Method of analysis of a family interview. *Arch. gen. Psychiat.*, 1961, *5*, 321–339.
5. Bateson, G., Jackson, D. D., Haley, J., & Weakland, J. H. Toward a theory of schizophrenia. *Behav. Sci.*, 1956, *1*, 251–264.
6. Haley, J. *Strategies of psychotherapy.* New York: Grune & Stratton, 1963.
7. Shaffer, L., Wynne, L. C., Day, J., Ryckoff, T. M., & Halperin, A. On the nature and sources of the psychiatrist's experiences with the family of the schizophrenic. *Psychiatry*, 1962, *25*, (1) 32–45.
8. MacGregor, R. Multiple impact psychotherapy with families. *Fam. Process*, 1962, *1*, (1) 15–29.

CHAPTER 17

Therapy for Underprivileged "Delinquent" Families

Clara Rabinowitz

This chapter attempts to suggest the way family therapy can be used to help disrupted lower-class families whose children have been characterized as "delinquent." A detailed description of the process of therapy with such a family will be presented here. The material drawn upon was collected during a study[1] made by the Wiltwyck School of families of seven- to fourteen-year-old boys who were living in the school because of acting-out behavior. The families in this study were of a very low socioeconomic class, mainly Negro and Puerto Rican, although several white families were included. Often one or both parents had for a long time been delinquent themselves, and in some cases a parent or a sibling was imprisoned or was residing in another training school. The research for the study was carried out through a program of family therapy, of which the writer was a team member. A full description of this study may be found elsewhere (1).

These families also included female siblings who acted out sexually and whose attitudes toward marriage and sex would seem to lead them into inevitable difficulties. The position taken by this study was that these sex difficulties do not belong in a special category and that the "symptom," no matter what it may be, is but a particular aspect of a much larger configuration of feeling, thinking, and experience, which is directed by the particular family system. To deal with the symptom, the therapist must get to know the whole interacting human mosaic of which it is an integral part. Within such a context, the single actor, the individual offender, is often submerged into the larger show with its patternings of people acting together. The "disturbed family," rather than the "disturbed person," becomes the center of therapeutic attention.

For this reason, the basic therapeutic method with the girls with sex problems was essentially the same as for children with other symptoms. Although the family described here consisted of a mother with three boys, the writer feels that the treatment method used with this case is equally

[1] Study supported by N.I.M.H. Grant No. OM745 (R1) MHPG (1).

179

applicable to work with families whose special problems center on the sexual acting-out of their young daughters.

Before starting the history of the treatment of this family, it might be well to give an impressionistic account of the kind of world such families present to an outside observer. Researchers participating in the Wiltwyck study were struck by how little these families seem to be recognized by their members as groups of people who belong together. Parents seem to disassociate themselves from each other and from their children. They seldom have conversations with each other or with a child. If a child has difficulties, they take the attitude, "That's his lookout. What have I to do with it?" Often the court, which "took him away," or the school, which was "prejudiced," becomes the focus of angry blame. The parents do not see themselves as having an executive function in guiding and controlling the children's lives. They do not show lack of affection, but neither do they show affection in any distinct and recognizable ways. Both enjoyment of family life and any positive valuing of family relationships are notably absent. Data collected from control families which do not have acting-out children indicates that they tend to be different from the study families; for one thing, they have a greater capacity to enjoy family life. Conversely, the children from delinquent families do not seem to think of themselves as "belonging" to their families. In fact, they might as well belong to anyone, so little do their lives reflect conscious direction by their parents.

If we can see acting-out as a possible resolution of the child's struggle to remain in touch with a parent and still to get out of a family system which allows him few alternatives, it is possible to conceive of the child's defiance as congruent with a struggle for survival as an individual. Our task as therapists is to catch this aspect of a child's struggle by helping him or her to bring it into the family for transformation into its potentially creative construct.

Concerning the experience of pleasure within the family, these families seem to lack any conception of the happiness possible in being a parent or being a child. The very young—recipients of the family's nurture principle (2), however irrational—will behave spontaneously and as if they are the center of life about them. But all too soon they lose the valid sense of "I" and "me," as they are subjected to ill-conceived control and emotional neglect.

The quality of consciousness in these families is dictated by their mode of existence, which has been evolving throughout a lifetime. Although they maintain a family form, they do not develop a family consciousness. Our role is to disturb the static and malevolent mode of existence. The necessary degree of "disturbance" and the particulars of the method will need to be fashioned by the quality of consciousness confronting us in each particular family.

It is not the purpose of this paper to go into social and historical reasons for this, except to say that presently there are many families which, because for generations they have belonged to society's backwash, and because the human personality has ways of adapting to circumstances that may be injurious to mental health, appear to breed problem children. Society and the individual parent have had a constant interdependence, as in every human endeavor. It becomes apparent that the delays and resistances toward forward movements in society have ground down masses of people until they have become immobilized or have had to forego the experience of struggling for change, which is essential for personal and family growth. There is now evidence that even with "good" training or rehabilitation programs, many participants give up quickly. They have not developed sufficient skills or sufficient "will," for lack of a better word, to take on the new opportunity without some assistance; that is, the impediments toward learning may be experiential and/or psychological. Fortunately, these are, for the most part, temporary and amenable to change.

What follows is a description of an attempt to help one extremely deprived and disorganized family to take the opportunity for change. An effort will be made to present the course of therapy chronologically, but it has obviously been necessary, out of the huge mass of material available, to select only those events which seemed to the writer most relevant in the treatment history of this particular family.

THERAPEUTIC METHOD

The method of intervention used in these families was a variety of conjoint family therapy. (The process of family therapy has not yet been codified, any more than has individual therapy, into any preferred style or method.) Three therapists usually worked as a team with one family; the child's caseworker at the Wiltwyck School was one member of this team. On occasion, with the family's permission or invitation, a session was conducted in the home. This was usually an occasion for a party of sorts, and the event often evoked a warm interaction, which moved the family-team process a notch closer to "you and us" and farther from "we and you." From time to time, with the family's consent, other professional workers were included for a session: a probation officer, a school guidance teacher, a religious adviser close to the family, or a friendly relative.

As mentioned in Chapter 15 each session was usually divided into three stages. In Stage I, everyone met together. In Stage II, a therapist and the child's caseworker met with the children, while another therapist met with the parent or parents. In Stage III, everybody came together once more. The sessions would usually last about one and a half hours, and were held once weekly. After the family had left, the professional staff would meet to evaluate and criticize the session.

CASE STUDY: THE PETERS FAMILY

The Peterses were a Negro family with three boys. At the time of treatment, the father was in prison for a federal crime and for burglary. He had previously been imprisoned for similar offenses, all committed since his marriage. Mrs. Peters was in her forties—a large, stout, good-looking, angry woman, who nevertheless kept up an agreeable facade. She was a high school graduate, very intelligent; she had no siblings. With us, she was affable and expressive until any personal talk came up; then she would be stonily silent and remote, or cuttingly and quietly angry. Frank, the oldest boy, was a tall, lanky thirteen-year-old. At that time he was living in a training school for delinquents (not Wiltwyck), which permitted him to come for the weekly sessions. Jack was nine years old, quite tall and very fat. He was committed to Wiltwyck shortly after Frank left home. Both boys were removed from home for participating in setting fire to a public building. Jimmy, seven, was small and terribly thin; he looked and acted "crazy." In the substandard, poorly-cared-for home also lived the senile maternal grandfather.

Sample Scene from an Early Session, Stage I. [2]

This scene is typical of the interaction between the three boys and the mother at the beginning of therapy. Jimmy cannot sit still, talks irrelevantly, and is generally disruptive. After a while, he pulls a top from his pocket and begins to play with it. Jack eyes it enviously and soon manipulates it away from Jimmy, spinning it himself. Frank rouses from apparent sleep to quick alertness. Being pretty much the obvious leader of the brothers, he takes it easily from Jack, returning it after some brief play. Meanwhile, Jimmy is begging for his top and Jack is wheedling to hold it for keeps. The mother is silent. After this has gone on for a while, a therapist says, "Jimmy, I guess you want Mamma to settle this?" Jimmy looks fearfully at his mother, and she looks back dispassionately. No one speaks. Shortly afterward, Jimmy helplessly submits to Jack.

In the early sessions, the hierarchy and power operations among the children followed the pattern of the interaction described above. The mother's hands-off policy with the children was also characteristic. In fact, this kind of non-interference in the lives of the children is typical of most parents in the study. They leave their children too much on their own, unprotected and feeling that to count on their parents would be futile.

Behavior of Children during Therapy

Frank's characteristic manner in the sessions was to hang back in his chair, feigning sleep and answering a polite "Yes" or "No" or "I don't know" to a question from a therapist. He might rouse himself momentarily to join with his brothers, if their play interested him. Any reference by a therapist to his state of mind, problems, interests, or concerns, if persisted in, brought tears and quiet weeping.

Jack was harder to figure out. He, like Jimmy, acted psychotic when his demands were denied or when he appeared to feel threatened. At such times, he would sputter and rush out of the room, locking himself in the bathroom. When things bothered him at the school (when the other kids called him "Porky," when he could not keep up with the class, or when he

---

[2] The therapy team with this family consisted of the writer, Mrs. Mary Lopez Watkins, and Charles King.

could not conform to routines), he would act up disruptively or run away. He was not learning and could not read or do any sustained activity. In the sessions, however, we began to see that Jack's running away was also a great controlling device. It would end any effort to understand his aggressiveness or his obvious panic. Later on in treatment, we learned that he was afraid that his mother would get mad at him if he said he was frightened of anything, or if she learned of his "badness," or if he said anything which he thought she might disapprove of. He also seemed to be unable to tolerate any talk about him on the part of the other two boys. At these times, he would turn up his eyelids, grin irrelevantly, and assume a generally fantastic appearance. He would also hang on to his mother after the sessions or, if he sat near her, during them. At times she would tolerate this, but more often she would push him off. Jack could not bear to have her out of the room, and whenever she left he appeared compelled to go and find her.

Jimmy would jump about perpetually, calling attention to himself. He would interpret every (to us) innocuous act on the side of horror and violence, of which he was obviously in terror. Only when one of the therapists would show some discomfort with his behavior would the mother call out to him to stop. In fact, these were the only times she would interfere directly with any of the children's disruptive behavior. Usually she would merely fix a child with a malevolent look, and this would momentarily interrupt what was going on.[3]

Mother's Attitude toward Children's Difficulties

In one early session, we raised some questions about how life had been at home since Frank and Jack had been away, how they felt about being away from home, and how Jimmy and the mother experienced their weekly homecoming. We decided to break up the session when only monosyllabic and noncommittal replies were forthcoming. In Stage II, during the conference with Mrs. Peters, she said she felt that it was a good idea to have the sessions. However, she still did not tend to include herself in the picture of the children's problems. She felt that these problems were due to the interference of her own mother, who undermined her authority when the children were little. The grandmother, she said, would indulge them, but would criticize her for "spoiling" them; and she frequently

---

[3] This kind of silencing operation is well described by Zuk (3). He summarizes the aspects relevant to this mother and her children as follows: "Step 1. A forceful, consistent, subtle and frequent resort to silencing strategies levelled against an immature, dependent personality (for example, a child) by one or more closely related personalities (for example, parents) who are multiply-motivated: at one level, by the wish to possess an object on which to project their own unwanted feelings of being bad or inanimate. Step 2. The 'public' message conveyed by the silencing strategy is: 'I will not conform or be compliant to your likes, but I will agree to a certain isolation by silence because that is better than an outright dissolution of our relationship' [this would seem to apply to Frank and Jack], or, 'I will not conform or be compliant to your likes, or be *isolated in silence*, but I will agree *not to make sense* because that is better than an outright dissolution of our relationship." This would apply very much to Jimmy's behavior and talk.

prosphesied that they would come to a bad end when she, the grandmother, died. Jack and Frank were, in fact, arrested some weeks after the
grandmother's death. Although the mother could perceive that the children had already begun their difficult ways while the grandmother was
alive, she preferred to see these difficulties in terms of the prophecy, as
something fore-ordained. She declined responsibility in a similar way by
blaming the court for taking the children away. She had wanted no part of
that plan and saw no need for it.

At the time of these early sessions, the mother was unable to examine
what was going on between herself and the children, now that the grandmother was gone. Her cold attitude toward any consideration that concerned the family continued, as did her distance from the children. She
felt that their getting into trouble was their business, and that their not
communicating verbally in the sessions when she was present had nothing
to do with her, because "away from here they talk and carry on with each
other." She said they had a right to talk of only what they wanted to, and
that this held for her, too. She was entirely unaware that they might get or
take their cue from her.

Children's Behavior When Mother Was Not Present

In early sessions, when the children were seen apart from their mother,
there would often be an upsurge of spontaneous interaction. This would
die down as soon as the therapist began to participate actively, either by
trying to join a game or by attempting to talk about the family or a
particular child's situation. However, after being temporarily subdued, the
children would go on as if the therapists were not present—that is, they
would not talk with us directly. It was as if they were still complying with
the mother's command for silence toward us, while at the same time they
continued their independent activity. (Following Zuk's observation, they
seemed to be saying, "I will not conform to your likes, but I will agree to a
certain isolation.")

Often Frank and Jack would become quite competitive with each
other. Neither of them felt he was favored by the mother; each felt the
other was. Jack and Frank talked about their truancy while they lived at
home. Jimmy would get into the act in a "me too" manner. The older
boys boasted about how each could "truant" better than the other. It
appeared that the message on one level was that each was trying to prove
that he could make the mother the madder and get her attention that way.
On another level, the meaning appeared to be that one must cope with
authority by controlling or outwitting it.

Throughout these periods, Jack and Jimmy would run in and out to
"find Mother" (although they had been shown the room she was in), or to
"go to the bathroom," thus creating a milieu of disruption and disconti-
nuity. This was a common experience during that part of the sessions,
requiring a strenuous effort on the part of the therapists to keep order and
control. It was seen, in retrospect, to reflect the inability of these children
to carry on any sustained activity as individuals or as a group of siblings. It
certainly prevented others from having any meaningful connection with

them, and was in this way a barrier to fuller development of their thinking, planning, coping, experimenting, etc. To bring something meaningful and different into this situation meant to tackle it head on and repeatedly until the children were themselves able to experience some loss from the lawless, noisy interaction and some gains from learning to communicate more successfully, whether by expressing a thought fully or by hearing another person out. The recorded tapes of these periods are full of calls for order on the part of the therapists, demands that only one person speak at a time, requests that the children delay going out of the room. In Stages I and II, the therapists frequently intervened to ask why a child did not listen to his mother or brother, or to point out that the consequences of asking the mother's permission to run to the bathroom too frequently might lead her to refuse the request on some occasion when the child really had to go.

Mother and Children in Early Stage III Session

In Stage III of one early session, the mother was asked, as was our wont, if she would tell the children what went on in her session. This had previously been presented as a method we had found helpful to other families in their efforts to get a different understanding of each other. Because the children were still not ready to speak with any freedom in their mother's presence, their therapists briefly described the highlights of the meeting with them. In this instance, the children's competitiveness for the mother, and the fact that none of them felt she favored him, were noted. The mother smiled and elaborated on how Jackie would cling to her, how manageable Frankie was. She did not mention Jimmie. After her own session she merely said, "We talked about the family."

Attitudes of Family Members toward Father

During Stage I of the next session, we raised the issue of the father's existence. The mother told us the story of his imprisonment. The children said very little about him. The mother said that she and her husband had not been living together even before his latest arrest, and that she had decided not to take him back. Quite incidentally, in explaining the reason for this decision, she reported that her husband had shot at her and missed. We tried to get each child's understanding of the father's act. Frank "didn't see it" because he was "asleep." Jack admitted to being "scared." Jimmy talked wildly about it, at the same time appearing to describe a TV show (which Jack and Frank later said made Jimmy keep them awake, even though they would try to reassure him that the events were not real). We wondered why the shooting had been such a secret, and why the children even now spoke so cautiously about it. The mother blandly averred that there was nothing to discuss, that all the children had been witness to it, even Frankie, that the bullet hole in the wall was still there, and that the children still talked about it. "What is there to say?" became her refrain.

This talk about the father appeared to stimulate Jimmy to greater disruptiveness and incoherence. When we picked the shooting as a subject to follow up in Stage II, the child was in panic. His therapist held him close and guessed that Jimmy was still very scared of what had happened, and that maybe the TV shows reminded him of the shooting. Jimmy was encouraged to tell about it, with the reassurance that the mother would not get mad at him. (We had interpreted for ourselves that the mother had made a move toward opening up a sore subject, even if she was not yet ready to do more than break the silence, and we wished to see what would come of the opening she gave us.) With much terrified crying, Jimmy told us that he lived in perpetual fear that his father would return from prison. This time, Jimmy said, he was sure that his father would kill his mother and, more than likely, him too. He said he had to keep jumping around to keep himself from remembering about his father and the shooting; and when the jumping did not prevent him from remembering, he had to run in the street and hit a grown person, preferably a big boy or a man. Only then did Jimmy feel he could control the situation. Although he felt that it was somehow up to him to stop his father, he also believed that his father would be victorious. During this session and subsequent ones, the basis for Jimmy's preoccupation with, and fear of, violence became clearer. Also, Jack's hanging on to his mother and his intense anxiety about her whereabouts became more understandable to us.

Shifts in Family during Therapy

This session marked a breakthrough. While all the children were more or less constrained during Stage I, responding very cautiously in their talk about the father and the shooting, a few personal reactions did come out. It was Frank who, so to speak, let the cat out of the bag about Father. The essence of Frank's guarded remarks was that Father could be fun. Father had taught them how to shoot and hit a target. Jack and Jimmie amplified this, describing how he taught them to make guns. (We had known before the sessions how the father's way of relating to the children had implicitly encouraged their truancy, stealing, and aggressiveness.) The children were unaware of their contradictory feelings about the father, but at least they were able to come out with a positive valuing of him, in spite of the code of silence imposed by the mother on that subject.

A digression is necessary here to describe the kind of change in therapy which this whole scene presaged. It is impossible, without the use of the recorded tapes, to recreate the atmosphere of any session—its ebb and flow of mood and subject, the switches of feeling, thought, behavior, or speech on the part of the various participants, and all the other nuances of the live interaction. It is even harder to depict the movement which took place from session to session. However, certain shifts were large and noticeable enough that, at least impressionistically, they can be described.

In this instance the therapists were struck by the fact that the family began to come into a different relationship with them. During the early sessions family members acted more consistently as a *group* in the distance they kept from us, the outsiders, and in their efforts not to give themselves away. During the later sessions they began to respond more *individually* to our cues or to cues coming out of their own private development. In this session in particular, when the material about the father emerged, the solidarity of the family in the face of therapeutic intervention began to break down. The children were on the one hand restrained and cautious, taking their clue from the mother. At the same time, they became somewhat released from her encompassing direction, and were able to come out with feelings about their father which were not the same as they were "officially" supposed to have. And even though the mother still controlled herself and held to her position of "What is there to tell?" she nevertheless did report something about the father's role in the family. The children were not entirely freed from her continuing command for silence relative to family problems, but they did respond to some *new* element in her behavior and themselves, and were able to lead with a *new* facet: father was not all bad.

Thus, in these family sessions one is able to watch for a breakdown in the rigidity of the patterns. Sometimes the change will start with one member, sometimes with another. Important as this is to note and to nurture therapeutically, it is equally urgent to watch for the ways this is received by other family members: who picks it up and carries it further; who receives it, only to counter it or block it; and how this is managed, however subtly or covertly.

Reaction of Family to Open Discussion of Father

At the end of the session just reported, after the older children had said their goodbyes, the mother turned to us and said, referring to Frank, "That boy will sell you down the river for a nickel." When we pressed her to explain what she meant, she said, "I'll not tell you any more. I'll leave that to him." We interpreted this curious remark of the mother's as a reaction to the events of the session. She had found she could no longer dominate the children by her silence, and her fear and anger had taken this form.

During Stage I of the next session, the family greeted us with tense quiet. To break into this, we returned to the mother's statement at the end of the previous session, in which she expressed her feeling that Frank had betrayed her, and asked her what she was alluding to. She glared. Frank, now in the spotlight, wept more bitterly than usual. We wondered privately whether the mother's open anger toward Frank might not have been precipitated by his having led off in the previous session with how much fun Father could be, and that she had interpreted it to mean, "He is my favorite parent." It did not seem useful, however, to present this in the family group, because it was evident that there was too much unknown business between the mother and Frank, and that it could not be gotten at with the mother so angry and Frank so scared. We called for a Stage II earlier than usual.

In Stage II, the mother was responsive to the writer's guess that Frank had done something which she took as a betrayal, a going over to the father. She explained that the father, prior to his latest imprisonment, was living away from the family, and that whenever he would telephone, Frank would report who had been in and out of the house. In other words, the mother felt that she was being spied on by a child for whom she felt she had done so much, in the face of the father's complete abdication.

Here, while we were aware that we had only a partial view of the mother's experience with Frank's dealings with his father, it was possible to feel and to show compassion for her suffering, and also to convey that we knew that an act has many different meanings, depending on whether one is the actor, the person for whom the act is intended, or the observer. We suggested that perhaps Frank and the children's therapist would be able to discuss this action and help us, in Stage III, to understand his view. The mother then went a little further in her talk about her own mother, how she had tried to be different from her own mother with the children.

In Stage II, Frank was finally able to say that he did not feel about his action the same way his mother did. He saw only that he was giving his father what his father seemed to want of him. Surprisingly, Frank brought a secret of his own into the open. He said that he loved his father and felt bad about not seeing him. He knew his father had done wrong things (about which he was quite fuzzy), but when his father got out of prison he intended to find him, even if it took the rest of his life, because he wanted to know for himself what his father was really like.

With the family reassembled in Stage III, the children's therapist reported that what had felt to the mother like betrayal and spying, seemed to have been experienced and meant by Frank in a very different way: Frank wanted both to keep his mother and to stay in touch with his father. By telling his father the things the father wanted to know, Frank was using the only way he knew to hold on to his father. We also pointed out that Frank was unaware of how his mother might interpret his behavior. We talked about a child's natural concern for a parent—regardless, often, of his parent's behavior; how a child's feeling of security often depends on his having access to the parent. The tension in the family gave a bit during the session, and the children talked more freely about less intimate matters, such as their doings at school. Frank told us how he had witnessed the boys in the school group outwitting a counsellor. (He obviously got a good deal of vicarious pleasure from this, though he himself did not participate.) Jack talked less despairingly about his inability to diet and told how he was being helped with the problem at school. At the end of the session, Frank was openly affectionate to his mother, and she appeared a bit more responsive.

Efforts to Involve Mother Herself in Therapy

After this session we were ready to use our separate meetings with the mother to focus on a basic issue: how distant she had generally been from the children, how little family business got aired in the therapy, and how little she had been able to let the children know what her feelings were, despite her deep desire and efforts to give them a better life than she had had. In doing this, it was now possible to use specific data from previous sessions. We also communicated our observations about how the children had become closed in on themselves through various fantastic notions about their experiences in the home. We illustrated this with Jimmy's preoccupation with fear and violence; Jack's shame at not being considered a person in his own right by the mother, and his need to hang on to her physically, in order to be sure that she was available to him, as well as to "protect" her; Frank's need to fall asleep in order to close out contact with a world he felt he could not control (by now a less necessary device for him). The mother continued to act defensive but added that she and the children were now talking more at home.

The Sibling Subsystem in the Family

In a subsequent Stage II with the children, we observed that, although Frank was the leader, Jack had protective feelings for him. In a number of sessions, Jack had told us how he used to follow Frank "to keep Frank out of trouble." Jack pleaded with us to let him come home when Frank returned. (Frank was due for earlier discharge by the school, because he had not gotten into difficulties and was carrying his responsibilities.) Jack wanted to be home with Frank, because then he could "hang on to Frankie." When he saw trouble coming he would "hit Frankie and holler and then run for home," so that Frank would have to follow him. In this way, Jack felt he could help Frank avoid trouble.

Thus we discovered that Jack felt responsible for Frank. At the same time he felt that he had gotten into trouble because of Frank, who, he told us, had taught him how to steal. Because of his feelings about Frank, Jack had to keep a close watch on him to prevent him from getting into trouble, and that was why he was present when the building was set on fire, the final act for which both boys were removed from home.

Gradually, Frank's anxiety about his return to the family emerged and increased. He wept each time it was mentioned, although he did want very much to go home. He was terribly afraid that he might not be able to keep out of trouble, though he meant to try very hard; and he was also afraid that Jack might get into trouble again because of him. He was also frightened by the whole new set of feelings related to assuming the role of the "good" family leader.

The mother accepted Jack's version of Frank's responsibility for his getting caught, but she missed completely the nuance of the nine-year-old's premature sense of responsibility for Frank, and of Frank's precarious conception of being the children's leader. Such feelings are typical of the sibling subsystem which is a basic process in the lives of these families (1). It is characterized by a great sense of responsibility on the part of one sibling for another, usually before he has had the necessary experience and judgment to meet the problems he feels forced to take on. The compelling desire to nurture each other contains, at the same time, a contradictory and disruptive force: while siblings protect each other, they also indoctrinate each other into delinquent ways and compete antagonistically with one another. Then they suffer from guilt and anxiety which arise from these aggressive and contradictory feelings about each other.

Role of Mother's Boyfriend

A time came when it seemed possible to broach more directly another touchy subject, the mother's boyfriend. She had told us in a preliminary session that she had one, but she did not mention him again or permit any talk about him during the separate sessions with her. The children, meantime, had spoken of him in their own sessions. Frank, again showing much deep feeling, said he liked and respected "Uncle Harry." To himself, and when the family was alone, Frank called him this, but the boy was uncertain what to call him or how to behave toward him in the presence of other people. Knowing that Harry was not their real uncle, he said he was ashamed to call him that, though he would like to. Jack said he liked Harry, too, and told us that Harry taught them things. He was a mechanic, could fix things, and shared his knowledge with them. Jimmy, although he appeared to respond warmly to mention of Harry, talked in a kind of private language, which we thought might reflect this young child's confusion over relationships in the family. This kind of irrational talk was what we had come to see as his response to any emotionally charged or frightening subject.

The mother's marriage had never been dissolved. She had limited her talk about her husband to saying that she knew immediately after the marriage that it was a "mistake." She had several times given way to his urgent demands to be taken back after other imprisonments. However, after the shooting which took place before his latest arrest, she decided that she would not take him back again. She was more evasive about any talk of divorce. We offered the possibility of agency help to look into this and let the matter go for the moment. We did suggest however, that perhaps she could talk with the children about her feelings for Harry and her decision about the father, because they were confused about their relationship with Harry. She insisted that this did not concern them, taking the position that she did not neglect them for him, and that she tried to be discreet when Harry stayed over.

When the children began to be freer in the family sessions, we questioned the mother about her continuing exclusion of the father and Harry in her talk. We also wondered why, if Harry were such a big part of the children's lives—as they appeared to feel he was—he was not brought into the "meetings," as the family called the sessions. Mrs. Peters openly expressed the anger which we could only guess at earlier. She did not see what her private life had to do with any of this. She was not coming to these meetings for herself, and she did not think that her relations with Harry were of concern to the children.

We could only say that we were aware of her discomfort at our whole procedure, but that by long experience we had learned that the majority of children released from Wiltwyck would return to the courts, if the families were not included in the work. We wondered why she was so fearful of participating more fully. We were well aware of how much the children meant to her (and here we cited examples of the clues she gave us for this observation), and yet she seemed to strain so much not to show it openly. Why? Could it be that this had something to do with her relationship to her own mother? Perhaps she felt that she had failed both as a mother and as a woman, in the light of her experience with her own mother. Perhaps, too, she did not dare to divorce Mr. Peters because she would then be free to choose again, and feared she would repeat the "mistake."

Her manner became cold and stony, as it had been early in the work, but she did yield a bit when we reiterated a guess that she felt she could do nothing "right," that she felt stuck and, feeling so, had to act stuck. We told her that we believed that Frank and Jack were really bright children, capable of understanding much that we had talked of, even if they only brought to it children's judgments. We observed that the children were greatly improved in their behavior at their schools and in the sessions. Had she not noticed it? She agreed and said that when the children came home on visits, she questioned them about what went on at school and that it jibed with what they told us. She had never thought her children were bad. We said we thought that even "good" children can get into difficulties when their parents, out of ignorance, fear, or too many troubles, do not become the family leaders they are capable of being. We thought her boys had a way to go, but that they could make it if she would come out of her "seclusion." We told her that the children had begun to question their not getting the guidance they wanted, especially in regard to their conflict between their fondness for Harry and their embarrassment over his presence in the home.

We talked some more with the mother in this vein before bringing up the subject in the family session. We told her that we thought that the questions from the children should come to *her* and not to us, because what she had to say would be important, and we expressed confidence that she would find the answers as she went along. We pointed up a problem which is common in this group of families, the importance of giving children an example of love-sex-marriage responsibility. We said that while we did not doubt that mutual respect and responsibility could exist without legal ties, this did not obviate the necessity for telling her children about her plans relative to Harry and the father, in terms commensurate with their ability to understand. In other words, we talked of the importance of presenting children with socially acceptable models in family life.

When confronted with these problems, Mrs. Peters reflected her ambivalence. She balked at the implication that her kids were not getting the "best" under the circumstances and, at the same time, revealed some concern.[4] Unable to take any step as yet, she retreated to her affable "but-I-won't-give-an-inch" attitude.

Subsequently, in a Stage III session we discussed the father's future in the family and had asked why Harry was not coming to the family meet-

---

[4] There has been criticism about "imposing on deprived families middle-class values." This is indeed an important ethical question, but we might well ask what these middle-class values are in reference to legal marriage and the family. What other values are there? Do we propose to impose still a new set of values on these families, separating them even further from society by making them the vanguard of a "new morality"? Naturally, when we speak of offering the children a model relative to love, sex, and marriage, we do not concern ourselves with dogmas attached by religion to these matters, nor with the uses and abuses of legality (such as the muddled legal status and cost problems of divorce, or the doubtful regulations in some public housing which exclude unwed mothers). There is a good discussion about the way ethical concepts survive or change in a recent book by Howard Selsam (4). Selsam also mentions Wallace (5) in considering why some customs endure and others do not.

ings. Frank grinned. Jack said, "Why don't we ask him?" Jimmy got nervous and began to be noisy. The mother said she didn't know if he could leave work. One of the therapists stepped in to say that if she would ask Harry, we either might be able to arrange an evening session, or we could meet in her home for a time. The mother said she would let us know before the next session. There was some more talk about the father on the part of the children. We said we wondered if they couldn't try talking with mother about this subject, and left it at that.

Including Boyfriend in Therapy Session

The next session was something of a turning point; "Uncle Harry" did come to a session. His work did not permit regular attendance, but he offered to try and make it even at a loss of pay if we needed him. He turned out to be a mild-mannered, soft-spoken, kindly man who, in contrast to the mother's past behavior, was concerned about the children's conduct during the sessions and firmly called them to order. The children, even Jimmy, joked with him and responded with respect and obvious affection for him. We let Harry know how glad we were to meet him and, putting this as lightly as possible, said that we were wondering why he and Mrs. Peters were making like a family but not really clinching matters. Harry said, "I'm ready. It's up to her." The mother looked uncomfortable; she was openly enjoying Harry's being accepted by, and participating in, the group, but did not commit herself.

The topic turned to Frank's impending discharge. The mother showed more concern than usual. We aired Frank's fears and asked Harry how he saw things. He agreed with the mother that it was too bad that Frank had to return to the same neighborhood school for the present. Mother talked vaguely, once more, of moving. Harry felt that the negatives could be balanced out by his efforts to back Frank up in seeking a different kind of life and avoiding his previous companions. We agreed. Frank was attentive and commented appropriately and spontaneously.

We did not split the session up this day, responding to the new, more unified mood of the family group. This, too, we commented on. The family was left to its farewells with Frank and Jack, and to its own affairs. The atmosphere was warm and friendly.

Changes in Children Toward End of Therapy

Subsequent sessions were considerably different in character, having mainly to do with the children. Frank was full of his coming return home. His "sleeping" had given way to active participation and the appearance of what might be called an open, boyish quality. He still delighted in a joke on his supervisors, but was much more concerned with his own legitimate wants. His eventual discharge was taken in stride and marked by very deep efforts to avoid invitations to join former neighborhood pals, who were often in trouble. He wanted to join youth organizations, for which he perhaps had felt ineligible in the past, and to follow up an interest in carpentry created by Harry. He was helped to ask his new teachers, whom he still eyed suspiciously, for book titles and advice. In an effort to help him sustain these gains, a male student caseworker was assigned to him as a big brother, who would keep in touch with him after the sessions ended and before another agency program could be instituted. Frank seemed to be enjoying his life. This is worth noting because characteristically absent in the families studied was the sense of gratification that comes from finding new skills and new methods of coping, with the accompanying feeling of inner security in the self. This, of course, was mirrored and cued off by an absence of family pride, family fun, family celebrations of any kind. Poverty was the offered excuse, but poverty was in reality only a limiting factor. There was often no noticeable attempt at even simple recognition of birthdays, anniversaries, or holidays.

The change in Jack was more gradual and, in a sense, more critical, since his behavior was the more disruptive and difficult to live with. The external symptomatology—the eyelid-twisting, the panic tantrums, the aggressive running out on every difficult encounter—began to disappear within the first months of family work. Then, in the joint sessions, he began to urge us to let him take the subway trip home alone.[5] We would refer him to his mother in an effort to help her take over appropriate authority. At first his mother quashed his suggestion. We intervened, with the prupose of getting Jack to explore his reasons for the plan and to express them. In answer to his mother's objections that he could not read and therefore would not know where to get off, he insisted that he was a careful watcher and had begun to know the signs of his particular station, that he was "grown up enough," and that he wanted to "try." Later, Jack figured out a method to substitute for his still limited reading ability. He had counted the stops and had learned when to expect the correct one. We interpreted this as Jack's effort to try himself out in taking more responsibility for himself. In the end, the mother was able to give up her too tight hold over him (in contrast to more appropriate ways of protection) and let Jack try coming alone to the meetings. Jack followed this success with the startling announcement that he had decided to learn to read and to do his other school work, "because it will help me get a better job when I'm big." He also began to display a more wholesome concern with his weight.[6]

Jimmy's problems had still a different dimension. His birth had come at a time when the mother had given up hope for a marriage and home independent of her own mother, with whom it had been necessary for her and/or the children to live periodically, and at a time when she was already defeated in the struggle to free herself psychologically from her parents.

---

[5] Wiltwyck children on a visit home or for an overnight stay preceding a therapy session were brought to New York City from the upstate residence school by bus, and were usually met by some family member. This plan was instituted to enable the family and the child to interact, and the experience was often the basis for work in the sessions.

[6] This kind of change in a child—or in an adult—usually presages a transformation from a consciousness which puts upon the other person the burden for his disabilities to an acceptance of responsibility for coping with what belongs to him (relative to his age-ability level). It is also a move away from a view of the world, and especially its authority figures, as hostile and threatening.

This had left Jimmy more open to traumatizing and emotional neglect, and less eligible for the grandparents' attentions. Harmful as the grand-parents were in some ways for the mother and children, they did offer some semblance of structured family life. There was also some suspicion that Jimmy had suffered organic damage, due to an early accident—a possibility later ruled out. Thus, while Jimmy's restlessness diminished considerably, and while his behavior began to conform more to a seven-year-old's, he continued to express irrelevant ideas and to refer to imaginary happenings.

Jimmy also continued to be an outsider to his mother. However, as the tumult in the sessions died down, and as the mother began to take over activity that belonged to her, she also began to involve herself in our concern over Jimmy. While at first she limited her attentions to paralyzing Jimmy with her "look" or a verbal command, she moved on to blaming his teachers, as did Jimmy, and to criticizing him for the tales he told about seeing "monsters." She felt that she had explained away these irrational ideas. But there was evidence that, like most mothers in the group, she did not ever make a plain, reassuring statement of fact to him about the nonexistence of the object of his fears.

The developments noted here in the lives and behavior of the children obviously had an effect on the mother's behavior. Toward the end of the sessions, the mother began to take more responsibility for Jimmy. She told us that she had long ago taken him to a hospital where certain further studies were recommended. Now, she said, she planned to follow these up. By this time, also, Frank was living at home, and the mother was able to initiate discussion of her experiences with him and to express her appreciation of his efforts and success. She was able to consider, with Jack and with us, whether Jack was ready to return to her.

The problem of the process of change in family therapy is an interesting one. In individual therapy, there is always the question of how one begins to detect, measure, and encourage change. In family therapy, there is an added dimension. The process is no longer limited to the stimulation and help initiated within the me-you relationship between patient and therapist. The new and powerful element is the dynamic-for-change which enters because each person in the session, not excluding the therapist, has begun a development which impinges on that of every other person, so that each forces the others to respond in different ways. By this means, each person stretches the others' potential for growth and is stretched by each in turn. In such a process, it is sometimes the children who move quickly and push the parents into new positions. Sometimes it is the parents who must move to unlock rigid positions of children. In the Peters family, it appeared to be the children's growth which "forced," if you will, the mother's.

Discussion of Treatment of Peters Family

To generalize from the year or more of interaction between the Peters family and the team—only the highlights of which have been presented here[7]—one may say that the aim of family therapy intervention is to reorganize the relationships within the family in such a way that each individual can develop appropriate roles for interacting with others, within which his own struggle for growth may proceed. Parents must find roles which allow them to guide and direct their children; and children must find roles which allow them gradually to take more responsibility for themselves.

The process of therapy may be described as one in which the staff enters the family system, hopefully better prepared to cope with it than the family. The technical problems of handling each case must be dictated by the staff's assessment of how the family system works and what is going on in the interpersonal activity of all participants. Hopefully, again, the team can bring an expansive use of (*a*) whatever professional–technical (psychoanalytic, psychological, casework, sociological) knowledge each has about personality, pathology, and the relatively new understanding about communication and society, and (*b*) what each person on the team has been able and willing to learn about himself through living in the world.

RELEVANCE OF THE WILTWYCK STUDY TO FAMILIES WITH ACTING-OUT GIRLS

In applying the family approach to understanding families with young girls with sexual problems, perhaps the only generalization we can make is that these children who become delinquent (break laws) or who act out sexually (break social codes) are, first of all, children who have grown up in milieus with certain definite, if not easily delineated, patternings of thought and behavior. One could say about the patterning of the Peters family that the mother, in reacting to the restrictiveness of her own mother, consciously sought to break away from this pattern and thus took too little control in mothering her own children. Confused, however, by her unaware, too-close tie to her parents, she had taken over their views of child-rearing and became in her own eyes a wrong-doer, despite her conscious efforts. Actually, she was a wrong-doer in a sense which she was not able to assess consciously; she wronged herself through a marriage which was calculated to bring freedom but, having been executed in unaware defiance of her parents, brought only more dependence on them. Her long other-family training experience prohibited interpersonal exploration by verbal communication, a characteristic lack in such families. Thus this mother, without knowing it, silenced her children. While she tried, on one level, to be a good parent and saw herself as such, she turned away helplessly from her children's misguided efforts to grow up. The children,

---

[7] In this overview, only the main events of the therapeutic work were included. A forthcoming book will analyze and interpret the content of sessions with different families, tracing the development of each person's form of behavior and thought in its impact on that of each other person, in an effort to clarify the family style of communication and interaction.

situated in an outer environment where aggression and acting on impulse were the chosen methods of coping, could not develop appropriate experience or judgment soon enough to protect themselves.

Let us posit that young girls in families where verbal communication is limited, and where models of parenting have been influenced by severe conditions of poverty, also develop styles of thinking which compel them to reach for balance in certain ways. Among the families of the Wiltwyck study were young girls of twelve to sixteen who already gave signals of what might follow. Some lived with mothers who had a long series of "boyfriends" living in the home; some had mothers who were prostitutes. One girl of sixteen, who came from a large family in which all the siblings were out-of-wedlock births, had already been assaulted by neighborhood boys. In the ensuing court action, it came to light that the "stepfather" had also attempted to assault her. She knew much about sex and claimed she wanted none of it. Her mother, however, had picked this oldest daughter as the one to "protect," and treated her to a continuous admonishment about the dangers of men, was constantly suspicious of her, and when the "stepfather" was ordered out of the home, took the girl as a target for accusations of "badness." The girl's thirteen-year-old sister was already about to give birth, the father being a married man in the area. This sixteen-year-old was a bright girl; she had already been a mother-substitute for five or six siblings, and was "destined" to become an umarried mother on several counts. On one level one might say that her mother was virtually giving the girl orders to act out sexually. Then there was the model at home and on the street. The girl would blandly say, "All my girlfriends already have babies." Most of all, there was her feeling that "I want a baby of my own, but I don't want to marry, not now anyway."

In another very large family where the parents had been married in childhood (the mother had been thirteen, the father seventeen) the pattern between the parents was extreme violence, on the one hand, and extraordinary dependency of the illiterate father on the natively gifted mother, on the other. The mother's mood would swing from brutal retaliation against the father to maternal nurturing of him. The oldest girl, lovely in appearance and bright enough, "never" wanted to marry. Her fantasy of the future was to become a dancer, though she had no noticeable interest or experience in dancing, to live in luxury and drive beautiful cars. By her own description, validated by her mother and sister, she could get lots of fellows to admire her but would "get rid of them soon." The younger sister, here, was more mentally ill than well, but she too, said at the outset, "I don't want to marry unless *I* can beat *him* up." Both girls felt the mother was weak and foolish "to take it"; yet both, along with seven younger siblings, were terrified lest the mother leave the father and the family break up. Both also felt that men were inferior to women, a view encouraged by the mother's reliance on the girls.

I cite these vignettes to point up the statement, made at the beginning of this paper, that in itself the "symptom" relative to sex can only be understood in the context of a much larger picture. To our way of think-

CHAPTER 18

The Sexually Delinquent Female: Observations in Therapy

Jerome E. Jungreis[1]

The broad areas of understanding and treating acting-out behavior have elicited considerable interest in recent years. In the delinquency literature, however, sexual acting-out per se has received considerably less attention than stealing, truancy, assault, and similar behavior. Much information is available on the intrapsychic and familial forces that generate unmarried motherhood, but references to sexual delinquency without resultant motherhood are comparatively meager, although it is probable that promiscuous sexual acting-out without pregnancy is far more prevalent. Our popular culture is becoming more accepting of a variety of sexual experiences among adults, but we still regard promiscuity among teen-age girls as symptomatic of personal maladjustment. Indeed, very strong family feelings are communicated regarding such behavior.

This chapter, building upon the knowledge already available, will (a) relate observations of a number of families in which a female teen-ager presents sexual acting-out behavior, (b) compare these findings with a select number of references, and (c) integrate and refine the combined findings.

The study on which these observations are based grew out of the practicum part of the special training program described in the Preface of this book. The trainees were senior caseworkers who were receiving training in family counseling and treatment, with a preceptor as co-counselor demonstrating the effectiveness of family group treatment with families who have a sexually-acting-out, delinquent daughter. In the course of the twelve months of this work, seven senior caseworkers, carefully selected by their agency for training in conjoint family treatment, saw a total of 33 families. Of these families 24 were seen for at least five family counseling sessions of one and a half hours each, with some of the families seen over 35 times. Three of the 24 families were considered atypical, in that homosexuality rather than heterosexual acting-out was found to be

author is indebted to Mrs. Susan Freeman, of the Philadelphia Child Guidance
for her help in the preparation of this paper. At the time, she was with the
Service of Philadelphia.

ing, it is limiting to see the life dilemma of a single person in terms
symptom only.

REFERENCES

1. Minuchin, S., Auerswald, E., King, C. H., & Rabinowitz, C. The study an
ment of families that produce multiple acting-out boys. *Amer. J. Orthops.*
1964, *34* (1), 125–133.
2. Minuchin, S. *The acting-out child and his family: An approach to family t*
Mimeographed, 1961; for publication.
3. Zuk, G. H. On the pathology of silencing strategies. *Fam. Process*, 1965, *4*
4. Selsam, H. *Ethics and progress.* New York: International Publishers, 1965
5. Wallace, A. R. *The wonderful century: Its successes and its failures.* N
Dodd Mead, 1898.

either the main form of, or a significant part of, sexual delinquency. Since the caseworkers were all highly skilled and experienced, we have assumed that they can be considered expert observers. Our findings are the result of their clinical evaluation of the families, as organized on special rating scales developed for this study.[2]

The families seen were predominantly white, lower-middle-class families, in which the fathers were skilled or semi-skilled workers. The number of children in these families roughly paralleled the population norm. Thirteen of the designated patients (namely, the acting-out daughters) were the oldest child in the family, and five others were the second-oldest child, but the oldest daughter. These figures are significant, and can be speculated about in conjunction with our other unusual findings. The families were not prone to regard the sexual delinquency as requiring outside intervention until after at least a year and a half of such continued behavior. Most often, the problem had agitated the family for two to three years before help was sought. In six of the families, the problem girls had had one pregnancy each.

In these families we observed a number of characteristics that are common to almost all families seeking help for their children. What was different, though, was that while these families showed evidence of serious disorganization as families and disturbance in other members besides the designated patient, the teen-age daughter is the one around whom family concern and cohesion focuses. For example, in only 5 families did observers find no serious psychopathology in other family members. It should be noted that of these 5 families, 3 were seen only briefly. In the remaining 19 families, at least one other member was considered seriously disturbed; in 6 of these 19, every member was seen as quite disturbed. Psychopathology included psychosis, alcoholism, and gross failure of a child in school performance. Thus 19 of our original 24 families showed serious psychopathology in other family members, but the family chose to express concern about only the sexually delinquent one. The parents seemed relatively unconcerned about pathology in the other family members, or at least tolerated it without special interest. Only the sexuality of the daughter aroused the interest of both parents and, to a lesser extent, of the girl's siblings. The fathers, who otherwise appeared to be generally passive and not deeply involved in family life, showed remarkable concern with the daughter who was exhibiting sexual delinquency. Indeed, as we observed these so-called "passive" fathers with greater precision and over a longer period of time, we became aware of the subtle and active roles that they played in influencing the family.

This observation corresponds very closely with another one: in 20 of the 24 families, the designated patient was seen as the family scapegoat. She was seen as the only source of family stress, the one who is upsetting everyone, and the one but for whom everything would be fine. Thus, the

---

[2] Copies of these scales are available on request from Alfred S. Friedman, Ph.D., Philadelphia Psychiatric Center, Ford Road and Monument Avenue, Philadelphia, Pa. 19131.

sexually delinquent girls seem to help their families suppress awareness of pathology in other members and give them a common bond of interest. There was evidence that this bond of interest and unity was badly needed. Of the 24 families, 22 showed little sense of family unity and common purpose outside of their interest in the designated patient. Almost all of the parents admitted sexual problems in their own marriage, though 21 of the 24 wives saw their husbands as adequate. We were particularly struck with the fact that 42 percent of the husbands worked on a nonstandard work day, and were seldom at home to spend time with their families. These families, interestingly enough, readily accepted the father's absence as reasonable. Seventeen of the families were over-involved with various in-law relationships, and almost all of the families showed little if any comforting by the parents, either of each other or of the children.

The acting-out girl seemed to assume the role of the family "id." The lack of pleasure, stimulation, and comforting coming from the parents, and the lack of such affect in the parental marital relationship, possibly placed too heavy a demand on the girl to supply pleasure and parenting to the family. It may have been partly to escape from this excessive demand from the parents, as well as from the threat attached to these impulses within the family, that the daughter felt pressured to act out sexually outside the family.

There is some evidence to indicate that the family was involved in perpetuating the sexual delinquency. For example, in 20 of 24 cases the parents showed far more concern about the social indiscretion of the daughter's sexual acting-out than about the inherent meaning or implication of such behavior to the girl, or about the violation of a strongly held superego taboo. Many parents did not even talk directly about their daughter's delinquency, but talked mainly about her defiance, lying, staying out late, and other such behavior.

Observations of the parents in their family roles confirm the family's over-involvement in the daughter's problem. While the fathers were typically seen as passive, dependent, needy, and wanting their wives to assume mother roles for them, they were also seen as seductive to their daughters. The majority of the fathers and almost all of the mothers showed exaggerated interest in the girl's dating habits even before there were signs of promiscuity. All the mothers had excessive emotional investment in their daughters preceding the sexual acting-out, while simultaneously they saw the daughters as very much unlike themselves. The mothers' own neediness and dependency, while not superficially apparent, came out in the observation that their struggle with the daughter seemed to be mostly over who shall make the other one the parent.

Finally, the observers achieved high correlation in their consensus about the characteristics of the designated patient herself. She was described as immature, doing poorly in school regardless of intelligence, having poor or no peer relationships, attractive yet pseudoseductive, and basically not very sexual.

Our study did not investigate individual intrapsychic dynamics in depth, but rather the family interaction in role conflicts. For example, the daughter's behavior certainly revealed many interesting family paradoxes. She was not found to be the oversexed, erotically-charged woman seeking sexual release. On the contrary, she appeared to be much less a sexual creature than the average girl her age. Another interesting paradox is that despite her obvious immaturity, poor schoolwork, etc., both parents saw her as a mother figure and a highly sexualized one at that. While the parents had a poor relationship with each other, they were banded together in their common concern about the daughter's potential and actual sexual behavior. In these otherwise disorganized families, something quite different occurs in reaction to their daughter's sexual behavior. The passive father becomes a part-time tiger. He may indulge in temper outbursts and rages, and become punitive, authoritarian, restrictive, and critical toward his daughter. The dependent mother now evidences concern for her daughter. Most of the time the parents find it infinitely easier to complain of the daughter's running away, lying, or stealing than of the sexual threat that is involved with the running away or other such behavior. On the manifest level, the anxiety of the parents is around social conformity, not the intrinsic taboo on promiscuous premarital intercourse. Another striking paradox is the evidence of serious psychopathology in other family members and their relative indifference to this psychopathology. Only the sexual acting-out seems to arouse concern. In a general way, we can say that the sexual acting-out is seen by the parents as a threat to the family homeostasis (1). The siblings do not seem to be as threatened as the parents, and their anxiety is apparently more a reflection of the parents' anxiety than their own. Thus, we see a convergence of multiple family factors ending up with a focus upon the oldest daughter. That is, because both parents are weak, the entire family becomes emotionally needy and puts pressure on the oldest daughter to assume the mother role.

If the father's choice of a marital object was a mother figure whom he can sexualize, it would be reasonable to suppose that his projecting the same role onto the daughter would have similar unconscious sexual associations. If the mother's unconscious need for dependency upon her own mother were associated with unconscious homosexual strivings, these too can be focused upon the daughter. The only way out for the daughter, then, seems to be a direct heterosexual expression as a sexual female, not as either a homosexualized or a heterosexualized mother figure. The daughter's over-determined asexual appearance and behavior had previously helped the family to prevent an oedipal threat to the father or a homosexual threat to the mother. Now the acting-out upsets the homeostasis. Mother and father are faced with having to give up the fantasied, sexualized mother object.

The implications of the acting-out as related to other problems in the family are not quite clear. The rallying of the parents around a central concern and the father's typical switch from passive underachiever, with minimal involvement with the family, to aggressive head of the family seem to be focused only on the daughter's acting-out. These changes do not seem to spill over into concern for other disturbed members of the family.

If there is one general statement we can make about these families, it is that the symptoms of the daughter are clearly a concomitant of intra-family forces that must involve *both* parents. We may also assume that the symptoms of the siblings relate to other, parallel problems with *both* parents. It may be assumed too, as a corollary, that converging and inter-locking fantasies and projected roles of both parents are necessary for symptom formation. Conflicts between marital couples do not exclude interlocking fantasies about a child. In fact, it may be hypothesized that the conflict between the parents is related to immature fantasies that have become fixed upon the child, who is more tractable and needs a role, rather than upon each other, who started marriage already fixed in their role expectations of each other.

Having conceptualized some of the family dynamics from our own experience, we now compare them with formulations from other sources:

The first comparable study is by Johnson and Szurek (1), who used material from their experience over a ten-year period to explore the etiology of sexual acting-out. The "superego lacunae" theory stressed in this paper regards a specific superego defect in the child as a duplication of a similar suppressed distortion in the parent's personality. Specific points are made in relation to the girl's sexual acting-out. These refer to inconsistent attitudes in the mother, who may herself have developed a reaction formation against sex to handle her own poorly integrated inpulses. These mothers, in their accusations and detailed questionings of their daughters, actually give unconscious permission to the teen-ager to act out. Little is said in this article about the father's role.

In addition to the Johnson and Szurek study, three others offer a fruitful basis for evaluating our own findings: the studies by Blos, Robey, and Tessman and Kaufman—reported in Chapters 10, 12, and 13, of this book.

As we relate these four studies to our own material, we are impressed with the degree to which additional knowledge about the family, particu-larly the parents, enriches and deepens the formulations made by these writers. In some instances, our study suggests that dynamics other than those suggested in previous studies may be operating. For example, Johnson and Szurek state that the superego defect in the child duplicates a similar defect in the parent's superego that the parent cannot express openly, but can covertly encourage in the child. We too have noted that the parents do not convey a superego prohibition against promiscuity. Instead, they tell the child of the shame she is causing them. Also, they are excessively involved in, and aroused by, the daughter's dating even before acting-out appears. The parents' own poorly integrated impulses and inconsistent attitudes, our study suggests, may well be due to having to give up the fantasy of the daughter as a sexualized mother figure, on the one hand, and to relief from the threat of incestuous acting-out on the other. Their excessive interest in her dating habits may give the daughter unconscious clues to the way out of the dilemma which they all share.

It is also possible to suggest that, while the other siblings may be acting-out in other ways, these lacunae are more acceptable to the parents as gratification of the parental impulses. However, with the other children a different kind of unconscious parental teamwork is operating, in which one parent secretly encourages the acting-out while the other parent takes over the superego function for the partner and child. We have all noticed, in our general clinical work, that one of a marital pair may be consciously attracted to the other because of the real or imagined control that the other will bring to bear on his or her impulses. With the delinquent daughter, however, neither parent can be the strong one. Both are threatened by either her growing up and becoming more seductive to them or her acting-out outside the home, and causing them to face renunciation of a cherished fantasy. Hence, the parents in these families can better tolerate other kinds of acting-out in the other children; they have their unconscious teamwork operating. Siblings may well have their own brand of fantasies about the designated patient, as filtered through the parents' lens and their own needs and experiences. More attention may profitably be paid to such sibling ideas.

The father, as we see him, is not just "passive, weak, and ineffective," nor is he just a pawn of the mother and daughter; he has a complementary relationship that fits his own unconscious drives as well as those of his spouse and daughter. Not only are the mothers fixated on traumatic abandonment, replaying the old game by letting the husband take away the daughter-mother figure as described by Tessman and Kaufman; we would add that, for reasons not determined, the father has some need to replay the game of taking away the daughter-mother from the wife-mother—possibly in part as revenge against his wife-mother's abandonment of him. In all of these formulations, the daughter's position is also not entirely that of a passive reactor, but one who fosters all these family roles for many reasons. One is the enhanced status she gets from the importance her parents place on her. This last statement has clear therapeutic implications, in that the family therapy presents a narcissistic threat to the daughter, who is presumably asked to change her family role. This ambivalence about status and roles, already noted in the parents, is equally applicable to the daughter. These interlocking dynamics form some of the elements of the family homeostasis.

As we review the paper by Robey, we find many elements that are consistent with our findings. There is a disturbed marital relationship, deprivation, and pressure by the family for the daughter to assume the maternal role. As in Blos's second constellation, the girl's running away from home is seen by Robey as an attempted resolution of potential incest with the father. Here, too, we must point out that Blos's first constellation, that of the acting-out as a resolution of potential homosexual incest with the mother, is also operating. Thus we find that Blos's first two formulations are not either/or, but parallel operations. However, on the basis of our findings, we would hesitate to describe the regressive homosexual threat as pre-oedipal and the daughter-father incest threat as oedipal. Actually, we found the regressive threat of homosexuality equally coming from the mother and the regressive threat of incest from the father, who is looking for a regressively gratifying mother figure, not a genital wife figure. Our own view would be to see mother and daughter in a struggle over who is to be the sexualized mother object for the other and for the father. Each participant—mother, father, and daughter—both wants and fears what the other is prepared to offer: they are all locked together by their ambivalent feelings of wanting to be the special person to each of the others and to fulfill the others' role demands, but at the same time fearing the implications of those roles. For the mother and father this refers to the desire and threat of the adult genital heterosexual role; for the daughter it is the desire and threat of the incestual and homosexual implications of the triadic relationship. Essentially, we see these families as fixated at an early level of psychosexual adjustment, certainly pre-oedipal. Finally, we did not directly observe Blos's third constellation, namely, acting-out in the service of the ego. However, we would suspect, in view of the serious pathology noted in other family members and the hints of underlying psychotic depression in the designated patient, that this dynamic might well be operating.

One observation that struck us as unusual was the fact that frequently, shortly after the family group treatment began, the sexual acting-out ceased. One can speculate that the therapists had become "parents" to the entire family, without the sexual charge attached. The pressure on the daughter to continue parenting was reduced. She could now feel more free to act her age and not assume the unconscious role needed by her parents. For herself, her importance as the designated patient bearing the family symptoms maintains her narcissistic self-image of being very important and special to the family. The family implicitly borrows the therapist-parents' superego taboo in return for the implicit deal, in the mind of the family, that the therapists will assume responsibility for all of them.

One of the great benefits of family counseling is the increasing awareness of the interlocking dynamics of the primary triad and of the entire family. Our understanding of individual processes is enriched through a perception of complementary roles and relationships, each of which supports the others. This added dimension is a sobering one, as it adds greater complexity to an already intricate intrapersonal structure. Added knowledge, however, can in the long run only serve to increase our effectiveness in the helping process.

Since this is apparently the first report in the literature of a systematic effort to conduct conjoint family treatment with cases of female sexual acting-out, we consider that we have developed some useful insights into the problem, but we certainly recognize the need for further intensive work in this field.

REFERENCES

1. Johnson, A., & Szurek, S. A. The genesis of antisocial acting out in children and adults. *Psychoanal. Quart.*, 1952, *21*, 322–343.

Index

Index*

Ackerman, N., 37, *42*
Acting-out. *See also* Delinquency
  as attempt at ego continuity, 106–7
  in female delinquency, 100, 106–7
  running away, 127–37
  sexual. *See* Sexual delinquency
Adams, H. M., 71–72, *77*
Adolescent adjustment reaction, 51–56, 92
Adolescent development, normal, 52, 139
Adolescent rebellion, 54
Adolescents, deprived. *See also* Poverty culture
  attitudes toward marriage, 54–55, 56
  characteristics, 55–56
  developing ego strength, 60–63
  development of heterosexual relationships, 53
  developmental problems, 52–55
  family constellations, with case histories, 161–69
  group discussions with, 58–63
  improving self-image and social skills, 59–60
  parent-child relationships, 53–54
  peer-group relationships, 54
  self-image, 55–56
Adolescents, pregnant unwed. *See* Unmarried mothers
Andry, R. G., 40, *42*
Auerswald, E., 171, *178*, 179, 189, *197*
Ayres, B., 53, *63*

Bacon, H. K., 39, *42*
Barry, H. A., 39, *42*
Bateson, G., 172, *178*
Benedek, T., 53, *63*
Bennett, I., 40, *42*
Bernstein, B., 72, *77*
Bernstein, R., 71, 72, 73n, 74, *77*
Block, H. A., 114, *125*
Blos, P., 54, *63*, 102, 103, 106, *110*, 113, 118, 139, *150*, 202, 203
Borgatta, E. F., 121, *126*
Bott, E., 17, *21*
Bowlby, J., 40, *42*
Brammer, L. M., 14, *21*
Brown, T., 114, *125*
Bruch, H., 30, *33*
Buber, M., 7
Butman, J. W., 115–16, 121, *125*
Bychowski, G., 119, *126*

Calhoun, A. W., 65n, *77*
Campbell, A. A., 69n, *77*
Castration complex in promiscuity, 94
Chicago, Community Services Project for the Unwed Pregnant Adolescent, 78–86
Child, I. L., 39, *42*
Chilman, C. S., 62, *63*
Cloward, R. A., 36, *42*
Cohen, A. K., 39, *42*
Cohen, J., 56, *63*
Community Services Project for the Unwed Pregnant Adolescent (Chicago), 78–86
Couch, A. J., 164, *170*

Dame, N. G., et al., 116, *125*
Day, J., 173, 177, *178*
Delinquency. *See also* Delinquency, female; Delinquency, male; Sexual delinquency
  and family system, 34–41
  female vs. male, 100, 106, 114
  parental failure in, 19–21
  parental sanctions of, 38–39, 48–49, 97–98, 117–18, 200, 202–3
  peer-group culture, 35–36
  theories of, 34–37
Delinquency, female
  promiscuity. *See* Promiscuity; Sexual delinquency
  the runaway girl, 119, 127–37
  sexual delinquency. *See* Sexual delinquency
Delinquency, male, object-centeredness in, 89, 106
  regressive phenomena in, 104–5
Delinquency, sexual. *See* Sexual delinquency
Delinquent behavior. *See* Delinquency
Delinquent female, family patterns of behavior, 37–38, 195–97
  motivation, 119–20
  and schizophrenics, comparison of families, 123–25
Desertion, effect on family, 28–29
Deutsch, H., 139, *150*
Development and maturation, role of family system in, 13–21
Divorce, effect on family, 29

Ego continuity, and acting-out, 106–7
Empey, L. T., 35, *42*
Erikson, E. H., 13, *21*, 52, *63*, 166, *170*

*Italicized page numbers indicate bibliographic reference.

207

Ernst, C., 119, *126*

Families of delinquents, characteristics, 37–38, 171–74
of female vs. male delinquents, 123–25
See also Family constellations; Family structure; Family system
Family constellations, 161–69
case histories, 162–69
classification by developmental arrest of patient, 161–62
interactions, chart of, 164–65, 169
Family language, 172–73
Family Life Education Program, Family Service, Philadelphia, 51–52, 58–63
Family structure, 22–32, 173–78
broken family, 27, 28–30
fatherless families, 27–30
mental health implications, 22–32
middle-class family, 23–25
patriarchy vs. matriarchy, 30–32
three-generation family, 25–27
two-generation family, 23–25
uncompleted family, 27–28
Family system, and delinquency, 34–41
division of labor according to sex, 15
dysfunctions, 18–21, 45–50
fusion factors, 164
interactions, 13–16
parents-children system, 16–18
sibling system, 16, 18
spouse system, 16
subsystems, 16–18
Family therapy, assumptions about human nature, 6–7
interviews and the therapist, 5–12
in low socioeconomic groups, 171–78, 179–97
"me-you" language, 172–73
means of challenging family structure, 176–77
Multiple Impact Therapy, 3, 162, 177
overlapping interviews, 162
relation to family structure, 173–78
of underprivileged "delinquent" family, 181–95
Female delinquency. *See* Delinquency, female; Promiscuity; Sexual delinquency
Flynn, F. T., 114, *125*
Fraiberg, S., 139, *150*
Freud, A., 105, 108, *110*
Freud, S., 138, *150*
Fries, M. E., 15, *21*
Fusion factors in family functioning, 164

Geismar, L. L., 53, *63*
Giffin, M., 118, *125*
Glover, E., 100, *110*
Glueck, E., 39, 40, *42*
Glueck, S., 39, 40, *42*
Goddard, D. R., 19, *21*
"Going steady," 91
Greenberg, N. H., 122, *126*
Gregory, I., 39, *42*
Guilt, relation to promiscuity, 94

Haley, J., 172, 173, *178*
Halperin, A., 173, 177, *178*
Hathaway, S. R., 116, *125*
Healy, W., 37, *42*
Hecker, F. J., 14, 20, *21*
Heims, L., 142, *150*
Herskovitz, H., et al., 40, *42*
Herzog, E., 71, 77, 120
Hess, R., 172, *178*
Hollingshead, A. B., 128, *137*
Homans, K. G., 13, *21*
Homosexuality, following incest, 141, 143
promiscuity as defense against, 94–95, 102–5
Howard, A., 40, *42*

Identity confusion in promiscuity, 95
Illegitimacy, 64–77, 120–23. *See also* Unmarried mothers
incest anxiety as cause, 20
motivations, 97, 122–23
psychodynamic factors in, 121–23
statistics on, 64–71, 120–21
in strict middle-class family, 4–5, 122
Incest, 138–49
case examples, 142, 144–45, 146–47, 148–49
girls "unchosen" for incest, 138, 140, 142–45
homosexuality following, 141, 143
overt, 138, 140, 141–42
prohibited by one parent, 138, 140, 145–47
psychodynamics of, 140–41
role of mother in, 141
stimulated incest fantasies, 139, 140–41, 147–49
Incest anxiety, causes, 20
factor in female delinquency, 119
in families of schizophrenics vs. families of delinquents, 124–25

Jackson, D. D., 172, *178*
Johnson, A., 38, *42*, 118, *125*, *126*, 201, 202, *204*
Johnson, M. A., 108, *110*
Jones, E. C., 121, *126*

Kahn, A. J., 75, 76, 77
Kassenbaum, G. G., 164, *170*
Katan, A., 139, 140, *150*
Kaufman, I., 37, *42*, 58, *63*, 119, *126*, 129, *137*, 141, 142, *150*, 202
Keller, S., 40–41, *42*
King, C. H., 171, *178*, 179, 189, *197*
Kris, E., 14, *21*

Lakin, M., 122, *126*
Lee, R. E., 127, *137*
Litin, E., 118, *125*
Loesch, J. G., 122, *126*
Lorr, M., 169, *170*

McCord, J., 40, *42*
McCord, W., 40, *42*